Socialist Women and the Great War, 1914–21

Socialist Women and the Great War, 1914–21

Protest, Revolution and Commemoration

Edited by

Corinne Painter, Ingrid Sharp and Matthew Stibbe

BLOOMSBURY ACADEMIC
LONDON • NEW YORK • OXFORD • NEW DELHI • SYDNEY

BLOOMSBURY ACADEMIC
Bloomsbury Publishing Plc
50 Bedford Square, London, WC1B 3DP, UK
1385 Broadway, New York, NY 10018, USA
29 Earlsfort Terrace, Dublin 2, Ireland

BLOOMSBURY, BLOOMSBURY ACADEMIC and the Diana logo are trademarks of
Bloomsbury Publishing Plc

First published in Great Britain 2022
This Paperback edition published 2024

Copyright © Corinne Painter, Ingrid Sharp and Matthew Stibbe, 2022

Corinne Painter, Ingrid Sharp and Matthew Stibbe have asserted their rights under the
Copyright, Designs and Patents Act, 1988, to be identified as Editors of this work.

Cover image: © 1928, Chaim Soutine EVA

This work is published open access subject to a Creative Commons Attribution 4.0 licence
(CC BY 4.0, https://creativecommons.org/licenses/by/4.0/). You may re-use, distribute,
reproduce, and adapt this work in any medium, including for commercial purposes,
provided you give attribution to the copyright holder and the publisher, provide a
link to the Creative Commons licence, and indicate if changes have been made.

Open access was funded by Knowledged Unlatched.

Bloomsbury Publishing Plc does not have any control over, or responsibility for, any
third-party websites referred to or in this book. All internet addresses given
in this book were correct at the time of going to press. The author and publisher
regret any inconvenience caused if addresses have changed or sites have
ceased to exist, but can accept no responsibility for any such changes.

Every effort has been made to trace the copyright holders and obtain permission
to reproduce the copyright material. Please do get in touch with any enquiries
or any information relating to such material or the rights holder. We would be pleased
to rectify any omissions in subsequent editions of this publication should
they be drawn to our attention.

A catalogue record for this book is available from the British Library.

A catalog record for this book is available from the Library of Congress.

ISBN: HB: 978-1-3501-1034-2
PB: 978-1-3503-4350-4
ePDF: 978-1-3501-1035-9
eBook: 978-1-3501-1036-6

Typeset by RefineCatch Limited, Bungay, Suffolk

To find out more about our authors and books visit www.bloomsbury.com
and sign up for our newsletters.

Contents

List of Illustrations	vi
Glossary and Abbreviations	viii
Notes on Contributors	x
Preface	xiii

1 Socialist Women and the Great War, 1914–21: Protest, Revolution and Commemoration *Matthew Stibbe, Ingrid Sharp, Clotilde Faas, Veronika Helfert, Mary McAuliffe and Corinne Painter* — 1

2 Socialist Women and 'Urban Space': Protest, Strikes and Anti-Militarism, 1914–18 *Matthew Stibbe, Anna Hammerin, Katharina Hermann and Ali Ronan* — 31

3 Socialist Women and Revolutionary Violence, 1918–21 *Veronika Helfert, Clotilde Faas, Tiina Lintunen and Mary McAuliffe* — 65

4 Suffrage, Democracy and Citizenship *Ingrid Sharp, Manca G. Renko, Ali Ronan and Judith Szapor* — 99

5 Life Trajectories: Making Revolution and Breaking Boundaries *Corinne Painter, Veronika Helfert, Manca G. Renko and Judith Szapor* — 133

6 Commemorating Revolution, Commemorating Women *Mary McAuliffe, Ingrid Sharp, Clotilde Faas, Tiina Lintunen and Ali Ronan* — 169

Notes	201
Further Reading	251
Index	253

Illustrations

1.1 Photograph of a group of women campaigners for the ten-hour day in Crimmitschau, Saxony, taken on the final day of the twenty-two-week textile workers' strike of August 1903 to January 1904. 3
1.2 Members of the Irish Women Workers' Union on the steps of Liberty Hall, Dublin, during the lock-out strike of 1913–14. 20
2.1 Anti-war demonstration on the Quaibrücke in Zurich, March 1915. Willi Münzenberg (wearing a flat cap) is standing directly in front of the banner which reads: 'Girls! Boys! Join the Free Youth'. 36
2.2 Women working in an arms factory, c. 1917, place unknown, Germany. 38
2.3 Women and children queuing for bread in First World War Vienna, exact date unknown. 40
2.4 The women's hunger protest in Söderhamn, Sweden, on 11 April 1917. 53
2.5 Women's 6,000-strong hunger march, here passing along Vasagatan, one of Stockholm's central thoroughfares, en route to the Milk Central, 26 April 1917. 54
2.6 The events of 17 June 1918 in Zurich, when Rosa Bloch-Bollag led a delegation to the canton council, as presented in the *Schweizer Illustrierte Zeitung*, No. 26, 29 June 1918, 322. 55
2.7 British delegation at the second international conference held by the Women's International League for Peace and Freedom, Zurich, May 1919. 61
3.1 Propaganda poster against the Munich Republic of Councils, 1919. 71
3.2 Finnish Red female soldiers Tyyne Backman and Rauha Sinisalo, photographed in a studio on 20 April 1918. Sinisalo (on the right) was executed ten days later. 77
3.3 Still image of Irish woman May Connelly after she was punished by the British by having her hair forcibly cropped, 25 November 1920. 84
3.4 Cartoon mocking Red female soldiers in the Finnish satirical paper *Nya Fyren*, no. 5–7 (1918). 91

3.5 'Wen wähle ich?' ('Who do I vote for?'). German propaganda poster, 1919, promoting the Majority Social Democrats while warning against the dangers of the Spartacist movement represented by a dishevelled and armed woman in the front row. 92
3.6 Cartoon 'Kommunismus' in the Austrian satirical paper *Die Muskete*, 13 March 1919, equating the socialization of property with free sexuality and/or women with property. 94
3.7 Irish socialist and revolutionary Margaret Skinnider, 1915. 97
4.1 Ive Šubic: 'Slovenian woman, you are free and you will vote for the first time', poster, 1944. 109
4.2 Clara Zetkin (1857–1933) with Rosa Luxemburg (1871–1919), 1910. 112
4.3 Election of the Budapest Councils, April 1919. The second woman from the left in the back row is Jolán Kelen. 118
4.4 Clara Zetkin (1857–1933) with Lore Agnes (1876–1953) (left) and Mathilde Wurm (1874–1935) (right). 128
4.5 Ellen Wilkinson (1891–1947), MP, speaking at Labour's London May Day Celebration in Hyde Park, 1939. Wilkinson was Labour Party MP for Middlesbrough East (1924–31) and Jarrow (1935–47) and Minister of Education (1945–7). 130
5.1 A woman addresses a communist demonstration in Vienna, 1929. 139
5.2 Käthe Leichter (1895–1942). 149
5.3 Angela Vode (1892–1985). 158
5.4 Idrija in 1934. 161
6.1 Boleslaw von Szankowski's portrait of Countess Constance Markievicz, 1901. 179
6.2 'The Ripening Tide' poster, 1976. 179
6.3 *Girls 1918*. 182
6.4 *Fellman's Field* (in Finnish *Fellmanin pelto*). 183
6.5 Peace Crusade Choir, 2018. 184
6.6 Rehearsal image from *Women of Aktion* by Bent Architect, 2018. 187
6.7 Revolutionary women of Easter 1916, Dublin, autumn 1916. 194
6.8 The '77 women' of 1916 quilt, Richmond Barracks Exhibition, 2016. 194

Glossary and Abbreviations

AHRC	Arts and Humanities Research Council (UK)
BBC	British Broadcasting Corporation
BDFÖ	Federation of Democratic Women (post-1945 Austria)
CO	Conscientious objector/objection (to military service)
CPGB	Communist Party of Great Britain
Cumann na mBan	(Republican) Council of Women (Ireland)
Decade of Centenaries	Period of commemoration of the centenary of several important events in Irish history between 1912 and 1923/2012 and 2023
EFF	Election Fighting Fund (UK)
FRSI	Federation of Revolutionary Socialists International
HLF	Heritage Lottery Fund (UK)
IAW	International Alliance of Women (successor to the IWSA)
ICW	International Council of Women
ILP	Independent Labour Party (UK)
Inghinidhe na hÉireann	Daughters of Ireland
IRA	Irish Republican Army
ISK	Militant International Socialist League
ITGWU	Irish Transport and General Workers' Union
IWFL	Irish Women's Franchise League
IWM	Imperial War Museum (UK)
IWSA	International Women's Suffrage Alliance
IWWU	Irish Women Workers' Union
JSDS	Yugoslav Social Democratic Party
KPD	German Communist Party
KPÖ	Austrian Communist Party
MI5	The Security Service (UK)
NCAS	National Council for Adult Suffrage (UK)
NCF	No-Conscription Fellowship (UK)

NMI	National Museum of Ireland
NUWSS	National Union of Women's Suffrage Societies (UK)
SDAP	Austrian Social Democratic Party
SPD	German Social Democratic Party
SWI	Socialist Women's International
USPD	Independent Social Democratic Party (Germany)
WHAI	Women's History Association of Ireland
WIDF	Women's International Democratic Federation
WIL	Women's International League (UK)
WILPF	Women's International League for Peace and Freedom
WPC	Women's Peace Crusade (UK)
WSPU	Women's Social and Political Union (UK)

Contributors

Clotilde Faas is currently a PhD candidate at the University of Neuchâtel, Switzerland. Her research focuses on women's involvement in the German revolution in Berlin and Munich between 1917 and 1920. She is under the supervision of Professor Kristina Schulz at the University of Neuchâtel and the co-supervision of Professor Belinda Davis at Rutgers University in New Jersey.

Anna Hammerin is an independent researcher, focusing on bringing to life previously untold or lesser-known stories and historical accounts of her native Sweden in the late nineteenth and early twentieth centuries. As project coordinator for the AHRC-funded 'Everyday Lives in War' First World War Engagement Centre led by Professor Sarah Lloyd at the University of Hertfordshire, Anna came across her own family connection to the Swedish hunger uprisings of 1917 and the town where it all started. Söderhamn was the birthplace and home of both her grandmother and mother, and her grandfather was Söderhamn's policeman from 1917 until his death in 1938. Anna is currently working on a documentary film based on her research, interviews and oral-history recordings.

Veronika Helfert is currently a Postdoctoral Fellow at the Central European University Vienna/Budapest, working on the Research Project 'ZARAH: Women's Labour Activism in Eastern Europe and Transnationally, from the Age of Empires to the Late 20th Century'. Her research interests are women's and gender history, the history of protest and revolution, women's suffrage, and labour history in the twentieth century. Her recent publications include the monograph *Frauen, wacht auf! Eine Frauen- und Geschlechtergeschichte von Revolution und Rätebewegung in Österreich, 1916–1924* (Vandenhoeck & Ruprecht, 2021).

Katharina Hermann is a PhD candidate at the University of Bern, Switzerland. Her research focuses on gender relations, political protest and social cohesion in Switzerland during the First World War era, with particular emphasis on women's activism in the run-up to and during the *Landesstreik* (general strike) of November 1918.

Tiina Lintunen is an Adjunct Professor and works as a University Lecturer in Contemporary History at the University of Turku, Finland. She is also the Head of the Department. Her research interests include the Finnish civil war, war propaganda, history of Nationalist Socialist Germany, and the function and methods of the state police in the Nordic countries.

Mary McAuliffe is a historian and Director of the Gender Studies Programme at University College Dublin, Ireland (UCD). She recently published a biography of the Scottish-born Irish revolutionary and feminist, Margaret Skinnider (UCD Press, 2020), and was co-editor, with Miriam Haughton and Emilie Pine, of *Legacies of the Magdalen Laundries; Commemoration, Gender, and the Postcolonial Carceral State* (Manchester University Press, 2021). She is currently pursuing research on gendered and sexual violence during the Irish war of independence and civil war (1919–23).

Corinne Painter is Lecturer in Intercultural Studies at the University of Leeds. Her current research focuses on how power dynamics and political activism are expressed through women's life writing. Her recent publications include *Writing Lives: A Female German Jewish Perspective on the Early Twentieth Century*, a monograph published with Peter Lang in 2019.

Manca G. Renko is a historian currently working on the ERC Eirene Project ('Post-War Transitions in Gendered Perspective: The Case of the North-Eastern Adriatic Region') at the Faculty of Arts, University of Ljubljana, Slovenia. She has published on gender and intellectual history, and her current research is focused on women in the aftermaths of the First and Second World Wars.

Alison (Ali) Ronan is an independent scholar. Her PhD ('A Small Vital Flame', Keele University, 2009) focused on local, national and international networks of anti-war women in Manchester in 1914–18. She has worked on a number of community-led projects since 2014, uncovering local activists, socialists and suffragists in the North-West of England and using archival research to create documentaries, booklets and exhibitions. Currently, she is working on a project to restore the five unsuccessful contenders for the 2018 Womanchester statue into the radical histories of the city and working on another community led-project about pioneering women doctors in Manchester and the North-West.

Ingrid Sharp is Professor of German Cultural and Gender History at the University of Leeds, UK. She has published extensively on women's organizations and female activists during the period 1914–24 and the revolutionary upheavals of 1918, and on various forms and expressions of war resistance. She is co-editor, with Matthew Stibbe, of a previous volume of essays for Bloomsbury, *Women Activists between War and Peace: Europe, 1914–1923* (2017), and with Christa Hämmerle and Heidrun Zettelbauer, of a special issue of the journal *L'Homme, Zeitschrift für europäische Geschlechtergeschichte*, on '1914/1918 revisited' (2018). She is also editor of the anthology *A Cultural History of Peace in the Age of Empire* (2020), which appears in the Bloomsbury series *Cultural Histories*.

Matthew Stibbe is Professor of Modern European History at Sheffield Hallam University, UK. He has published widely on twentieth-century German, Austrian and European history, including in-depth studies of civilian internment during the First World War era. He is co-editor, with Ingrid Sharp, of a previous volume of essays for Bloomsbury, *Women Activists between War and Peace: Europe, 1914–1923* (2017), and is currently pursuing research into state of emergency regimes during the 1914–18 period and beyond. His book *Debates on the German Revolution of 1918–19* is due to be published by Manchester University Press in 2023, in the series *Issues in Historiography*.

Judith Szapor is Associate Professor in the Department of History and Classical Studies of McGill University, Montreal, Canada. She has written on Hungarian intellectual, women's and student movements in the twentieth century, and the intellectual migration from Central Europe. Her second monograph, *Hungarian Women's Activism in the Wake of the First World War: From Rights to Revanche*, was published by Bloomsbury Academic in 2018. Her current research project explores the impact of Hungary's 1920 *numerus clausus* law on Hungarian Jewish women and families.

Preface

This volume is born of many conversations both in person and online, within and across the various chapters. As well as the authors represented in the volume, the conversations were shaped and developed by scholars, activists and practitioners who attended a series of in person and hybrid workshops at the Universities of Leeds (2018), Sheffield Hallam (2019) and Neuchâtel (2021), which were funded by these institutions, as well as a series of online workshops throughout summer and autumn 2021. These workshops were central to the volume, which grew out of the discussions in Leeds and Sheffield and then took shape at Neuchâtel, where ideas for the introduction were shared and fed into the finalized version, and through the online editorial meetings.

Our initial discussions were influenced by Kathleen Canning's published work and further shaped by her contributions to the 2019 workshop, which she was able to attend in person as a visiting professor at Sheffield Hallam University. Jude Wright, Producer and Co-Director of the socially engaged theatre group Bent Architect, reflected on her practice of bringing untold stories and unheard voices to the stage, and scholars Philippa Read and Hanem El-Farahaty contributed their knowledge of French and Egyptian women activists at the Leeds workshop. Although the COVID-19 pandemic of 2020 onwards and conflicting demands prevented them from being part of the published volume, their contributions helped to shape it.

Parts of Chapters 4 and 5 were written within the EIRENE project, which is funded by the European Research Council (ERC) under the European Union's Horizon 2020 research and innovation programme (Grant Agreement No. 742683: Post-War Transitions in Gendered Perspective: The Case of the North-Eastern Adriatic region).

For the front cover, we chose the 1928 painting *Eva*, by the Belarusian-Jewish expressionist artist Chaïm Soutine (1893–1943), who worked for most of his adult life in Paris and died whilst in hiding from the Gestapo in German-occupied France. In 2020, *Eva* became a symbol of the peaceful pro-democracy protests in Minsk and other Belarusian cities that were largely led by women and began in reaction to the suspected falsification of the presidential elections there in August, handing a disputed victory to the incumbent, Alexander Lukashenko, over his main challenger, the now exiled opposition leader Sviatlana Tsikhanouskaya. As the German journalist and author Elisabeth von Thadden puts it in her excellent feature article about another prominent Belarusian dissident, Olga Shparaga, in the weekly newspaper *Die Zeit* in June 2021, Soutine's *Eva* 'depicts the open face of a dark-haired woman, her neck framed by the contours of a black dress, her arms folded across her chest. A subject that shows herself publicly. The successor of the invisible woman.'[†]

Corinne Painter, Ingrid Sharp and Matthew Stibbe
Leeds/Manchester, April 2022

[†] Elisabeth von Thadden, 'Die Sichtbare: Die Revolution in Belarus hat ein weibliches Gesicht – Eine Begegnung mit der europäischen Philosophin Olga Shparaga aus Minsk', *Die Zeit*, No. 24, 10 June 2021, 53.

1

Socialist Women and the Great War, 1914–21: Protest, Revolution and Commemoration

Matthew Stibbe, Ingrid Sharp, Clotilde Faas, Veronika Helfert, Mary McAuliffe and Corinne Painter

The German Women's Paper, the *Central-Blatt*, of which Frau Marie Stritt, the President of the Bund [*deutscher Frauenvereine*], is editor, gives an account of a most interesting women's meeting held lately in Berlin on the subject of the women textile workers, who, with the men, have been so many weeks on strike in Crimmitschau. Fraulein Alice Salomon, a well-known worker in the woman's cause, had just returned from a visit to the scene of the strike, and spoke feelingly on the evils to health and to social and domestic conditions caused by the eleven hours day, which (with the two hours often taken up by going and returning from work) kept the workers thirteen hours away from their homes. We learn also from her reports that men's wages, being rarely higher than 13s. to 16s. a week, all married and single women are forced to work these long hours in the factory ... A certain Herr Tietje, however, representing the factory owners, attempted to prove to the audience that the conditions demanded by the workpeople would destroy the textile industries. A most animated discussion followed his remarks, and he was vigorously opposed by Mr. Jutz, an editor and Miss Bohn, who spoke for the Socialists. The meeting finally carried the following resolution:- 'That this meeting expresses its hearty sympathy with the demands of the Crimmitschau textile workers for the reduction of the hours of the working day. It considers this demand doubly justified, because women, both married and single, form a large percentage of the workers. This meeting further protests against the attitude of the judicial officials, whose actions tend to increase the hostility, and regrets the continued refusal of the factory owners to consider proposals for a settlement of the dispute; and this meeting requests the Reichstag and the Bundesrat to fix a legal maximum of ten hours for women working in factories'.[1]

This description of a feminist meeting in Berlin in January 1904 is interesting on a number of different levels. It came just five months before the foundation of the International Women's Suffrage Alliance (IWSA), the first major cross-border pressure group for the female vote, at a conference, also held in Berlin and again involving Marie Stritt, in June 1904. It was written by Dora B. Montefiore, a London-based British-Australian member of the militantly pro-suffrage Women's Social and Political Union (WSPU) who later aligned herself with the international socialist views of Ellen Wilkinson and Clara Zetkin and joined the Communist Party of Great Britain (CPGB) in 1920.[2] It concerned calls to support 7,500 women and men striking for the ten-hour day in Crimmitschau, a relatively obscure textile town in the Zwickau district of Saxony, which at the turn of the century had a population of around 20,000 and no significant organized women's movement at local level. By the time the piece was published, the strike had collapsed, being called off on 18 January 1904. Hundreds of strikers were fired, and those who were spared dismissal were forced to go back to work under the same terms and conditions that they had had to endure before August 1903. All this was achieved because the factory owners had resorted to a lock-out, backed by the local military, police and judicial authorities, who declared a 'lesser' state of siege in the town, enabling bans on public assemblies and 'seditious' literature.[3]

For labour and gender historian Kathleen Canning, the 'legendary Crimmitschau textile strike of 1903[–04]' is significant above all because it demonstrated the 'fluid boundaries between factory and family in women's working lives, as they fought to set their own rhythms of work'.[4] The ten-hour day was both a long-standing demand of the German labour movement, and a campaign which had a specifically gendered meaning in the context of Crimmitschau, where the majority of women workers were married and had to take an extended lunchbreak to see to their domestic duties, and where 58 per cent of the strikers from August 1903 to January 1904 were women. The relevance of gender-specific needs at work was being asserted over the supposedly universal issue of pay. 'One more hour for our families!' was the slogan which they used to justify their demand not only for a reduction from eleven to ten hour shifts, but for a guaranteed two-hour midday break.[5] This was all the more remarkable as 'half the women were unorganized' – in other words, not members of the (male-led) trade union for textile workers.[6]

As we will show in this volume, the battle over who or what might have the sovereign right to determine female productive and reproductive lives at both micro and macro levels was not just a phenomenon of the mid-1900s and early

1910s. Rather, it gained renewed intensity during the years 1914–21, when the First World War and its brutal three-year aftermath haunted the continent of Europe. Once again, albeit now on a much larger transregional and transnational scale, unorganized working-class women, and some who belonged to official trade unions or unofficial shop steward movements, asserted the right to self- and co-determination of the political – with the added dimensions of their growing consciousness as consumers and de facto single parents raising children in the absence or death of soldier-husbands; as revolutionaries, street protestors and co-combatants in the struggle against wartime militarism and militant post-1918 counter-revolution; as citizens, members of left-wing political parties and voters; and as (self-) emancipated sexual beings determined to cast off many of the conventions of 'bourgeois' morality. This understanding of and claim to participatory rights in the creation of the social, the productive and the reproductive, and the forging of personal and community-based interconnections between all three, too often dismissed by socialist men as 'unpolitical' or 'pre-political',[7] as too bodily and/or too emotional, or as lacking in strategic purpose or plan, has yet to garner the scholarly attention and critical scrutiny that we believe it deserves. Our volume meets a long overdue imperative to place socialist women at the heart of understandings of the political in the era of the Great War.

Figure 1.1 Photograph of a group of women campaigners for the ten-hour day in Crimmitschau, Saxony, taken on the final day of the twenty-two-week textile workers' strike of August 1903 to January 1904. Source: Alamy.

Through five further multi-authored chapters and drawing on case studies from Austria, Britain and British-ruled Ireland, Finland, Germany, Hungary, Sweden, Switzerland and Yugoslavia, the volume shows that the involvement of socialist women as opponents of war and militarism, as advocates of social and political change, and as participants in industrial and street protests, was a core feature of European history in the years 1914–21. Their contributions ensured that, alongside the continent-wide strike wave of 1903–5 and the upheavals in Tsarist Russia in 1905–7, the First World War and its immediate aftermath marked a key moment in the development of a new mass democratic politics and new visions of national and global citizenship. The volume is at the same time intended as a critique of much of the previous literature on this subject, which is heavily skewed towards actions by men and primary accounts written by men. This preference, we would argue, reflects, among other things, a seldom examined but nonetheless historically rooted prejudice against the involvement of women in modern revolutions, except in the purely allegorical form made famous by French artist Eugène Delacroix's 1832 painting 'Liberty Leading the People' (*La Liberté guidant le peuple*).[8] It is a conscious and unconscious method of exclusion that can be found as much in the conventional historiography of modern European revolutions as it can be in the hidden assumptions and languages of gender present in many left-wing political organizations of the nineteenth and early twentieth centuries, such as trade unions, workers' councils and socialist or Social Democratic parties.

'Wild, wacky and wrong' are the words chosen by Sheila Rowbotham to denote how men have typically castigated female revolutionaries.[9] The genealogy of this deep-seated prejudice can be traced back to the era of the French revolutions of 1789, 1830 and 1848, and, in the British case, to the period between the radical movements of the 1780s and 1790s and the Great Reform Act of 1832, as Nan Sloane has also recently argued.[10] It was at this point that the 'convention that women were not qualified for politics and needed to be trained or educated before they could participate or express an opinion' first became the dominant factor in the gender politics of modern revolutions and counter-revolutions.[11] Needless to say, it was a way of thinking that reared its head anew at various moments in the late nineteenth century, and again in the wake of the First World War. Sometimes women activists themselves bought into the 'wild and wacky' label. The Austrian Social Democrat Marianne Pollak, for instance, in a 1928 article on the actions of women 'barricade brides' in the revolutionary year 1848, mentioned their participation in a raid on a bank building, as well as their work sewing badges and reading revolutionary leaflets, while suggesting that when it came to organized political or military struggles, 'they did not join in'.¹² Men, however, were at the forefront of suggestions after 1921 that women insurgents in Austria were not only lacking in self-control, but an all-out abomination. Similarly in Ireland, after the 1922–3 civil war, female militants were seen as 'hysterical women', who were 'unlovely, destructive minded, arid begetters of violence' and largely responsible for the horrors of the fighting, although as Maryann Valiulis points out, this position is not supported by events of the period.¹³ At its most insidious, the male gaze can be found in the fearful image of the 'dangerous' female revolutionary masses developed by the German criminologist Hans von Hentig in his 1923 article 'Die revolutionäre Frau' ('The Revolutionary Woman'):

> Experience teaches us that in revolutions the woman exceeds the man in determination ... The woman, once rebellious, knows no fear; this is rooted in her divergent sense of morality. The morality of the women extends to her small circle, her family and not the state or society, two entities to which she mostly does not share a strong relation ... Because the organism of a broad part of women succumbs to periodical flows, that leave deep marks in their mental state, a mass consisting of women is much more explosive than a mass consisting of men.¹⁴

Strategies adopted by socialist women in the years 1914–21 for combatting such chauvinistic-reductive arguments about their moral and biological 'unsuitability' for revolution included their involvement in work-based strikes, food riots and street demonstrations. However, as our five further chapters make clear in different ways, this was simply the outward manifestation of a variety of more hidden yet equally important methods for demanding economic and social resources and claiming sovereignty over their own lives and the lives of the nations and communities in which they lived, many of which have since been erased from the historical record. These include: smuggling and distributing illegal literature and (less frequently) money and arms, often at night; running underground printing presses and arranging forbidden private gatherings and reading circles that were often disguised as 'trivial' meetings of women for harmless gossip; hiding deserters and men on the run; standing up for teenagers when they were arrested or brutalized by the police; and supporting strikes through carrying out reproductive tasks such as caring for pre-teenage children and ensuring their education at times of enforced school closures. They also involved 'memory-work' – in other words, female-specific and self-empowering ways of working through and communicating lived experience for future generations of women (and men).[15] Indeed, by bringing scholars with expertise in gender-based historical research in different national contexts into dialogue with one another, our separate chapters aim to highlight the different forms that socialist-oriented and anti-militarist political action could take, and make women's agency in creating and sustaining the various revolutionary contexts visible.

Understanding these developments as historical phenomena also requires substantial critical engagement with historical methods and sources, including interrogation of how masculinities as well as femininities were constructed during this period. The German socialist (and later communist) Martha Arendsee judged, perhaps a little harshly, that proletarian women's participation in strikes and protests during the First World War was 'always more an emotional decision [made in the moment] than the outflow of a socialist worldview with a consciously desired end goal'.[16] This also makes women's participation more difficult to see in the surviving records, as it did not always conform in gender-normative terms to the political category 'worker' as constructed in the official programmes, minuted meetings and informal rites of socialization to be found in male-dominated socialist parties, strike committees and trade unions.[17] These gender norms could be casually and almost unthinkingly enforced by male socialist leaders for whom the 'amorphous', 'erratic' or 'uncontrolled' mass only acquired agency and purpose with masculine party leadership.[18] Socialist men usually had little interest in the 'specific deformations of women's conditions', as Frigga Haug puts it, and were unwilling to do the necessary 'detective' or 'memory-work' to identify them empirically, situate them historically into understandings of the material and cultural reproduction of human social relations, and integrate them meaningfully and sensibly into a general Marxist theory of the emancipation of both sexes.[19] The German revolutionary Rosa Leviné-Meyer, for instance, remembered an off-the-cuff remark made by her second husband, the former KPD (Communist party) general secretary and hard-line Leninist Ernst Meyer, who died suddenly in 1930:

> I was taught on many occasions to distinguish between the revolutionary value of organised and unorganised workers. Once I was carried away by the sight of a large demonstration. 'Too many housewives, women, youngsters,' Ernst coolly remarked.[20]

And yet, as Moritz Föllmer has shown, the supposed straightforward, historical-materialist thinking of 'disciplined' male workers within organized labour movements of the post-1848 period itself met a dead end in the revolutions of

1918–19, as men too found that they lacked a clear-cut script to help them make sense of the unexpected and unpredictable events happening around them.[21] Conversely, as some of this volume's authors have argued elsewhere, emotion-driven responses to human suffering and unorganized feelings of solidarity with those who suffered most from state-led violence and economic exploitation could also lead to some very clear and rational, utopian *and* strategic political reasoning about how to achieve the one immediate goal that really mattered in the here and now to socialists in 1914–21: ending the war and restoring peace on terms that benefitted workers, including women workers, young people, conscientious objectors and army deserters, not capitalists.[22] This was a goal that depended on creating new horizontal structures of protest and imagining new possibilities for everyone to become 'independent citizens who show solidarity'.[23] It required a de-centring of power, or rather a reclaiming of power at the margins, including the power to interpret what constituted legitimate and purposeful protest. It also entailed using strikes, demonstrations, illicit leafleting, police interrogations and court appearances to communicate lived, everyday war experiences from the edges.

One example here would be the 'communal strikes' across urban parts of Russia, Italy and Spain in 1917–22, written about in 1987 by Temma Kaplan for the second volume of the path-breaking feminist series *Becoming Visible: Women in European History*. According to Kaplan, these strikes – rather like the anti-eviction demonstrations in Budapest in the 1900s, or the Glasgow rent strike of 1915 which we discuss in Chapter 2 – were legitimized in the first instance as a protest against neighbourhood economic conditions that made it impossible to survive, even in a neutral country like Spain, during the war and immediate post-war period. By 'demanding food, fuel or housing at reasonable rent until they succeeded in mobilising the support from the men of the same social class', the women strikers hoped to 'force action from the side of those in power'.[24] However, in most accounts of Russian, Italian and Spanish history during the First World War era, just as in most accounts of Glasgow's 'Red Clydeside' in the 1910s and 1920s, or of the Swedish hunger riots of 1917 (also examined in Chapter 2), it is the subsequent challenges to authority made by their husbands, fathers and sons that are foregrounded and labelled political. The female 'neighbourhood', the characteristic public space in which urban and suburban working-class women did their politics – as 'protesters plain to see'[25] – was thereby rendered 'unpolitical' or 'pre-political', in other words, not part of the 'crisis' or the new society in the making. This is a phenomenon that we examine and challenge in Chapter 2 of the volume, using case studies from Germany,

Austria, Britain, Sweden and Switzerland during the years 1914–18, and again in Chapter 3, where we show how working-class women in post-war Austria, Germany, Finland and Ireland often laboured and lived in the same small neighbourhoods and again saw revolutionary activities as an opportunity to claim urban space.

Recognizing women's lived experiences and political subjectivities, and their reflection in the historical record, or rather lack thereof, as a methodological challenge for feminist and gender historians also requires acknowledging what Joan Wallach Scott refers to as the uneven relationship 'between the seemingly fixed language of the past and our own terminology'.[26] Acknowledging and working through such 'anachronistic' tensions, as Caroline Arni argues, allows a more critical approach to gender and makes historical conditions more susceptible to feminist analysis.[27] Where 'emotions' end and where 'reason' and 'long-term goals' begin, in other words, is both context-dependent from a historical point of view and at the same time inseparable from gender politics, in other words, from the problem of gendered divisions, hierarchies and blind spots within the concepts and analytical/political categories used by historiography itself to decide what is relevant to the study of revolution. In this respect, we also agree with the Austrian historian Gabriella Hauch when she writes that 'the separation of everyday life and the public sphere, of productive politics and reproductive routines, is an antiquated way of writing modern history'.[28] In this volume, we bring the two together as a critical part of our method for uncovering and reinterpreting socialist women's activism in the Great War era.

The liberal-progressive and the Socialist women's movements: overlapping temporalities and spaces

One of the key analytical categories used by historians to understand and conceptualize the political and social upheavals of the First World War era is sovereignty. The crumbling of imperial dominion, for instance, has been identified as a central part of the war experience in Eastern Europe, not least in the 'shatterzone' along the frontiers of the Russian, Austro-Hungarian, German and Ottoman empires.[29] The successes and failures of the Paris Peace Conference of 1919–20 have also been measured against the ability of the victorious Allies to reshape the European state system according to Western models of territorial sovereignty and stable borders,[30] while contrasts have been drawn with Leninist and other 'eastern' solutions to the national question in the borderlands and central regions of the former Tsarist Empire.[31] In this volume, we also recognize the matter of political sovereignty and the demand for new democratic polities to be central questions thrown up by the First World War. These were issues that US President Woodrow Wilson, British Prime Minister David Lloyd George and French premier Georges Clemenceau, with their tendency to 'conflate ... the individual with the white male', failed to resolve.[32] Race blindness was one of their key faults. However, we also challenge master narratives that, at Paris and in other arenas, privileged certain highly gendered versions of sovereignty – the ruggedly individualized, the bordered and the national – over others – female self-determination and transnational organization, sexual freedom for both sexes, and workers' self-government.[33] In particular, we ask what happens when we place working-class women, the very people whose voices were least heard during the peace negotiations between the victor powers, at the centre of discussions of sovereignty.

One immediate barrier to doing so is the thesis of a 'clean break' between socialist and progressive middle-class women's movements from the 1890s onwards, the former focused on collective rights, the latter on individual ones.[34] This 'clean-break' notion serves to highlight the biographies of some prominent women campaigners from both the socialist and non-socialist camps, especially those who took a notably doctrinaire position for (Zetkin) or against (Emmeline and Christabel Pankhurst) class-based models of sovereignty. Yet it also obscures the lives of hundreds and thousands of ordinary working-class women activists, who were less interested in issues of ideological demarcation or in campaigning for single causes such as the vote, and more willing to shift their positions pragmatically, in line with particular temporal, geographical and political contexts.[35]

In Chapter 5, we see how women's experiences of revolution and the choices they made to pursue their vision of a better world led them into conflict with authority figures, meaning not only representatives of state governments but also those who saw themselves as an authority on Socialism. Some of the activists we discuss in this volume thus identified only temporarily as socialists, for instance in the moment of revolution and the achievement of full adult suffrage in 1918–20 in Austria, Germany and Sweden, while others retained a lifelong self-identification as Marxists and party members first, and women only second. Some rejected nationalism and/or feminism outright, whereas others adopted a more fluid approach in contexts where (full) voting rights for women (in Yugoslavia, Hungary and Britain) or claims to national independence (in the

Slovene parts of Yugoslavia and in Ireland) were still contested after 1921. Above all, while some had already been involved in the workers' or women's movements before 1914 or during the years 1914–18, others were inspired to do so by the end of the First World War. Quite a few of the latter – often referred to, pejoratively, as *Novembersozialistinnen* (November Socialists) because it was only then that they joined the Social Democratic Party – remembered the autumn of 1918 as a revolutionary new beginning in their activist lives.[36] Chapters 3 and 4 in this volume tease out some of these fluidities and consider how they empowered women to enter the political sphere in new and unforeseen ways.

Our more flexible approach requires some justification as is at odds with the tendency in much of the current literature to shy away from complexity and diversity and to focus instead on the surface continuities in political and ideological separation of 'bourgeois' feminism and the women's socialist movement from the end of the nineteenth century through to the 1920s and beyond.[37] In the case of Germany in particular, the radical stance taken by committed Marxist Clara Zetkin against cooperation with middle-class suffragist, and later pacifist groups, is seen both as characteristic of this division, and as an appropriate way of defining who was and who was not a socialist. Thus Werner Thönnessen quotes Zetkin as writing in the Social Democrat magazine she edited, *Die Gleichheit*, in early 1901, declaring her firm opposition to any attempt to open up this periodical to 'bourgeois' voices and influences.

> The characteristic standpoint, that of class struggle, must be keenly and unambiguously stressed in a magazine for the interests of proletarian women. This must be done all the more keenly, moreover, the more the bourgeois women's libbers make it their business, by the use of general humanitarian phrases and petty concessions to the women workers' demands for reform, to bring intrigue into the world of proletarian women and to draw them away from class struggle.[38]

Zetkin's impact was felt far beyond Germany's borders, not least after she became secretary of the women's section of the Second International in 1907, after she helped to launch the first International Women's Day in 1911, and again after she organized a conference of anti-war women socialists in Bern, Switzerland, in March 1915.[39] Her influence could even be seen in post-1918 Denmark, where – in the words of Ann Taylor Allen – the country's first female Minister of Education, Nina Bang, who held office from 1924 to 1926, 'supported the Social Democratic Party's opposition to feminism as a movement that distracted working-class women from the class struggle'.[40] From there, according to Marilyn

J. Boxer, 'the concept ["bourgeois feminism"] spread around the world, and it persisted [until the late twentieth century] as a means to discredit nonsocialist women activists', leaving a 'divisive residue' in its wake which the European Left is still coming to terms with today.[41]

And yet as Gisela Bock argues, the lines between 'socialist' and 'bourgeois' women could be blurred on occasion even in the 1890s and 1900s and continued to be so in decades to come. Both feminists and socialist women prioritized the social question for much of the period before 1904, even though both actively embraced suffrage from the early to mid-1890s.[42] By 1908, all wings of the German women's movement – 'moderate' bourgeois, 'radical' bourgeois and socialist – had come to see the vote as a necessary, if perhaps not sufficient, step towards the full-scale democratization of society at national and international levels. Whether they held a largely positive or negative view of the militant tactics adopted by the WSPU in Britain, they were all influenced by the latter's core message that it could not be left to men alone to decide whether women should be given the vote.[43] True, at international level, the foundation in 1904 of the IWSA was possibly something of a turning point, as socialist women had to draw a line when it came to supporting a single-issue, cross-border pressure group for women's suffrage lest it alienate indifferent or actively hostile proletarian men.[44] Three years later, and partly in answer to the IWSA, the Second International formally created its own women's section under Zetkin at the first international congress of socialist women, held in Stuttgart. At this event, Zetkin went out of her way to denounce the specific form of suffrage about to be granted to women in Norway as 'reactionary' as it applied only to those with a certain level of income. In other words, she presented it as a setback for full adult suffrage, and for working-class women (and men) in particular. Furthermore, it was another reason to stay clear of feminist internationalism as a 'fake' liberation movement.[45]

However, other socialist women were less doctrinaire and/or had other priorities than distancing themselves from feminism. One example among many from the pre-war period would be Hannah Mitchell, a Lancashire seamstress and Independent Labour Party (ILP) member who joined the WSPU in 1903 precisely because she saw it as a vehicle for ending the 'life of drudgery that trying to make ends meet' brought to the mass army of female wage-earners.[46] She also contributed to the debate about women's special interests versus their common interest with men in the struggle for socialism, noting in an opinion piece for the ILP newspaper *Labour Leader* in January 1906 that working-class women did not need journals to tell them about food and clothes but about politics, since 'our lives are [already] one long round of cooking and sewing'.[47] 'I realized,' she later wrote in her memoirs, 'that if women did not bestir themselves the socialists would be quite content to accept Manhood Suffrage in spite of all their talk about equality.'[48] After the war and the granting of female suffrage in the UK, she remained loyal to the ILP but refused to join the mainstream Labour Party. According to Jill Liddington and Jill Norris, this was because 'she did not like the Party's constituency Women's Sections' whose main task – as she saw it – was to side-line local female activists by channelling them into organizing social events and taking on the role of '[o]fficial cake-maker[s]'.[49]

Views like those of Mitchell can also be found in the pages of the *Irish Citizen*, the newspaper launched in 1912 by the Irish militant suffrage group the Irish Women's Franchise League (IWFL, founded 1908), which provided a forum for suffrage and socialist women. Articles thus regularly appeared in this paper on the right to vote as well as on 'working-class women's conditions and their need for trade union organisation [and] equal pay'. It also made frequent calls to reform the legal system, especially when dealing with domestic and sexual violence against women.[50]

Another, somewhat different but equally striking case would be that of Sonja Lerch (aka Sarah Rabinowitz), a Jewish woman born in Warsaw in 1882 who took part in the 1905 Russian revolution by helping to organize workers and students' soviets in the Ukrainian port city of Odesa, one of the major sites of unrest at this time. Forced to flee to Central Europe in 1907, she retained her lifelong attachment to the secular, non-Zionist Jewish socialist movement, the Bund, and was eventually drawn to the anti-war Independent German Socialists (USPD) around Kurt Eisner in First World War Munich. A member of a pro-revolutionary reading circle and (briefly) a prominent strike leader in the Bavarian capital in January 1918 (see Chapter 2), she mixed with anarchists and pacifists as well as socialists, and refused to take up any doctrinaire positions. Instead, she channelled the possibility of protest into the specific, the immediate and the everyday – a form of pragmatism that Bundists referred to by the Yiddish term *Doigkejt* or 'doing in the here and now'.[51]

With a view to integrating these and many more concrete individual examples into our analysis, we follow Kathleen Canning in deliberately adopting a much more open and 'capacious' definition of 'socialist woman' in this volume than that offered by the 'inveterate Marxist' Zetkin.[52] We do so without wishing to deny Zetkin's own consistent rejection of feminism, a repudiation which was much more 'strenuous' than the approach adopted by the pre-war leaders of the German Social Democratic Party (SPD), August Bebel and Hugo Haase,[53] but with the intention – again, following Canning – of exploring *revolution* as a 'rupture in time and space' and a site of (gendered) political imaginaries and experiences transcending political loyalties, class divisions and pre-existing scripts.[54] In particular, we recognize the existence of important national, temporal and situational variations in how starkly the separation between the different wings of the women's movement was experienced and understood by contemporary activists from the 1890s onwards. Socialist women, in our definition, were those who wished to empower the working people of both sexes, the majority in society, against the privileges of the male propertied elite. They did not intend to leave the struggle against capitalist economic exploitation to men alone to fight, but nor did they wish to fight against men of their own social class (even though they often felt forced to do so owing to the latter's frequent lack of interest in issues of gender equality). The important thing was not their own origins, but their self-identification as women activists for the proletarian cause and for the rights of all workers. In the decade or so before the First World War, they also took on a distinct anti-militarist stance, meaning opposition not just to the present, and in their view, solely profit-driven, arms race between the European great powers, but to the increasing control of the military over ever greater aspects of civilian life within nations, including interference in strikes, threats to use martial law against anti-war street protests and peacetime conscription of young men. They were campaigners against (capitalist) war but did not necessarily consider themselves absolute pacifists, even though in Britain and Germany in particular pacifist and socialist women mingled side by side in the ILP and USPD.

In other contexts, such as post-war Slovenia, socialist women worked together with nationalist groups disputing Serb hegemony in the new Yugoslav state. Here and elsewhere in the former Habsburg Monarchy they formed Marxist reading circles in an attempt to reach out to non-party but fellow-travelling female (and male) academics and intellectuals. Already existing associations like the *Bildungsverein Karl Marx* in Vienna or the Galileo Circle in Budapest were places where they met with socialist men and women who were later organized in different parties and federations – be they Social Democratic, Communist or Anarcho-Syndicalist.[55] One example would be the Austrian Anna Frey, née Schlesinger, who was active in youth and student organizations, connecting young women workers with young intellectuals who were interested in the social question. Another would be the Polish-Hungarian revolutionary Ilona Duczynska, who moved between Hungary, Switzerland, Russia, Austria, Britain and Canada, and between organized political work (for communist and left-socialist parties) and more scholarly pursuits linked to the life-work of her husband, the economist and founder of the Galileo Circle Karl Polanyi (see Chapter 5).

In short, socialist women lived in the moment while working for a better future. They wished to bring an end to 'bourgeois' order, but this did not stop them from cooperating from time to time with, or even identifying themselves as simultaneously belonging to, communities of social reformers or political campaigners from the non-socialist or 'bourgeois' camp.

The battle *against* militarism and socio-economic injustice and *for* democracy and mass civic participation also led socialist women to campaign for the right of women of all social classes to vote and stand for election to state parliaments, without making this the be-all and end-all of socialist political activism or visions of democratic socialist citizenship. In some countries, such as Sweden, and to a more limited extent, Britain and Ireland, the very restricted male vote at the turn of the twentieth century 'encouraged Liberal-Socialist cooperation' in pursuit of a wider franchise.[56] In Ireland, Countess Markievicz, one of the main revolutionary leaders of 1908–22, argued, in 1909, that women should fix their minds 'on the ideal of Ireland free, with her women enjoying the full rights of citizenship in their own nation'.[57] For Markievicz, like so many Irish women of the revolutionary period, the three great causes of women, of workers, and of Ireland, were interlinked.

In Germany, although the battle for manhood suffrage was largely won at Reich level in 1867–71, unequal voting systems persisted at the level of individual states. The SPD, the principal party of the democratic left and of Zetkin until 1917, was committed from 1891 to introducing votes for women on an equal basis to men and saw this as a crucial part of its battle against the *Klassenstaat* (class rule/the ruling class). On 10 January 1908, several thousand socialist women demonstrated in Berlin in front of the House of Deputies (*Abgeordnetenhaus*) against the unequal franchise in Prussia, and on 22 and 24 January, a further 8,000 and 2,000 women turned up to hear Zetkin speak at two public rallies in favour of full adult suffrage.[58] In Austria, socialist women, disappointed that the universal franchise granted in 1907 applied to men only, emphasized the social progress that had been achieved in Finland since the introduction of female suffrage there in 1906.[59] In the Saxon capital, Dresden, a 25,000-strong demonstration in favour of universal adult suffrage 'without distinction of sex' took place on 1 November 1908, with women making up an estimated 5 to 10 per cent of the participants, according to a report in the *Dresdner Nachrichten*.[60] Around the same time, Zetkin was also invited by Dora Montefiore to address an audience in Britain on the subject of adult suffrage,

'[Zetkin] having been in Germany the leading woman to advocate in her paper, *[Die] Gleichheit*, the enfranchisement, more especially, of the working woman'.[61] And on 19 March 1911, the first International Women's Day, 'more than a million women – mostly, but not exclusively, women organized in the SPD and the unions – took to the streets in Germany demanding social and political equality'.[62]

The pre-war campaigns of socialist women for full adult suffrage are thus well documented and cannot be eradicated from the feminist historical record. Even so, Geoff Eley is right to note that the failure of most European socialist parties to engage positively with feminist movements before 1914 was 'extremely short-sighted', not least as it weakened their claim to be in the 'vanguard of democracy'.[63] This is borne out when we bear in mind that electoral successes for Social Democrat parties in Germany and the German-speaking parts of Austria (with a wide male franchise) and in Sweden and Britain (on a more restricted male franchise) were never going to translate into political power or social justice without support from a broader, more female-friendly and gender-aware, progressive base. In France and Switzerland, formation of such a progressive alliance was also hindered by the traditionally strong link between male left-wing republicanism and anti-clericalism, and by the deeply ingrained fear that enfranchising women would hand power to Catholic reactionaries.[64] Here and in other parts of Europe, as Marilyn J. Boxer puts it, socialist parties sought to win elections under the current rules, and therefore – in practice if not in theory – opted to campaign significantly harder for 'the votes of [those] men who envisaged no part in public life for women' than they did for female suffrage as a political goal.[65]

In fact, of all the countries mentioned in this volume, the real outlier before 1914 was Finland, which in 1906 became the first nation-state in Europe, and the first in the world after New Zealand (1893) and Australia (1902), to enact votes for women, in spite of its lack of a significant *organized* industrial workforce at this time. The key factor, as Jad Adams argues, was the extension of literacy into rural areas and the integration of women into the Finnish nationalist movement, which by late 1905 was ready to join forces with Social Democrats in launching a general strike in support of national autonomy from Tsarist Russia and voting rights for all adults.[66] By this time, '[e]ven the conservative [Finnish] Women's Association had ... come round to universal suffrage, moving away from its stance of enfranchising only the wealthy'.[67] At the other extreme, women did not obtain the right to vote at federal level in Switzerland until after a referendum in February 1971, another reflection, says Bock, of the influence of radical republicanism and anti-clericalism on anti-feminist politics there.[68] This was in spite of full adult suffrage having been on the programme of the Swiss Social Democrats since the 1890s and in spite of it having been listed as the second of nine demands made during the Swiss general strike (*Landesstreik*) of November 1918.[69]

Women also did not get the vote in Yugoslavia in 1918–21, and in Hungary, initial wholesale success was met with partial reversal in 1920 under the counter-revolutionary measures introduced by the reactionary regime of Miklós Horthy, which were directed primarily against the Left (as well as against Hungarian Jewry). Our decision to place working-class women at the heart of debates about sovereignty in the First World War era and the period to 1921 is nonetheless justified when we consider all the new and expanding, national and transnational spaces on which such women met during that time: food protests, unofficial strike movements, anti-conscription and anti-war campaigns, the revolutionary overthrow of defeated empires in 1917–18, and ongoing demands for the full and equal enfranchisement of all adults. Without wishing to ring-fence ourselves into taking a definite position in the now tired debate over whether the vote was 'won' through women's war work or through longer-term political struggles, we argue, in Chapter 4 of the volume, that the achievement of female suffrage, in whole or in part, in many of the countries we have placed under consideration was a revolutionary act. It was a temporal and spatial breach in the male-dominated order that also represented, in the political imaginary of the years 1918–19, a victory for an unscripted and non-doctrinal version of socialism. It brought many women to believe – some temporarily but others in deeper and more life-affirming ways – in the possibilities of a new era of democratic emancipation reaching into the spheres of citizenship and reproduction, social relations and military organization, as well as education, the workplace and communal politics. And as we show more fully in Chapter 5, this working-class female identification with democratic socialist revolution as a fluid and shifting construct was sustained and reproduced in many of women's personal biographies and life trajectories after 1921.

1905 – 1914 – 1917: overlapping moments in the development of a democratic protest culture

For many early twentieth-century observers of modern revolutions, the coming to power of the Bolshevik regime in Russia in late 1917 represented a turning point in world history. In the eyes of the Bolshevik leadership and its Western supporters, it provided a 'laboratory for new forms of political order', in other words, a space for creative thinking, not only about questions linked to sovereignty, violence, war and civil war, anti-imperialism and national self-determination, but about all aspects of human creativity, collective organization and social relations.[70] For socialist women, it was the next stage on from the granting of female suffrage in Russia, which had already happened under the provisional government between April and September 1917.[71] It also overcame the many limitations of Woodrow Wilson's fourteen points and, for some national movements representing peoples newly liberated from oppressive imperial regimes in Central and Eastern Europe – such as Béla Kun's short-lived councils republic in Hungary – it provided an alternative model of global order to that offered by the Western victor powers meeting in Paris in 1919–20.[72] Certainly we would not wish to deny the equally momentous impact of the Russian Bolshevik revolution (and of Kun's extraordinary five-month reign in Hungary) on the outlook of socialist women across Europe, and the different chapters in our volume give ample consideration to this. Nonetheless, the volume as a whole begins in 1914, not in 1917, and focuses not on Russia, but on other European contexts and spaces. Decentring the Bolshevik revolution, we believe, offers us another way of challenging established master narratives in the interests of uncovering female subjectivities and women's political agency during the entire period 1914–21. We declare it here as one of our major interventions in the debate on socialist women and revolution.

When the First World War broke out in 1914, many socialist women felt they had already been at war for at least a decade, albeit not against any particular nation, but against the militarism and economic injustices of the capitalist world around them. This had been brought to a head in the years around 1905–6, through the revolutionary uprisings of oppressed workers in Russia, the mass strikes across many other continental countries, and the refusal of the incoming Liberal government in Britain to consider votes for women. At this point, Europe witnessed the birth of what Amerigo Caruso calls a cross-border 'democratic protest culture'.[73] Socialists no longer sought to seize power through spontaneous, one-off blows directed against the class system such as a national strike or Paris Commune-style uprising, or through individual acts of terrorism, as happened with the murder of the King and Queen of Serbia by a group of army officers in 1903, but by organizing the downtrodden and dispossessed in a mass movement that would be too heavily populated for the state authorities to repress. History, as the Dutch socialist Henriette Roland-Holst put it, with specific reference to events in Russia in 1905 and their repercussions throughout Europe, had 'taken wings'.[74] Calls for the enfranchisement of all workers was a fundamental part of this transnational phenomenon, a fact that has too often been ignored in the debate about the long-term versus short-term causes of the revolutions of 1918–19 and the simultaneous partial or full achievement of votes for women in many of the countries under consideration in this volume: Britain, including Ireland, Germany, Austria, Hungary and Sweden.

Two key events in the first decade of the twentieth century in fact played a key role in persuading more women (and men) from the socialist camp across Europe to see full adult suffrage – in other words, the equal enfranchisement of all men and women, whether to be achieved by means of parliamentary legislation or extra-parliamentary force or both – as an indispensable weapon in the battle to overturn capitalist and authoritarian states: the first Russian revolution in 1905 and the granting of votes to women in Finland in 1906. Neither event is given sufficient weight in current feminist or socialist histories. The movement of ideas within international women's or revolutionary-utopian movements is instead often depicted as being largely west to east, at least until 1917, with much less emphasis on travel in the opposite direction.[75] This in turn reflects the bias towards middle-class organizations in much feminist historiography, the example of the IWSA, which held its one and only pre-war conference in an 'eastern' capital, Budapest, in 1913, being a case in point.[76] It also reflects a tendency to downplay the role of working-class street protests and industrial militancy in democratic nation-building in favour of progressive middle-class reform movements, both feminist and non-feminist.[77] And in some branches of the inter-war communist movement, whose influence can still be felt in many radical-left histories today,[78] it reflected a line of thinking that dismissed the 'mass' as a purposeful political force in its own right and assumed that the working class required visible and disciplined leadership in the form of an avant-garde revolutionary elite of the type provided by Lenin's Bolsheviks. 'For the revolution we need factory workers, organised in a party or at least in a trade union', former KPD leader Ernst Meyer told his wife Rosa Leviné-Meyer in the 1920s. While she remembered 'favour[ing] "the revolutionary unorganised"', he insisted that 'we could not rely on them for any action'.[79]

Our identification of 1905–6 as a critical juncture nonetheless chimes well with recent writing on the global history of twentieth-century revolutions. Caruso, for instance, refers to the appearance of a 'transnational moment of crisis around 1905', during which 'mass rallies and demonstrations established themselves as a new, conflict-laden, emotionalised and medialised form of political participation'.[80] Likewise, Stefan Berger has argued that integrating national and regional case studies of strikes and street protests in the first years of the twentieth century into European-wide and perhaps even global histories of popular opposition to authoritarian regimes can lead to significant new insights.[81] In particular, it can embrace a wide range of at times overlapping and at other times competing transnational impulses, such as demands for social justice, democratization and national self-determination, as well as for international peace, recognition of the rights of racial and sexual minorities, and an end to colonial and economic exploitation across the world.[82] Some of the impulses behind this broad movement for change were distinctly utopian, but utopianism itself did not necessarily rule out extremely practical thinking about everyday matters such as health, housing, education and use/ownership of public space.[83]

Conceptualizing the Great War era as part of a larger revolutionary period from 1905–6 in which crises of sovereignty and representation occurred simultaneously in many parts of the continent is also a useful means of de-centring (North-) Western Europe in narratives both of the Great War era and of women's international and transnational activism. Russian Social Democrat and Anarchist influences were very important in several of the countries discussed in this volume – in Finland and Sweden, but also in Germany and Austria, where many revolutionaries from the 1905 events in Petrograd and Odesa later fled, among them Sonja Lerch, whose story is discussed above and in Chapter 2. Pre-war Switzerland was home to numerous Russian revolutionary exiles, not least revolutionary women, who were able to study for degrees there from the 1870s, much earlier than in other parts of Europe.[84] This followed an earlier movement of French communards to Switzerland after the 'bloody week' (*semaine sanglante*) of May 1871, including the socialist-feminist Paule Mink, who, as the train she was hiding in left France, 'waved to a guard on the French frontier, and shouted, "*Vive la Commune!*"'.[85]

Vienna, Prague and St Petersburg were also sites of significant working-class protest and political unrest in the period up to 1914, with the 'right to the streets' increasingly being contested by working-class women as well as men.[86] During the textile strike in Lawrence, Massachusetts, in 1912, as Ardis Cameron has shown, the demands of the predominantly female and teenage, first-generation immigrant workforce were rooted in the 'convoluted yet ordinary web of female daily life' in the town, rather than the official structures of the syndicalist movement, leading to a special kind of militancy 'formed below the surface of official scrutiny'.[87] According to one highly troubled Lawrence judge, the women who had taken to the streets had 'lots of cunning and also lots of bad temper'.[88]

In Ireland, from at least 1900 onwards, while there were debates and arguments between suffragists, 'many of the more radical nationalist feminists were also socialists'.[89] This was manifest during the lock-out strike in Dublin from August 1913 to January 1914 (also discussed in Chapter 6), when the feminists of the militant IWFL, trade unionists active in the Irish Women Workers' Union (IWWU) and other revolutionary women, many of them inspired by the self-declared feminist and socialist leader James Connolly, co-operated in supporting and feeding the workers, male and female. As Senia Pašeta has shown, between 1910 and 1917 Irish feminists moved 'increasingly in a leftward direction, especially after the Labour Party and a number of trade unions and trade unionists began to openly support women's suffrage while the major Irish parties remained resolutely opposed'.[90]

Violent clashes also took place between male and female strikers and the forces of 'order' in Habsburg Trieste during the general strike in February 1902, Barcelona during the 'tragic week' (*Setmana Tràgica*) in July 1909, and the Emilia-Romagna and Marche regions of Italy during the 'Red Week' (*Settimana*

Figure 1.2 Members of the Irish Women Workers' Union on the steps of Liberty Hall, Dublin, during the lock-out strike of 1913–14. Source: Alamy.

Rossa) of June 1914.⁹¹ All of these developments of course raised fears among the ruling classes, and played no small part in the push for war in 1914 as a 'flight forwards' ('*Flucht nach vorne*') from present intractable political and social conflicts into an imagined glorious national/imperial future in which all enemies, big and small, external and internal, would be forced into submission or slain through total victory on the battlefield.⁹²

The impact of war on women's bodies and the fight back against militarism

Alongside the question of whom revolution is for, and how gendered subjectivities should be represented in historiographies of revolution, we see our volume as an intervention in the debate on the place of violence in the First World War and its aftermath. This is a subject which again has focused largely on men and male actors, whether as regular soldiers, paramilitaries or more loosely organized participants in 'communities of violence'.⁹³ '[P]erpetration of violence was overwhelmingly a male affair', as the editors of one very important anthology on twentieth-century European military and political conflicts put it.⁹⁴ The vulnerability of the male body to wartime trauma, whether of the physical or mental kind, and the cultural meanings attached to this vulnerability has also produced a large volume of literature.⁹⁵ Some veterans' groups have been shown to have developed anti-militarist tendencies in the inter-war years – and to have sought international solidarity with associations of ex-soldiers in other countries.⁹⁶ By contrast, the gender-specific violence that soldiers did to women – for instance in occupied territories – was and is often forgotten, or pushed into the realm of the symbolic and representational rather than the immediate, the bodily and the urgently political.⁹⁷ Only a small number of studies – notably Annette Becker's work on German-occupied northern France – have looked in concrete empirical and situational terms at these forgotten female victims of male wartime violence in the years 1914–18.⁹⁸ Moving beyond the First World War itself, the complexities of women's participation in the Irish revolutionary period (1919–21 and 1922–3) became victim to selective and gendered remembering; their contributions and experiences, and particularly the violence and traumas they suffered were denied, downplayed, overlooked or indeed simply forgotten. However, there has been a shift among gender historians of the revolutionary period, and in recent decades several studies on gendered violence against women have been published.⁹⁹

Other gendered aspects of the extreme physical and developmental harm done to human bodies during the war have waited even longer to be recognized by scholars as political phenomena that were closely entangled with, and directly impacted on, the core questions of sovereignty and democracy. Food scarcity – or what Mary E. Cox calls 'nutritional deprivation' – was a shared experience for many European women and their children in the Great War era, including in neutral countries.[100] The bundle of authoritarian state measures that had begun in 1914 under the heading 'emergency war regime' soon turned into what the Austrian *Arbeiter-Zeitung* (the chief Social Democrat newspaper) described as a 'nutrition regime' (*Ernährungsregime*).[101] While the physical impact on bodies was already evident in 1915–16, the situation grew worse in the last two years of the war. In revolutionary Russia, in Finland, and in the defeated nations of Central Europe, food scarcity was in fact at its worst in the years immediately following the war, with full recovery only evident after 1924. While violence in the sense of mass killing of the enemy (*Tötungsgewalt*) and 'action deliberately aimed at causing physical harm to another' was most intense on the Western front,[102] the violations done to the bodies of women, children and the elderly also had measurable physical, and therefore political, consequences. As Cox shows, tangible 'generational injury' had been inflicted even before the end of the war.[103] In 1917, for example, 'nearly one third to one half of women between twenty and forty years old in [the Saxon city of] Leipzig [in Germany] suffered from CED' (Chronic Energy Deficiency), meaning that they 'were not only unable to engage in normal household activities but also unable to seek employment outside of the home, engage in market activities, or pro-actively search for supplemental calories for their families beyond the government ration'.[104] We touch on this topic again in Chapter 3.

While standard means of measuring and categorizing different levels of Chronic Energy Deficiency in adults and children were not drawn up until much later in the twentieth century, by the United Nations Food and Agricultural Organization and other bodies, and are still prone to variation,[105] the political and historical implications of war capitalism, meaning manufactured food scarcity for the low-paid masses and bigger and bigger profits for the few, were already evident to the German revolutionary Karl Liebknecht by the end of 1915. Several months before his arrest and imprisonment by the Prussian state for anti-militarist activities in May 1916, he used an anonymized article for *Die Jugendinternationale*, the organ of the International Socialist Youth organization, to take up the point that the war, by worsening hunger and exhaustion among the poorest, 'by eliminating and preventing the exchange of ideas [and] by preventing the spread of news, is able to hold back the effect of individual thought and actions, and to control the outcome of processes which in themselves would be expected to excite the masses to the highest degree [against the system]'.[106] To Liebknecht's continued outrage, majority Social Democrat parties and trade union bosses were still in late 1915 supporting their countries' respective war efforts, and thus 'the wholesale military slaughter of the working class for the benefit of Capitalism and absolutism'. But he continued to express confidence in (unorganized) women and young people, who, he suggested, had 'retained [their] internationalist spirit in spite of the general collapse' of the Socialist International in 1914.[107] His work is important because it was an early recognition of what Sheila Rowbotham refers to as 'the significance of specific contexts in shaping the forms and content of protest'. For him during the First World War, just as for Rowbotham in the early 1970s,

> It was evident that women's economic, social and cultural circumstances had changed and changed again over time, and there was no such thing as a universal immutable condition of women.[108]

This volume of essays also shows that socialist women became increasingly visible and active as challengers of militarism, and in particular of the intensified militarization of public spaces and prioritization of military needs in the allocation of scarce resources, as the material and social content of their lives was subject to rapid changes in the period from 1914 to the early 1920s. Not only the content, but also the (largely unorganized) forms of protest they took part in were in constant flux during this time, reflecting the shifting 'relationships between work for wages, domestic labour and family structures'.[109] But rather than taking Liebknecht's pronouncements as the last word on this subject, or even the pronouncements of leading female international socialists like Rosa Luxemburg and Clara Zetkin, we aim instead to uncover the voices of the thousands of unknown and hitherto largely unwritten about working-class women who helped to shape both the form and content of the peaceful and/or violent democratic protest culture of these years, whether within or beyond the bounds of organized left-wing parties and trade unions.

In part, we do so by following the work of social psychologists like Stephen Reicher in seeing the crowd as a purposeful collective with specific and often gendered aims.[110] We also reassess and add a gendered dimension to the transnational impact of political violence in Europe after the end of the First World War. While the histories of revolutionary movements are still written as a male story, we give voice in Chapter 3 to the multiple ways in which women were involved in and impacted by violent events in Finland, Germany, Ireland and Austria. Some women, as the Irish and Finnish cases highlight, were drawn into the wars on their doorsteps, and military service could be a means of empowerment and ensuring a better income. Women were involved in combat, in the auxiliary forces, and were doing clandestine work. This little-known activity needs to be cast alongside the sexualized and gendered violence employed by counter-revolutionary (and sometimes revolutionary) forces to target socialist women and their sexual and bodily integrity – a phenomenon that has received much more scholarly attention, albeit often as an addendum to male-on-male post-war fighting and bloodshed.[111]

Biographies, networks and life trajectories

Just as women's war with the militarism and patriarchal world around them did not begin in 1914, or end in 1918, for many socialist women, the fight for a better world continued for the rest of their lives. They maintained the struggle for better working conditions, education, health care, and political power, and for some, as right-wing forces seized control in authoritarian movements across Europe, they fought for the right to exist. Many of the women whose life trajectories are explored in Chapter 5 led transnational lives, traversing geographical boundaries in pursuit of their vision, or escaping persecution. The revolution could not be contained, and neither could they as they persisted in their revolutionary activism wherever they found themselves. By examining their biographies, their beliefs and the longevity of their convictions come to the fore, challenging Leninist party apparatchiks such as Martha Arendsee (quoted above) and many male labour historians who have criticized and continue to criticize their activism as spontaneous and purely driven by the immediate and the irrational.

The impetus that had led them to socialist causes in the revolutionary moment in the latter stages of the First World War placed them in a perpetual state of opposition and defiance against the regimes that sought to exclude them. It is only through examining their later life trajectories that we can understand their motivations, aims and experiences. Their oppositional stances brought them into resistance movements and into danger, often resulting in exile or imprisonment, as the women found new ways to continue to live by their values under very difficult circumstances. Many women joined a variety of resistance movements, fighting capitalism, fascism, Stalinism and war, and we can see how they were central to these movements through their underground activities but also through supporting their comrades. For some of the women discussed in Chapter 5, this work would also lead to their deaths as they sacrificed everything to the struggle.

Alongside more violent resistance activity, transnational networks of the labour movement had to be and were reconfigured after the First World War. Social democrats and communists met under the new auspices of international politics. The first International Congress of Working Women (ICWW), for example, took place in Washington, DC, USA, from 28 October to 6 November 1919 upon invitation of the American Women's Trade Union League (WTUL) at the same time as the International Labour Conference. Twenty-eight official delegates were mandated to represent particular organizations, and more than two hundred women in total attended the congress. Women from neutral or Allied states (and almost only from Europe) were invited, but not representatives from revolutionary Russia or the defeated Central Powers. However, among the official delegates were women from the successor states to the defeated imperial powers of Germany and Austria-Hungary, such as Poland and Czechoslovakia. One of them was the Czech socialist Marie Majerová, who, together with her comrade Luisa Landová-Štychová, proposed a revolutionary reorganization of women's position in the labour market, including the socialization of domestic work.[112] The International Federation of Working Women, which was founded by the ICWW, held two more conferences (1921 in Geneva, and 1923 in Vienna) before being dissolved. Social democrat women dedicated to improving women's labour rights nonetheless continued to network internationally, for example in the women's committee of the International Federation of Trade Unions (IFTU), which held its first congress in 1924 in Vienna. Here the Austrian social democrat and trade unionist Anna Boschek was an important figure.[113] Revolutionary communists organized themselves separately. They participated in the International Conferences of Communist Women, where Austrian Anna Hornik-Strömer was a key player,[114] or in the Red International of Labour Unions (RILU or Profintern), which held its founding congress in Moscow in summer 1921.[115]

Those who opposed these individual activists and networks endeavoured to silence them, erasing their work from the historical records or creating conditions that made it impossible for them to exist openly or speak plainly. Yet, by reading against the grain, evidence of women's ongoing activism is visible. Chapter 5 is by no means a comprehensive examination of all biographies and networks, but it presents some key examples to highlight the possibilities of this type of research and indicates new directions that it can take. To reclaim these women's biographies and networks is to challenge their erasure and to recognize their role in twentieth-century struggles to build a better world.

Commemorating revolution, commemorating women

In much of the one hundred years since these revolutionary moments, academic works, mainstream scholarship, remembrance ceremonies, commemorative statues and events, museum exhibitions and other sites of memory have focused almost exclusively on the male experience. In looking at the transnational commemorative landscape from 2012–21, the predominant events have been those which commemorated the First World War, 1914–18, and the Russian Revolution of 1917. For those European countries impacted, to a greater or lesser degree, by this war, the memory of the 'lost generation' remains powerful.[116] The narratives of high politics and war, and of the soldier who went to the front, who fought for his country, who died far from his home, who returned home injured, remains powerful whereas in this 'theatre of memory', women are tenuous shadows. The traditional historical narrative does not leave them much space, specifically insofar as it favours the public arena – politics, war – where they barely seem to appear'.[117] However, this emphasis on the glory, drama, trauma and sacrifice of the First World War and Russian Revolution masks the many smaller yet impactful revolutionary moments which occurred throughout Europe at this time.

Acts of collective remembrance are gendered, and we have to remain aware of why, what, how, and for whom commemoration occurs. It is also the case, however, that commemorative practices do not remain static; they shift, change and adapt to the changing political and/or cultural demands of societies and communities. Thus, as memory scholar Oona Frawley notes, it is important always to consider

> what stories are we telling ourselves? Who is doing the telling and who is included in those stories? Conversely, who is not speaking and who is excluded? How ... is the past being narrated to us – and which 'us' is being addressed? What audience have these stories found and reached, and what are their courses? What forms of narration are being deployed, and in what forums? And, crucially, what are the social contexts into which these narrations are inserted?[118]

The development of the discipline of gender history and the influence of second wave feminism have, over the past five or more decades, demanded a corrective to male-centric narratives and commemorations, albeit unevenly throughout Europe. Telling the stories of women's involvement in war and revolution often began through recovery projects, driven by a desire to shine a light on those female activists 'hidden from history'.[119] Feminists, and increasingly, academic scholars began to tell those stories of suffrage, socialist and militant women. However, these early histories, more often than not, delivered a focus on liberal, middle-class, educated, political women – to the exclusion of the narratives of working-class women. In many ways, scholarship on the experience of women in war and revolution centred on the domestic, on motherhood, on mourning or suffering and trauma. Women's experience of war work, for example, was only examined later, particularly the experience of working-class women.[120]

The question remains: has who and how we commemorate changed over the past hundred years, and if so why and how? In Chapter 6, using case studies from Ireland, the UK, Germany and Finland, we seek to explore what stories are now being told, by whom, in what way, in what forums and what contexts, during the centenaries of these revolutionary moments. What has the impact of five or six decades of gender history scholarship, of feminist activism, and of intersecting understandings of class histories been? What are the important stories we now tell ourselves, about ourselves, in the twenty-first century? Can commemorative practices be said to have become more inclusive of women, and if not, why not?

Feminist methodology: curious conversations

Gender-aware approaches to history include methods as well as aims and questions, and the process, the 'how', is as important as the end-product. The research methods we used to produce this book embrace feminist methodologies inspired by Cynthia Enloe's concept of feminist curiosity, which entails paying close attention to women's lives, especially those operating at the margins, to see how ideas about gender inform power relations.[121] Enloe's approach asks us to be 'on guard against treating all men or all women as homogeneous – in their ideas, actions or their experiences'. This is because such an approach 'is certain to produce unreliable analyses'.[122] She also urges us to resist uncritically adopting terms and definitions that cannot adequately capture the lived experience of historical agents, in particular marginalizing and erasing women's realities.[123] One characteristic of feminist methodologies is their ability to overcome the dichotomous and hierarchical thinking inherent in either-or positions and instead embrace complexity. Thus we do not need to decide whether women won the vote as a result of the revolution or because of decades of campaigning, or whether socialist and liberal-progressive women worked together or remained firmly apart. Our findings show that both statements can be true: while the separation in terms of priorities, methods and experience of protest is very real, there were areas and times in which the women worked together and made common cause.

Above all, we have embraced Enloe's concept of collaborative work across disciplinary and national boundaries and employed the model of the conversation both to identify the themes of our study and to reflect on their significance.[124] This has informed our approach to the historical sources we have used, bringing a consciously sceptical curiosity to see what is hidden and omitted from contemporaneous accounts and asking what this reveals about normative gender discourse in the past and the present, and pre-conceptions about the nature and scope of revolutionary activism. It has also informed our approach to sharing our scholarship and bringing different areas, as well as levels of expertise and knowledge, into conversation with one another in order to create knowledge in an inclusive and collaborative way. In particular, the practice of listening with an open-minded willingness to revise our views in response to new perspectives and examples – and 'a readiness to be surprised'[125] is embedded in each of the subsequent chapters of the book. While the lead and named authors have been central to structuring and shaping particular chapters, each of the themes has benefitted from the intellectual generosity of the collective in challenging, critiquing and expanding the arguments put forward. In this way, the final versions are a product of debate, discussion and compromise and represent a development in our individual as well as collective thinking. While the chapters on protest and strikes, violence, suffrage, life trajectories and commemoration can be read as stand-alone units, they are also in dialogue with one another and contribute to the internal coherence of the volume as a whole.

The study is not intended to be comprehensive and there is further scope for bringing scholars into conversation about the gender dynamics of revolutions both outside and within Europe, incorporating revolutionary activism in India, China and Egypt,[126] or looking in more detail at the experiences of socialist women in Eastern, Central and Western European states not included in this volume. However, by integrating scholarship from different national contexts and diverse disciplinary traditions into productive and open-minded conversation using a gender lens, we have been able to uncover commonalities and identify thematic links and connections between the socialist women who are our subjects. Above all, it is the anomalies, the complexities and curiosity about the things that do not fit that have prompted us to look very carefully at the diversity of women's experiences of revolution in the period 1914 to 1921. Taking account of and indeed centring the stories and the fluid and shifting subjectivities of the women in revolutionary contexts as messy as post-war Hungary, Yugoslavia, Finland and Ireland has allowed us to see the scope for both tension and cooperation in how socialist women interacted, to challenge ideas about the periphery and the centre, and to think more critically about who or what is relevant to the study of revolution. In this way, we have been able to move beyond a master narrative that legitimizes one version of Socialism or revolution over another, to look beyond constraining scripts and narrow definitions, and to ask instead what the lived experience, political subjectivities and recorded actions of socialist women can tell us about the nature of revolution in early twentieth-century Europe.

2

Socialist Women and 'Urban Space': Protest, Strikes and Anti-Militarism, 1914–18

Matthew Stibbe, Anna Hammerin, Katharina Hermann and Ali Ronan

'The revolution has a female face'. So reads the title of a book originally written in Russian and first published in 2021 in German translation by Olga Shparaga, a former philosophy lecturer at the European College of Liberal Arts in Minsk. Now a Vilnius-based activist and educational spokesperson for the Belarusian coordination council led by exiled former presidential candidate Sviatlana Tsikhanouskaya, Shparaga presents a feminist reading of her country's recent history of strikes and protests. For her, the demonstrations in Minsk and other Belarusian cities following the falsified presidential elections in August 2020 represent a 'revolution in progress' in which women have played and continue to play a 'central role':

> On 12 August, after three days of post-election terror unleashed by the [Lukashenko] regime against the peaceful marchers, they formed their first chain of solidarity … [They] led Belarusian society out of its paralysis and initiated the large-scale demonstrations in the weeks that followed. To this day they take part in the dissidents' protests, assert the right to a political voice, and insist that the link between state violence and domestic violence be recognised.[1]

This chapter argues that the European-wide food protests, strikes and anti-militarist demonstrations that preceded and accompanied the revolutions in Russia in 1917 and Central Europe in 1918–19 also had a female face, one, moreover, that is perfectly visible if one knows how and where to look and is sufficiently motivated to do so. It is not an attempt to essentialize these revolutions as female, to the exclusion of men and male actors. Nor is it an attempt to deny the role of class in explaining wartime strikes and protests, and in shaping the cultural meanings ascribed to them by contemporaries. It is, however, intended as a counter-narrative to mainstream accounts which tend to be based solely on male scripts and subjectivities, and then, uncritically, to universalize from the particular. It also seeks to challenge scholarship that, either by default or by design, has gendered the revolutions that ended the First World War as male first and foremost.[2]

In what follows, we establish a countervailing method for uncovering the voices of European women protestors, strikers and anti-militarists during the years 1914 to 1918 which involves placing particular emphasis on the 'small-scale', the 'everyday', the 'non-hierarchical' and the 'innovative'. We are influenced here by the 'spatial turn' in recent histories of social movements, particularly German historian Julian Aulke's study of urban spaces in the German Revolution from November 1918.[3] As Aulke shows, spatialization of protest and conflict can be an especially useful way of bringing to light voices of people who are usually dismissed as 'unpolitical' and placing them at the heart of narratives of revolution. This can also be applied to the pre-revolutionary period before 1917–18. According to Aulke, 'it is especially the time around the beginning of the 20th century, with its high point in the revolutionary era, when the masses, located in the public space of the streets and squares, begin to identify with the rapid dynamism and new qualitative dimension' of politics beyond established parliamentary parties and trade unions.[4] In this chapter, we aim to recapture some of the hitherto overlooked 'dynamism' inherent in socialist women's experiences of the spatial dimensions of wartime protest.

One particular aspect of wartime protests that has been largely neglected in the previous scholarship is the close ties of solidarity between working-class women and teenagers of both sexes, all of whom were increasingly visible in public spaces. True, in his famous 1907 pamphlet *Militarism and Anti-Militarism*, which was translated into several languages before the war, the German revolutionary Karl Liebknecht had already claimed: 'He who has the youth has the army.'[5] This was a reference first to fears that under Prussian state-of-siege legislation, the military could be called out in a peacetime strike-breaking capacity, and second to hopes that young working-class soldiers might refuse to perform such a role if the anti-militarist propaganda of the social democratic Left could reach them first. But in 1914–15, as even Liebknecht was forced to concede, the military all over Europe had been surprisingly successful in mobilizing most seventeen- to twenty-one-year-old men into the armed forces, and whisking hundreds and thousands of them away to war, including tens of thousands to their deaths. Particularly after 1916, as we will show, it was the thirteen- to sixteen-year-olds and their mothers who were now in the vanguard of national and cross-border struggles against *wartime* militarism.[6]

More generally, we are interested in the new informal alliances that socialist women formed across the 1914–18 period, and deliberately foreground these over the emphasis in many other studies on formal (and often pre-existing) local, national and transnational networks.[7] The Marxist urban geographer Edward W. Soja has written that urban streets are the 'vulnerable point' in the capitalist system, a space that can bring together 'landless peasants, proletarianized petty bourgeoisies, women, students, racial minorities, as well as the working class itself'.[8] However, we will argue that a gendered and historical perspective can add to this by recognizing urban spaces as points of vulnerability for masculine tropes about the need for 'order', 'discipline', 'hierarchy' and vertically structured forms of solidarity only. We illustrate this by focusing on four case studies: Germany (including the German-speaking parts of Habsburg Austria), Britain, Sweden and Switzerland. Germany, Austria-Hungary and Britain were of course belligerents from August 1914 onwards, while the other two countries remained neutral throughout the period under review. However, what all of these different cases have in common is that the framework for political protest had to take place in the context of a war-induced state of emergency, understood both in narrowly legal terms – the suspension of key civil rights such as freedom of speech, association and assembly under state-of-siege laws and wartime defence regulations – and in a discursive sense. Indeed, while for men, the wartime 'emergency' was often understood in abstract terms, as a matter of mobilization and related labour shortages, conscription, falling birth and rising death rates, requisitioning, economic planning and so on, for women and children, it increasingly came to be about something more immediate – having enough food to eat on a daily basis and daring to hope for peace while knowing that the real enemy, death or life-changing illness through 'severe nutritional deprivation', industrial accidents or lack of fuel and medicines, was advancing ever closer to their, and their children's, doors.[9] In Germany alone, as one recent study reveals, 'between 1914 and 1917 the accident rate ... for wage-earning women tripled and for minors doubled', while 'the accident rate for men actually declined'. This reflected 'the failure to train women and juvenile workers with no experience in the production of metal and chemicals' and the fact that men already 'had some experience of this type of work'. And yet

> In many cases the women themselves chose the most dangerous jobs because they paid better. Women also often preferred night shifts because they left free time during the day to stand in food lines with their families.[10]

Two other considerations shape our approach to socialist women's history in the chapter. First, although protests and strikes grew in intensity in the last two years of the war, we begin in the winter of 1914–15 because this is when urban working-class women first began to demonstrate their potential to spearhead opposition to war outside of formal hierarchies, particularly, but not only, as Ute Daniel argues, in the German case.[11] The link between more famous personalities in the already well-networked international socialist women's movement – such as Clara Zetkin, Alexandra Kollontai and Margaret Bondfield – and the now barely remembered female activists who engaged in underground activities or street protests in favour of peace will be laid out in the first section of the chapter, on the March 1915 Bern conference and the run-up to it. However, in the remaining three sections – on protests, strikes and anti-militarism – the largely anonymous and forgotten female activists of urban and suburban neighbourhoods will be at the centre of our analysis. Their voices, in other words, will provide the foundation for our argument in favour of a new, de-hierarchized understanding of protest during wartime. In particular, we are interested in highlighting the potential that anti-war protests brought for new types of solidarity beyond the centre – between peace campaigners, women munition workers, army deserters, fatherless teenagers, disabled ex-soldiers, missing foreign persons and POWs stranded thousands of miles away from home. These solidarities in turn called forth new ways of envisaging what a just society might look like.

Secondly, in choosing to focus on examples of urban protest drawn from neutral as well as belligerent countries, we are conscious that we are making a contribution to the urban history of the Great War more generally.[12] As Pierre Purseigle has noted in a recent essay, understanding how cities and their predominantly civilian populations experienced the years 1914 to 1918 requires us to 'pay particular attention to the geography of belligerence'.[13] However, in addition we would contend that a feminist approach to urban geographies of war forces us to rethink the historical and gendered meaning of the term 'belligerence' and the related concepts 'militarism' and 'anti-militarism', in order to embrace territorial spaces that, while neutral or at least not *at war* in official terms, were still involved, at state and international levels, in the (co)-construction of military norms and in the accompanying reproduction of material and social relations. As we shall see below, this also made urban and suburban landscapes in Switzerland and Sweden far from neutral spaces when it came to the gendered politics of wartime protest and the articulation of new solidarities among, between and beyond socialist women activists.

The International Socialist Women's Conference in Bern and the Bern Peace Manifesto

European-wide socialist opposition to the First World War can be traced back to the International Socialist Women's Conference that took place in the Swiss capital Bern from 26 to 28 March 1915. Only around twenty-five delegates were able to attend this event: seven from Germany, six from Russia, four from England, three from the Netherlands, two from Switzerland and one each from France, Italy and Poland.[14] Most of them came as private individuals, without a mandate from their respective national organizations. However, Clara Zetkin, the conference's chief instigator and chair of the women's section of the now defunct Second International, enjoyed the backing of the 'Gruppe Internationale', a revolutionary opposition group within the German Social Democratic Party (SPD) led from September 1914 by Karl Liebknecht, Rosa Luxemburg, Leo Jogiches and Franz Mehring. They encouraged her to establish contact with like-minded activists in other European countries. For instance, with their knowledge, she sought out links with the Swedish Social Democrat women's leader Anna Lindhagen, a city councillor in Stockholm and editor of the journal *Morgonbris* (Morning Breeze). The latter took a firm anti-war stand and in December 1914 published an appeal by Zetkin – first written in November 1914 – for women of all countries to oppose the war and campaign for an immediate peace without annexations.[15]

Zetkin also responded positively to a call from female anti-war socialists in Britain in January 1915 for cross-border contacts to re-establish peace and made a trip to Amsterdam in February–March 1915 where she met members of the Dutch section of the Socialist Women's International (SWI), including Mathilde Wibaut and Henriette Roland-Holst.[16] A January 1915 'Open Letter to the Women of Germany and Austria' was signed by 180 British female anti-war activists, including representatives of the British Section of the SWI, among them Independent Labour Party (ILP) members Margaret Bondfield, Marion Phillips and Ada Salter. The latter also made sure it appeared in the ILP newspaper *Labour Leader*, edited by the pacifist and No-Conscription Fellowship (NCF) founder Fenner Brockway. Together with Mary Longman, secretary of the British section of the SWI, Bondfield, Phillips and Salter attended the March 1915 Bern conference, where they represented the anti-war ILP, the Women's Labour League and women trade unionists.[17]

Zetkin's choice of the Swiss capital as the venue for this conference was no accident. Although Switzerland was not a belligerent nation, the outbreak of war had diverse impacts on its society and politics. As a neutral country in the centre of Europe, it was an important refuge for deserters and draft-dodgers and attracted pacifists and socialists from all over the continent. Indeed, Lenin and Nadeschda Krupskaja, Inessa Armand, Willi Münzenberg, Angelica Balabanova and others spent some years in Switzerland during the war.[18] There was also a home-grown anti-war movement with especially strong links to Germany. Thus extracts from Zetkin's November 1914 appeal to socialist women of all countries to position themselves against the war was first published on 1 December 1914 in the Swiss Social Democrat women's newssheet *Die Vorkämpferin* (*The Female Pioneer*), its German equivalent, *Die Gleichheit* (Equality), being unable to print it at all due to censorship restrictions.[19] Shortly thereafter, it was published in full in the *Berner Tagewacht*, a Swiss daily newspaper which was then still available for purchase in Germany.[20] Meanwhile, *Die Vorkämpferin*, taking advantage of the lack of pre-publication censorship in Switzerland, sponsored a number of women's peace assemblies in the winter of 1914–15. After an anti-war demonstration in Zurich on 18 December 1914, it reported that as well as large numbers of men, 'over one thousand women' had taken part.[21] Another demonstration, held in March 1915 under the slogan 'Girls! Boys! Join the Free

Figure 2.1 Anti-war demonstration on the Quaibrücke in Zurich, March 1915. Willi Münzenberg (wearing a flat cap) is standing directly in front of the banner which reads: 'Girls! Boys! Join the Free Youth'. Reproduced with permission of the Schweizerisches Sozialarchiv, Zurich, Switzerland.

Youth' and organized by the then leader of the Swiss Socialist Youth, Willi Münzenberg, inspired Zetkin to call for similar action to revive the SWI on an anti-war basis.[22] This was the background to the deliberations at Bern at the end of March 1915.

Most accounts of the Bern conference focus on the split that emerged between a 'pacifist' majority of twenty-one led by Zetkin and a radical, proto-Bolshevik minority of six led by Inessa Armand, which consisted of five of the six Russian delegates and the one delegate representing Poland.[23] The majority resolution put forward at the conference called on all 'women of the working classes' to unite in opposition to the war and in solidarity with their husbands and sons conscripted into the opposing armies. At the behest of the British delegation, it also announced that the SWI, 'notwithstanding the fundamental differences in the socialist and bourgeois conceptions of the peace question, expresses [its] sympathy with non-socialist friends of peace and in particular with the forthcoming International Women's Peace Congress in The Hague'.[24] By seeking to amend the majority 'pacifist' resolution and instead calling for a 'class against class' policy – in other words, a policy of encouraging armed proletarian uprisings across Europe in order to seize control of all governments on behalf of the working class – Armand is said to have anticipated the position adopted by Lenin and the so-called Zimmerwald Left in September 1915.[25] From this point of view, the Bern conference was a 'lost opportunity to have taken the first step towards the creation of a Third International'.[26] It may have been the 'first platform of the international anti-war movement', but in no way could it be regarded as being on a par with the manifesto of the Zimmerwald Left, because there were 'too many [ideological] inconsistencies attached to it'.[27]

The debate over whether the resolutions passed at Bern were truly socialist or not, in other words whether they paved the way for a decisive break on the part of the international socialist women's movement with pre-war Social Democracy and a shift towards Communist internationalism, or whether that break had to wait until the Zimmerwald meeting in September 1915, or later still to the founding of the Comintern in Moscow in March 1919, only gets us so far, however. In particular, it obscures two other important features of the Bern conference: first, its anti-capitalist thrust, and second, its specific appeal to proletarian women to fight for an end to the 'murderous' conditions not only in the trenches, but also on the home fronts, and to build new local, national and transnational networks to support this. A motion by the British delegation, which was translated into one of the conference's main resolutions, criticized what it claimed was the endeavour of individual capitalists and capitalist groups to drive up the prices of the necessities of life and of the entire army and navy, to depress wages and to worsen working conditions in general, but especially to worsen the exploitation of women and children. Against such practices ... the working people should fight with all determination regardless of the domestic political truce [in their respective countries] ... In all nations, the behaviour of capitalists stands in blatant contradiction to the lip service they pay to patriotism ... [In practice] they represent an international fraternity of profit-hunters.[28]

The image of the war presented here was, on the one hand, of an all-encompassing conflict that suited the interests of capitalists and arms manufacturers in every European country, not just belligerents, and conflicted with the interests of workers everywhere. On the other hand, it was also a view from the edges, laying bare the suffering caused by the war on a smaller scale, particularly as it affected women and children, and channelling the possibility of protest into the specific, the immediate and the everyday. As Toni Sender, one of the German delegates at Bern and a future Social Democratic Reichstag (parliamentary) deputy for the city of Frankfurt am Main, put it, the war had to be stopped and sovereignty

Figure 2.2 Women working in an arms factory, c. 1917, place unknown, Germany. Source: Alamy.

renegotiated for the sake of 'the wives of soldiers'. By this she meant the working-class women whose 'loved ones were in the trenches' and who, by 1915, were often faced with the choice of hunger/'near famine' for themselves and their children or 'working in munitions factories', in other words for the capitalist war machine.[29]

And what Sender said of Frankfurt is also confirmed in Sean Dobson's study of another German city, Leipzig, where, from 1915 onwards,

> the mortality of young women increased much more quickly than that of other groups, probably as a result of their high accident rate on the job, the fact that they had to work long hours while also caring for a family, (often without a man's wage), and their propensity to deny themselves food in favor of their children.[30]

Socialist women and anti-war protest

The delegates at Bern, and those who helped to distribute the conference's final Manifesto in flysheet form, understood that the domestic economic bargaining that fuelled the continuation of the fighting after the winter of 1914–15 had also made it harder to see the war from the (male-defined) centre of mainstream labour movements as a capitalist war fought against the material interests of the working class. More specifically, some skilled working men, especially in the metal industries, were paid higher wages (while being offered conditional exemptions from military service) in return for their loyal support for their country's war effort. Some working-class women also got better-paid jobs, at least in comparison with the kinds of employment they might have been in before 1914, although they were rarely paid the same rate as men for performing the same tasks.[31] Their bureaucratically organized and easily hoodwinked trade unions had joined majority Social Democrat party groupings in national parliaments in expressing cautious support for the war (or, in neutral countries, for emergency economic and mobilization measures). This meant, among other things, agreeing not to call strikes for the duration of the fighting. Many socialist women indeed abandoned their pre-war internationalism in 1914 and opted to support their nations' respective war efforts, arguing, among other things, that this would allow female workers to find their own political 'space' and social recognition as crucial members of the organized labour movement. Henriette Fürth, for instance, a pro-war Social Democrat activist in Frankfurt am Main, wrote in 1917:

We abhor war now as we have done in the past ... but we nevertheless give our sanction to the battle that has been forced upon us ... and are prepared ... to sacrifice all we possess, our body and soul, until the very last drop of blood has been spilt, so that ours will be a victory, a final victory bringing a peace in which Germany will bring to all the blessings of a civilisation and culture worthy of mankind.[32]

In the meantime, the poorest-paid and least unionized women – whether their menfolk were fighting and dying at the front or working long hours on the home front or both – were in the best position to see how higher prices, the no-strike policy and depressed wages for the majority were actually making the workers worse off, while allowing the war to continue indefinitely.

Those who did participate in anti-war protests after 1914 typically had some prior experience of class struggles, albeit less through the socialist parties and unions organized by men and more through community-based forms of confrontation with authority.[33] During the war, this also made them well-placed to experience feelings of solidarity with teenagers, war cripples and soldiers unwilling to go back to war after periods of leave, as well as enemy POWs.[34] Those women who stayed working in the traditionally female-dominated textile industry instead of moving into munitions, for instance, in parts of Saxony,

Figure 2.3 Women and children queuing for bread in First World War Vienna, exact date unknown. Source: Archiv der Bundespolizeidirektion Wien/Vienna.

Greater Vienna or Lancashire, 'did not share in the general improvement in women's wages and were badly hit by war-time inflation'.[35] This, together with the 'endless lines for food, hyperexploitation at work, hungry children and loved ones in danger at the front' or, in neutral countries, mobilized to defend the nation's borders, all bred a particular resentment among working-class women towards militarism and the soldierly and civilian elites who profited from it.[36]

This was one reality. Political persecution by the army and the state was another. After the winter of 1914–15, socialist women risked arrest if they involved themselves in anti-war or anti-militarist activities, and especially if they tried to establish contact with deserters in hiding or revolutionary groups in exile abroad. In Britain, for instance, this is what happened to members of the No-Conscription Fellowship, originally formed to oppose the introduction of compulsory military service into Britain, but from 1916 forced also to defend individual conscientious objectors threatened with jail after refusing to obey the new mandatory call-up.[37] As more and more pacifist men went to prison or into hiding, women assumed much of the campaigning work. Joan Beauchamp, for instance, who worked for the NCF and went on to become a founder member of the Communist Party of Great Britain (CPGB), and her fellow NCF members Violet Tillard and Lydia Smith were all prosecuted and the first two imprisoned towards the end of the war for publishing anti-war material, for failing to reveal the whereabouts of NCF printing presses and/or for refusing to pay fines.[38] Similar things happened to the eighteen-year-old socialist and anti-militarist Bertha Volk, a Swiss-born German national who was arrested in 1918 and sentenced to a six-month period of imprisonment followed by expulsion from Switzerland after distributing literature calling on Swiss soldiers not to shoot at strikers;[39] to the London-based anarchist Lilian Wolfe, imprisoned in 1916 alongside her partner Tom Keell for 'printing a leaflet against the war';[40] and to Florence Exten-Hann, a working-class anti-war activist and secretary of the South-East branch of the NCF, whose house was raided as late as 1919 'by police ... collecting information on "subversives"'.[41] The militarist system was certainly not on the side of proletarian women or those who campaigned alongside them to mobilize protest from the margins.

Beyond the world of illicit printing and campaigns against conscription, food riots were the principal arena in which anti-war sentiment began to take shape. They first appeared in major urban conurbations of continental Europe in autumn 1915 and grew in number and intensity as the war continued, even reaching the American cities of New York, Boston and Philadelphia in 1917.[42] They also brought home to independently organized women what Klaus

Weinhauer refers to as the 'power of localization', in other words the ability of micro-level protests to challenge state authority indirectly by encouraging previously marginalized actors to engage actively in the (re)ordering not only of 'food distribution' but of the related urban-political categories of 'space, time, experience and expectation'.[43] Although the police sometimes sympathized with the 'demands' and 'rightful concerns' of the adult women present, the appearance of young protesters of both sexes at street demonstrations typically made them more prone to use violence.[44] Following disturbances in Leipzig in May 1916, for instance, the local police called in the reserve army and issued an order banning all under-eighteens from gathering in the streets after 8pm, even though they were aware that the protests had been started by housewives in response to escalating shortages and food prices.[45] The events escalated into the police resorting to the sharp ends of their sabres, followed by press reports blaming the male teenagers for the police's 'upsetting abuse of older women and young girls'.[46]

Such 'objectifying' of working-class adolescents as 'wayward' troublemakers in fact brought young people and women food protesters closer together in a 'quest for [the rearrangement of] local order'.[47] Because in warring and even in some neutral countries, censorship measures meant that the local press was banned from reporting on events such as these, working-class women were also suddenly confronted with the immediate injustice of their teenage children being accused of having caused mayhem and physical damage through rioting, when in fact much of the rampaging was done by the police and military. In the aftermath of the Leipzig food riots, for instance, 106 minors, but only eighteen adults, were prosecuted after being arrested for public order offences by the police.[48] Censorship, meanwhile, became a personal, communal and family issue, as proletarian women, foreign POWs and war-weary soldiers on leave were brought closer together politically by the growing mistrust that all had for what was reported in the newspapers about teenagers at home and 'the situation at the front and in the army'.[49]

Under wartime emergency regulations, all forms of protest had to be organized carefully to prevent the police from being able to trace them back to the source. Simply being suspected of helping to distribute anti-war pamphlets, or of arranging for them to be published abroad, could lead to non-judicial arrest and detention.[50] It was also tiring and dangerous, as the work of distribution in urban areas usually had to be 'started each day after sunset' and was typically carried out by women walking the streets alone, irrespective of considerations of personal safety.[51] In Stockholm and other cities in neutral Sweden like

Norrköping, Gothenburg and Malmö, many of the women who came out in support of the localized hunger protests in spring 1917 complained of being manhandled and threatened by the police. Worse still was the threat of being *byråskriven* ('bureau-written' or entered onto the register of the national bureau for prostitutes), for a woman registered as a prostitute was forced to endure physical examinations twice per week and to accept limitations on her freedom of movement.[52] Furthermore, to be bureau-written meant to be 'dead to one's family'.[53]

In Berlin, several of the female Young Socialists detained on suspicion of disseminating banned anti-war literature were also accused of prostitution and/ or were held in 'protective custody' at Police Headquarters on Alexanderplatz alongside 'wayward' teenage girls arrested for 'soliciting'.[54] They were assumed to have been morally as well as politically misled and therefore faced a kind of 'double jeopardy' – as young women *and* as socialists – to which their male counterparts were not exposed. Yet illegally distributing leaflets or engaging in food protests symbolized more than a willingness to risk imprisonment, if that is what it came to. It was also about asserting one's physical and bodily presence in the (nocturnal) urban landscape and reclaiming it as political 'space' that belonged to women as much as men.[55]

This was especially important as, alongside state repression, women campaigners on the anti-war left also had to contend with the indifference and sometimes even the active hostility of men within the ranks of mainstream Social Democratic parties and trade unions. In part this was a hangover from ideological battles between left and right in the last decade before the outbreak of war, when conservative voices had used scare-mongering tropes such as 'strike terrorism' and 'disorderliness' to delegitimize labour protest and reinforce calls for state/ military intervention against 'unruly' or 'unpatriotic' trade unions. In response, as Amerigo Caruso has shown, the organized labour movement itself took up slogans like 'order' and 'discipline' in part as a 'defensive gesture against the [conservative] discourse about the irrationality of the masses'.[56] The war, however, and the decision by most Social Democratic parties to prioritize national defence over international solidarity, sharpened this tendency considerably, and made its gendered aspects more visible. Sophie Ennenbach, a senior functionary in the SPD in Frankfurt am Main since 1909 (and close collaborator of Toni Sender), remembered that after she refused to give information to the police about who might be responsible for the local distribution of flysheets containing the Bern Peace Manifesto, she was accused by male party leaders of bringing the party and its patriotic pro-war policy into disrepute:

In general, it was now hardly possible to have a personal conversation with a great number of party comrades without them losing all self-control. One forgot all friendliness, all courtesy and – only cursed the revolutionaries [*die Revoluzzer*]. On the other hand, it was equally unpleasant to hear the political tirades coming each day from the mouths of the press in their lead articles. All of this drove us to secretly get together with all the women who were trying to find a way out of all the horror.[57]

Ennenbach, Sender and other anti-war socialist women were eventually forced out of the Frankfurt SPD and into the Independent Social Democratic Party (USPD), founded in 1917.[58] But even before then, the fact that attempts were being made by the party to pressure them into silence meant that they had to organize and meet separately from the pro-war majority, a situation faced by many other anti-war leftists across Europe during this period.[59] Indeed, the situation in Frankfurt was probably more typical of the European-wide scene than that in Berlin, where the anti-war left was better organized and had already taken control of many of the local Social Democrat associations by early 1916.[60] A leading role here was played by socialist women from the German capital, including four who had travelled to Bern in March 1915: Martha Arendsee, Käthe Duncker, Agnes Fahrenwald and Margarete Wengels.[61]

In Frankfurt, one solution, which reflected Ennenbach's pre-war experience of organizing educational work among proletarian housewives and domestic servants, was to focus agitation on quite specific local issues, including industrial accidents in the city's munitions factories where women were employed in increasing numbers:

Who could forget the women with the sulphur-yellow, emaciated faces who … had survived an explosion in the munitions factory, how it would have rained torn-off arms and other parts of the body as the deadly pressure hurled upwards [seconds] before? And yet so many women willingly worked 'in the munitions' because at least it meant they 'earned something'.[62]

Female socialist anti-war activists also sought to show their solidarity with women food protestors gathered at major markets. In Switzerland, for instance, the war led to increasing inflation and shortages of essential goods. The country was highly dependent on food and fuel imports, and these were significantly disrupted by the Allied economic blockade of the Central Powers and counter-measures taken by Germany and Austria. Unemployment, especially in the first years of the war, and the missing salary of the men who were recruited for military service led to financial problems for working-class households. As the war continued, increasing numbers of middle-class families needed support too.[63] In 1914, 220,000 Swiss men were mobilized to defend the country's borders. Soon thereafter, the number of soldiers on active duty began to decline, reaching a low point of 38,000 in November 1916,[64] but significant numbers of men were still called up for several months' service in any given year. At that time, there were no family separation allowances and the jobs of these men were not secure.[65] The women left behind therefore had to shoulder a multiple workload to support their families while earning on average only 59 per cent of the salary of a male worker (and even less in female-identified industries like textiles, now in decline due to the war's disruption of traditional markets and supplies of raw materials from overseas).[66] These were the problems that brought the women to take to the streets. Indeed, working-class Swiss women, like their counterparts in Germany, Austria and Sweden, were far more likely to take part in outdoor protests against the continuation of the war and against local actions by military commanders and the police than they were in events to promote female suffrage.[67]

Cooperation between socialist women, suffragists and youth campaigners

Middle-class women dominated national suffrage societies in all of the countries under consideration in this chapter, but after 1915, they too could also be mobilized to challenge the police brutality and sexual double-standards that characterized military rule, bringing them into contact with socialist women.[68] One example is the petition launched by the *Verein Frauenwohl Groß-Berlins* (Women's Welfare Association of Greater Berlin) to the education ministers and parliaments of all the individual German states in September 1915 demanding the abolition of the celibacy requirement for women teachers, a lifting of the ban on hiring married women in schools, and legislation guaranteeing equality of pay between male and female school-teachers. Here again, it was the uneven consequences of the war and capitalism for marginalized groups that was at stake. A married or unmarried male teacher was able to retain a superior salary *and* stay out of the trenches, while a widowed female teacher with children might be forced (back) into the classroom at a low wage by the death of her husband and an inability to feed her children on his meagre war pension alone. Meanwhile, in a nod to male sensibilities, married women whose husbands were serving in the army were banned from the classroom, even if it made economic sense for them to be there, and unmarried women teachers had to remain celibate or risk instant dismissal (or an illegal abortion) if they became pregnant out of wedlock.[69] All in all, this made women second-class employees of the state, just as they were frequently second-class workers, with inferior rights and poorer wages, in factories. Exactly the same point was made by the pro-socialist League for the Protection of Mothers (*Bund für Mutterschutz*) in its petition against a proposed new Reich law restricting female access to contraception in 1916.[70]

In Glasgow, Scotland, it was an arbitrary increase in rents, combined with a long-standing failure by the city's landlords to carry out essential repairs to housing, that mobilized action from working-class women and middle-class reformers in the form of a rent strike. The secretary of the Glasgow Women's Housing Association was the suffragist and socialist activist Helen Crawfurd, who saw the potential to make rent a point of departure for political mobilization of working-class women against the war and against militarism.[71] Crawfurd was a former member of the militant pro-suffrage Women's Social and Political Union (WSPU) who had quit that organization in 1914 over its pro-war stance. Instead she joined the anti-war ILP in Glasgow and in 1915 helped to create a local branch of the pro-socialist United Suffragists, which had forty members by November.[72] Unlike the WSPU, the United Suffragists also invited men such as the East London MP George Lansbury to become members, thus cementing the link between the ILP, the UK-wide labour movement and the suffragist cause.[73] Crawfurd supported this alliance but was definitely on its more militant wing.[74]

The significance of the Glasgow rent strike for left-wing female activists should not be exaggerated; as June Hannam and Karen Hunt note, when it came to communication of ideas, 'even experienced socialist women' like Crawfurd 'did not break into the male dominated columns of the … socialist press [at national level] or even the local Glasgow *Forward*'.[75] Nonetheless, in addition to contributing to the cementing of pre-existing links between the ILP, the labour movement and suffragists at national level, it also marked the emergence of new bonds of solidarity between local socialists, anti-war campaigners and middle-class neighbourhood activists to replace older political networks that had been destroyed by the majority mainstream socialists' and feminists' support for the war. In this sense, it built on ideas already foreseen by Sylvia Pankhurst and the radical East London chapter of the WSPU in 1913, including use of the slogan: 'No Vote, No Rent', which was now, in effect, extended to 'No Peace, No Rent'.[76]

In Sweden, a country which like Switzerland was not actually at war during the period 1914–18, anti-militarism took the form of constant pressure on Prime Minister Hjalmar Hammarskjöld and his successors after March 1917 to engage in neutral mediation, both to bring the present war to an end, and to ensure that it was followed by a permanent peace. A starting point was the *Kvinnornas Fredssöndag* (Women's Peace Sunday) in June 1915, when about 88,000 women took part in 343 meetings all over Sweden in order to demand that the Swedish government proactively pursue an anti-militarist and pro-peace policy.[77] The above-mentioned Social Democrat women's leader Anna Lindhagen served on the organizing committee, as did working-class trade unionists Anna Sterky and Signe Svensson-Vessman, and suffragist/anti-poverty campaigner Agda Östlund.[78] An address read out at all of the 343 meetings on 'Women's Peace Sunday' called for a permanent peace based on compulsory arbitration of international disputes, the granting of female suffrage and democratic control over the foreign policy of all countries. Otherwise, the address noted, the post-war world would be stuck with the old militarist system, whereby 'states periodically enter a state of war with intervals of peace that would be used for rearmament'.[79]

Apropos the wartime economic exploitation of working-class families for the profit of big business, one form of localized protest that socialist women got involved with in Germany concerned work- and community-based campaigns to end *Sparzwangserlässe* (compulsory savings regulations) for pre-adult workers of both sexes. These were introduced arbitrarily in particular military districts where the local authorities feared that young people in work had too much money and were spending it on the 'wrong' things: gambling, smoking, alcohol. Under local regulations, a significant proportion of teenagers' earnings were paid into closed accounts controlled by the communal authorities, proletarian mothers not being trusted to act responsibly on their sons' or daughters' behalf. In Berlin alone, the number of such forced savings accounts had risen to 104,000 by 1 April 1918, containing 8.75 million marks.[80] Military commanders on the home front were seemingly unconcerned that such regulations risked further impoverishing working-class households, particularly those that relied on the wages of teenage members to pay the rent or to offset the absence or death of the father-husband. Young people and women who repeatedly distributed leaflets protesting against the war or the compulsory savings orders were closely watched by the police and were subject to arrests and house searches. This happened, for instance, in Braunschweig, where the local military commander introduced a savings regulation as early as 22 April 1916. A leafleting campaign, followed by street protests and a five-day strike involving, among others, 120 teenage girls from a local mill construction company, the *Braunschweigische Mühlenbauanstalt Amme, Giesecke & Konegen* (AGK), forced him to withdraw it after only two weeks, causing ripple effects in the neighbouring industrial towns of Halle and Magdeburg and as far away as Düsseldorf and Berlin, where similar *Sparzwangserlässe* had also been introduced.[81]

What particularly worried the authorities was the apparent 'failure' of parents – in most cases adult women workers – to keep their children away from the protests. When a crowd of 1,800 adolescents, among them 300 girls, gathered in the centre of Braunschweig on the evening of 3 May 1916, the police appealed in vain for the adult workforce to rein them in. The following afternoon,

> the police were replaced by the military. Hussars rode into the city at various points ... with rifle butts. In the meeting of the unions with factory executives, a sympathy strike by adults was considered. The next day, May 5th, the General Command withdrew the savings decree entirely.[82]

In Switzerland, too, the year 1916 saw the first food riots and the beginnings of cooperation between unorganized women protestors and disaffected young people, backed to some extent by the official socialist women's organizations.[83] Thus on 1 August 1916 (the Swiss national holiday), the Social Democratic Youth and the Social Democratic women's association of Zurich organized an anti-militarist assembly. The police forbade the demonstration, which was planned as a follow up to the meeting. But the young people and women decided to march through the city centre, anyway, calling what they were doing a *Spaziergang* (stroll) instead of a demonstration. The labelling of the march as a *Spaziergang* in fact reflected a tactic already used in protests before the war in Germany as well as Switzerland, and had become a part of what Amerigo Caruso calls the transnational 'democratic protest culture' of those years.[84] The point, as Caruso explains, was to assert the right of workers to 'occupy civic space' by taking a 'stroll through the streets and parks of their respective cities'.[85]

At first, the police in Zurich in August 1916 stood back but after some time they called for reinforcements. Without warning, they suddenly blocked the path of the marchers and confiscated their anti-militarist banners. While the police claimed that the violence was started by the protestors, the protestors stated that the police had provoked them by seizing their banners, using their sabres and conducting arrests. The public outcry that followed was huge. Two days later, the Social Democrats organized a big solidarity demonstration for the victims of police repression. The police action was also criticized in the city assembly (*Stadtrat*).[86]

When hunger protests broke out in the Swedish capital Stockholm in late April 1917 – an extension of disturbances that had already begun around two weeks earlier in the seaport of Söderhamn, more than 150 miles to the north – a similar process was observable. What started as neighbourhood protests by working-class housewives demanding bread and the lifting of ration cards, and by women factory workers opposed to rising milk prices, soon led to a confrontation between demonstrators and police in front of Sweden's parliament building, the Riksdag, with 'tens of thousands of people' taking part.[87]

Subsequent media representations of the events of 1 August 1916 in Zurich and 21 April 1917 in Stockholm at best presented women participants in the demonstrations as misled, and at worst airbrushed them completely from explanations for the rise in social discontent. Yet this did not mean that women food protestors were content to leave the riskier work of defending urban space to others. Reading between the lines of press reports on unorganized street protests, hitherto unpoliticized working-class women were often the instigators, especially when the issues at stake revolved around neighbourhood economic conditions.[88] Socialist women endorsed their actions by word and deed. Few of the demonstrators were consciously pro-Zetkin or supporters of the SWI, and in the Swedish case, fewer still were likely to have been aware that Lenin and other Russian revolutionaries had passed through Stockholm on 13 April en route for Petrograd. Indeed, one recent study concedes that 'Lenin's visit [to the headquarters of the Socialist Left Party] does not seem to have had any impact' on the street demonstrations later that month in the Swedish capital.[89] However, those neighbourhood female activists who had heard of Zetkin, whether in Switzerland, Germany, Britain, Austria or Sweden, understood that fulfilling the demands of the Bern Peace Manifesto required a focus on local and small-scale action, and on horizontal forms of collaboration between different groups of anti-war campaigners as a means of gradually building up to larger-scale industrial and urban protest. This is what we turn to in the next section.

Large-scale strikes and mass action

While Dan Diner has argued in his universal history of the twentieth century that urban street demonstrations in the winter of 1918–19 in Germany and Austria 'took on a pronounced social-revolutionary character and availed themselves of the language of class',[90] in fact it seems that this was already the case during the industrial stoppages of winter 1917 and 1918, a point also made by Veronika Helfert in her study focused in particular on the Greater Vienna region.[91] The intention was 'to force the end of the war through a political mass strike', and in this sense women workers were key to success.[92] They had less to lose than the men, since they could not be threatened with being called up to the army if they refused to go back to work. They were also less inclined to listen to the voices from the pro-war wing of the SPD and trade unions warning against strike action.[93] Anna Hornik-Strömer, one of the leaders of the January 1918 strike in Vienna and later a long-term activist in the Austrian Communist Party (KPÖ), wrote in her memoirs:

> The Austrian women and mothers were deeply impressed by the peace offer made by the Bolshevik government [in December 1917]. Finally, a belligerent power was extending its hand in peace, finally the murderous war would come to an end, finally women would be allowed to be human again. The striking workers from the munitions factories streamed back to their homes, laughing and crying for joy. 'Now the killing is finally over'. 'Now our sons and husbands are finally coming back!'[94]

Shop-floor agitation to join in solidarity with the Viennese workers had already begun in several German cities in the second half of January and was led by the USPD and the Revolutionary Shop Stewards. In Berlin, the Spartacist League (as the 'Gruppe Internationale' was now called) directly addressed women as well as male workers in a flysheet demanding 'What our Austro-Hungarian brothers have started, we have to finish!'.[95] Cläre Casper-Derfert, the only female member of the Revolutionary Shop Stewards' executive committee, described what happened next in the German capital after the strike there had started:

> On 29 January all gatherings were banned and on the [following day] the union building was occupied. Then the masses poured into the street. On 31 January there were huge demonstrations in all parts of the city. The police tried to break us apart on foot and on horseback and fired into the crowd. But we gathered again in the back streets and gave the police a hard time. On the same day the imperial government announced the intensified state of siege and the introduction of extraordinary courts-martial. The police were reinforced by 5,000 NCOs from the army. On 1 February the militarisation of all large factories was declared. A number of revolutionary workers' leaders were arrested, including Leo Jogiches, the organisational head of the Spartacist League.[96]

Although the strike collapsed in the early days of February, at its height more than one million workers across Germany came out. Alongside Casper-Derfert in Berlin, two women are known to have been elected to the strike leadership in Dresden, a further two in Mannheim and one each in Bremen and Gotha. In Hanover, women actually outnumbered men on the local strike committee.[97] Meanwhile, in Austria, two women had already been elected onto the fourteen-strong Viennese workers' committee on 18 January 1918.[98] Although an exact figure cannot be put on the total number of women participants in the German strike,[99] alongside the strikes in Vienna and Budapest it is clear that this was, as Ursula Herrmann puts it, the 'largest peace campaign ... with the greatest participation of women during the First World War'.[100] Full adult suffrage, including for women, is known to have been on the list of demands made by the strike leaderships first in Vienna and elsewhere in Austria-Hungary, and then in Berlin, Dresden, Kassel, Mannheim and Nuremberg.[101] But more than this, the strike wave represented the culmination of a fundamental change in the relationship between working-class women and the state which had already begun to take shape through localized food protests in 1915 and which was crucial in bringing about the revolutions in Central Europe in November 1918.[102] Thus in Halle, women accounted for 22.7 per cent of the strikers in the machine-tool factory Wagelin & Hübner, 32.6 per cent in the machine-tool factory Weise & Sons and 60.4 per cent in the machine-tool factory Auto-Schachtschabel. In Bremen, 52.5 per cent of those on strike at the Hansa-Lloyd-Werken were women. The proportions were even higher at the Universelle cigarette machine plant in Dresden (54.5 per cent), the machine-gun parts factory Quast & Co. in Berlin (57.1 per cent), the printing workshop Kühn & Sons, again in Berlin (64.9 per cent) and the tin packaging plant Singewald & Co. in Leipzig (90.7 per cent).[103] All of these cities, except Dresden, were strongholds of the USPD.[104] They were also places that since 1915 had seen a significant rise in the female workforce, and in female membership of the metal workers' union in particular.[105] The same applied in the industrial parts of Austria, where women already made up more than 23 per cent of strikes in 1916 and 1917, rising to as much as 53 per cent in January 1918.[106]

In Sweden, industrial unrest in 1917 was linked to growing food shortages caused by the Allied economic blockade and the counter-measures taken by the Central Powers, a rapid increase in exports to Germany at the same time as imports from North America were hindered by the United States' entry into the war, the government's inequitable rationing system amid dramatic price increases, Prime Minister Hjalmar Hammarskjöld's '[incorrect] belief that the right of Sweden to international trade would be upheld by international law', and a poor harvest in 1916.[107] Hammarskjöld himself was increasingly known as

'Hungerskjöld', as he was held personally responsible for the mismanagement of food distribution. On 30 March 1917, he resigned, and by May 1917, talk of revolution was in the air as hunger demonstrations grew in intensity. Most historians date the beginning of the 1917 hunger riots to the formation of a male-dominated workers' committee on 16 April in the coastal industrial town of Västervik, to the south of Stockholm.[108] This five-man committee (no women were elected to it) was charged with taking control of the protest movement and food supplies in the town – in conscious imitation of the soviets that had sprung up in Petrograd and elsewhere in Russia since March 1917. It issued a manifesto putting forward demands of the workers and the socialist movement: affordable food for all, distribution of land and seeds to grow potatoes, an eight-hour working day and release of those arrested during hunger protests. The Västervik manifesto then supposedly provided a model for similar hunger demonstrations throughout Sweden in the weeks that followed.[109]

Yet in fact, as Swedish journalist and author Ulf Wickbom has shown, the unrest started not in Västervik, but in the rural, suburban sawmill areas in the coastal area around Söderhamn, to the north of the capital. Here four women, soon joined by 200 others, gathered to stage Sweden's first hunger protest on 11 April 1917, marching six miles into the urban area of Söderhamn with demands for bread and the abolition of ration cards. These women – housewives and mothers – may not have been previously politically active themselves, but they were the wives and daughters of men who belonged to the socialist movement, so were politically aware. Indeed, to cite Olwen Hufton, a historian of women in the eighteenth and early nineteenth centuries, female-led hunger protests at times of revolutionary unrest cannot be understood by generalizing from the male experience but only by focusing on women's historically reproduced 'rôle in the family economy'.[110] It was during the years 1789–96 in Paris, at the height of the French Revolution, that working-class women (the *sans-culotte* wives) first understood how 'traditional notions of a moral economy' might be 'blended with democratic principle to produce vigilant market practice'.[111] The socialist women of Söderhamn, like their French foremothers, knew that they might fail in their efforts to go 'right to the top', but were still determined to 'confront authority ... as the innocent empowered to speak on behalf of their suffering families'.[112]

In fact, despite their fruitless demands to the Söderhamn Bread Bureau on 11 April for more by way of provisions, the Söderhamn women did not go home empty-handed; they returned with a new sense of their own political power and how to assert it, as a few days later, they staged a school strike, keeping their

Figure 2.4 The women's hunger protest in Söderhamn, Sweden, on 11 April 1917. Source: Photo courtesy of Bengt Herrman Private Collection via Arkiv Gävleborg, Sweden.

daughters and sons at home on the grounds that there was 'nothing to put in the children's lunch boxes'.[113] The School Board attended a gathering in the public meeting house in the presence of 600 (unnamed) women and three (named) men, where it agreed to the women's demands to change the length of the school day to allow the women to feed the children what little they could before they left home and after they returned. The protocol clearly states that the School Board's agreement to the demands 'was greeted with cheers from the women' in attendance.[114] This example was soon followed by other local communities, and the new school day was soon introduced across the entire region by the regional School Board. Thus the women were actually in charge of events and pushed through proactive social change in Söderhamn for a few weeks during April and May of 1917.[115]

The events in Söderhamn were also reported in the Stockholm and other Swedish regional newspapers – albeit in derogatory terms[116] – and from the date of the initial action (11 April 1917), Swedish women across the country started to conduct forced inventories of farms and shops, primarily of potatoes. Meanwhile, in a further demonstration of the growing inter-dependency between suburban and urban forms of women-led unrest, on 26 April, female factory employees in Stockholm – who had undoubtedly read of the Söderhamn

Figure 2.5 Women's 6,000-strong hunger march, here passing along Vasagatan, one of Stockholm's central thoroughfares, en route to the Milk Central, 26 April 1917. Source: Alamy.

events and the activities by other women these had triggered around the country, as well as the big demonstration in front of the Riksdag on 21 April – downed tools and set out on a march to the Milk Central to protest against the high prices for dairy products. They poured out of the Stockholm shoe factory, the Munich brewery, the Tobacco monopoly, the Barnängen textile factory, the Liljeholmens jersey factory and many others – until they were 6,000-strong.[117] A newspaper reported that even 'a large number of workers' wives and half-grown girls with braids on their backs' joined the large mass of women.[118] The Swedish hunger demonstrations are today considered to be the largest social protest movement in the country's recent history.

Similar events took place in Switzerland, building up to a large-scale demonstration in Zurich on 10 June 1918. Here an organized procession of women with around 1,000–2,000 participants, led by the socialist Rosa Bloch-Bollag demanded that the cantonal authorities in Zurich take action to mitigate the effects of the rapidly increasing inflation and poor food supply in the city.[119] The women tried to gain entry to the canton council meeting to put their demands, but were turned down. The police did not disperse the demonstration even though it had caused massive disruption to traffic. They argued that they

Figure 2.6 The events of 17 June 1918 in Zurich, when Rosa Bloch-Bollag led a delegation to the canton council, as presented in the *Schweizer Illustrierte Zeitung*, No. 26, 29 June 1918, 322. Courtesy of Schweizer Illustrierte/Ringier Publications, Switzerland.

found themselves confronted by a mob of 'agitated women' under the influence of 'mass suggestion' and that they could not have cleared the streets without acts of violence.[120] Once again, fear of the 'crowd', rooted in late nineteenth- and early twentieth-century psychology, was being used to deny political agency and rationality to women and young people in particular.[121] After being denied access to the meeting, the women marched again on 14 June, this time with the support of the Zurich workers' union. After the demonstration on 17 June, a delegation of women was invited to present their demands in front of the council. It was, as the social democratic women's periodical, *Die Vorkämpferin*, put it, a historic day. It was the first, and until 1970 the only time that women were able to address the Zurich cantonal council.[122] The events were also captured in the *Schweizerische Illustrierte Zeitung*, which published several photographs of the proceedings, making it clear that this was a delegation of women wage-earners, led by socialist Rosa Bloch-Bollag, who were presenting their 'complaints about the [mismanagement] of food distribution' to the cantonal authorities.

In Munich, a slightly different situation emerged. Here, the most prominent strike leaders were not workers at all, but the German-Jewish theatre critic and socialist journalist Kurt Eisner and next to him, an academically trained Russian-Jewish immigrant and Bundist, Sonja Lerch, born Sarah Rabinowitz in Warsaw, Russian-Poland, in 1882.[123] Sonja was the wife of Eugen Lerch, a Francophile man of letters and aspiring professor at the Ludwig Maximilian University, who in 1918 disowned her because of her political activism. Unbeknownst to him, she had already been a member of the workers' council in the Ukrainian port of Odesa during the Russian Revolution of 1905, before escaping to Central Europe via Constantinople and completing a doctoral dissertation at the University of Giessen in 1912 on the development of the Russian workers' movement.[124] In 1917, despairing at the inaction of other pacifist groups, she joined a USPD-friendly discussion circle in Munich led by Eisner, and in January 1918, she was one of the key figures, alongside Eisner and the revolutionary poet Ernst Toller, in the strike movement there. Indeed, on 26 January Lerch stood as the only speaker alongside Eisner when plans for the strike were announced 'before a crowd of 250 sympathisers' at the Kolosseum Beer Hall, and over the next five days she accompanied him as he sought to whip up support for the walk-out at various sites across the city.[125] In total, 8,000 women munitions workers downed tools in the Bavarian capital, and on 1 February 1918, Lerch and two other women strike leaders were arrested on charges of high treason: the sisters Betty and Emilie Landauer. In addition, three men were arrested for the same offence: Eisner, Carl Kröpelin and Hans Unterleitner. Several others followed, including the otherwise unknown woman worker Anna Niedermeier, who was held for one day on 15 March and willingly told her interrogators that she had joined the strike in solidarity with her co-workers in Germany and Austria and in order to force the governments there to make peace.[126]

Before her own case could be brought to trial, however, Lerch was found hanging in her cell at Munich's Stadelheim jail on 29 March 1918, in circumstances that have never been satisfactorily explained. Eisner blamed her apparent suicide on the actions of her estranged husband, who had demanded that she quit political activism and, shortly after her arrest, had it officially announced in the Munich press that he had instigated divorce proceedings against her.[127] But it was still far from certain whether she took her own life, or whether persons unknown had a hand in her death. At her funeral in Munich's New Israelite

Cemetery on 1 April 1918, the anarchist Josef Sontheimer interrupted proceedings to claim that she had sacrificed herself for the cause of revolution and was himself promptly arrested by police officers sent to keep an eye on proceedings and to prevent the making of political speeches.[128]

According to Sontheimer and others, peace was the salient political issue in the strikes of 1917 and 1918, with the Russian Revolutions of February and October 1917 the key inspiration. The last year of the war is also interesting because of the (often invisible) work that women did in supporting industrial action in the reproductive sphere. This can be seen in particular in respect to the nationwide strike or *Landesstreik* in Switzerland on 12 November 1918.[129] The stoppage was called by a group of leading socialist politicians and trade unionists, the so-called *Oltener Aktionskommitee* (OAK), in protest at the mobilization of the military in Zurich and Bern to safeguard 'order' on the first anniversary of the Bolshevik Revolution. This was a clear bid for control of the streets and urban workplaces. The OAK drew up a list of nine demands, which would have to be met before any return to work would be considered:

1. the immediate re-election of the national council on the basis of proportional representation;
2. active and passive suffrage for women;
3. the introduction of a universal duty to work;
4. the introduction of the forty-eight-hour week in all public and private enterprises;
5. the reorganization of the army in the sense of a people's army;
6. securing food supplies in agreement with agricultural producers;
7. old-age and disability insurance;
8. a state monopoly for imports and exports; and
9. the repayment of public debt by the wealthy.[130]

With the proclamation of the strike by the OAK on 11 November, to begin the following day, the women's action committee of the Swiss Social Democratic Party published a call in Zurich's main socialist newspaper, *Volksrecht*, for women to join the strike and be active in different ways: housewives should take care of the food supply and keep children away from the street to prevent clashes with police and military forces.[131] This measure was important because schools were closed during that time due to the Spanish Flu pandemic. But keeping the children from the streets was a difficult endeavour. Luckily the socialist teachers' association of Zurich had thought about that in previous discussions about their role in the event of a possible mass strike.[132] Together with the Social Democratic women workers' association, they organized special childcare during the course of the strike. They collected the children and led them to areas outside the city where they spent their days playing and receiving educational classes on socialism. Women also saw it as their task to talk to soldiers and 'explain' to them that they too were part of the working class.[133] This meant that they took on the role of mediators between the soldiers and the strikers, asking them not to shoot their brothers and sisters, and in so doing risked arrest and imprisonment for sedition, as in the case of Bertha Volk mentioned above.

Although Swiss women have often been written out of the historiography of the *Landesstreik*, and although the strike itself collapsed after just a few days, these examples show how crucial female participants were, both as strikers in their own right, and as performers of the kind of reproductive labour which allowed others to strike in the knowledge that their children were being looked after and that they themselves would still be fed.[134]

Anti-militarism and urban spaces

The two Russian Revolutions of 1917, the peace negotiations between the Bolsheviks and the Central Powers at Brest Litovsk from January 1918, ending in a formal treaty in March, and at the same time the prolongation of the war in the west, helped to intensify the anti-war activism of socialist women in the countries examined in this chapter. However, at the same time they brought to a head a growing division between pacifists on the one hand, and anti-militarists on the other, with implications for the immediate post-war period too. It therefore seems proper to end the chapter with a reflection on the extent to which wartime protest in urban spaces may have helped to sharpen, or conversely to render less relevant, the distinction between those socialist women activists who rejected violence altogether (sometimes referred to as 'absolute' or 'extreme pacifists'),[135] and those who felt that the physical attacks by governments and militaries against them justified the use of force in response (sometimes known as 'Bolsheviks', although this could be misleading and did not always imply membership of a Leninist group).[136]

The pacifist/Bolshevik division among socialist women may in fact have been less important than the common focus on militarism versus democratic revolution, in other words the notion that militarists in all countries – neutral as well as belligerent – were hell-bent on standing in the way of the movement to assert the sovereign will of the people for an end to war on terms that would benefit workers of both sexes. These sentiments were expressed, for instance, in a piece published in the Austrian Social Democrat women's newspaper, *Die Arbeiterinnen-Zeitung*, at the time of the January 1918 strike in the Dual Monarchy for 'peace, freedom and bread', in solidarity with the workers of Russia. Here the anonymous author reflected on what the struggle against militarism across Europe had come to mean in terms of the 'techniques' now deployed by the militarists to preserve their system:

> The unmasked horrors of military justice, the heart-breaking misery in the internment camps, the brutalisation of the militarised workers, which resulted in severe punishment for uttering any free word in defence of human dignity, the revelations that everyday experiences in the workplace brought with them, all of this trembles in the hearts of the male and female workers. Add to that the unreasonableness of the censorship. Every blank column in the Social Democratic newspapers had to lead to the assumption that some cruel truth had again been suppressed.[137]

War also turned urban streets into sites of heightened class conflict. First the police and military deployed sabres against food protestors, but by summer 1918, at least in Germany, they were using tear gas grenades, even though 'these weapons were in short supply and had actually been intended for [use against] enemy soldiers'.[138] In one case, recently documented by Christopher Dillon, security police in the Bavarian town of Ingolstadt used Bromoacetone tear gas to clear a crowd of several hundred soldiers and civilians who had gathered on 22 May 1918 in front of the town hall to protest against the war and against the abuse in custody of a local man who had gone absent without leave from the army after suffering shell shock. Ninety-seven people were arrested, among them thirty-five women.[139] Tear gas was used again at the *Türkenkaserne* in Munich on 7 November 1918 as a means of protecting the barracks from a revolutionary crowd.[140] For the Bavarian military, rapidly running out of material resources in 1917–18 and with the home front beginning to crumble, notions of self-preservation meant that the fight against the internal enemy had become as important, and almost as violent in terms of its 'technique', as the fight in the trenches. The same applied elsewhere, for instance, in Austria, Sweden, Switzerland and Britain. Here too, in the face of strikes and demonstrations in 1917–18, the home front increasingly turned into the 'inner front' in the battle to sustain militarism.[141]

Yet there were signs of hope that the struggle against militarism was also changing in response. In particular, socialist women as housewives and waged workers had displayed their international solidarity through their opposition to military training in schools, a precursor to the formation of school councils (*Schülerräte*) in schools in early post-war Austria which campaigned against the continuation of military drill in the curriculum,[142] and by planning for education of children in anti-militarism during strikes, for instance, in Switzerland in late 1918 ('He who has the youth, has the army!', as Liebknecht said). Hiding deserters and conscientious objectors, visiting men in prison and supporting their wives and children materially and emotionally were also activities that increased in volume in all countries in the last year of the war. In Britain, for instance, branches of the explicitly socialist and anti-militarist Women's Peace Crusade (WPC) were established in August 1917 in the industrial centres of Blackburn, Nelson, Manchester, Leeds, Birmingham, Leicester, Melksham in Wiltshire and Belfast.[143] In 1918, the Crusade ignited in the industrial towns of Hull, Reading, Norwich, Exeter, Rothwell and Market Harborough.[144] By September, there were 123 branches across the country with at least two branches having 'almost 1000 members'.[145] In North-East Wales, at a demonstration of the Wrexham WPC, the women had let out a great cry of 'Heddwch!' ('Peace!') while at a WPC rally in Burnley the Red Flag was sung.[146] In Glasgow, the Crusade visited over ninety local churches while in Nelson, more than 3,000 women had turned out for the Crusade organized by socialist Selina Cooper.[147]

In the ILP in Lancashire (then including the urban area of Greater Manchester) 'many ... shared [WPC member] Hannah Mitchell's opinion that "War in the main is a struggle for power, territory or trade, to be fought by workers, who are always the losers"'.[148] In Blackburn, the daughter of socialist anti-war activist Ethel Derbyshire remembered:

> I've been at the ILP rooms. They used to have dances of a Saturday night, and so many of the boys had got their calling-up papers and wouldn't go; and they knew that the military police were coming for them at such a time and they would be arrested. So they used to be all there at the dance, and they used to come for them, quite young boys, eighteen, nineteen, seventeen, and they'd wait, and they'd sing the Red Flag, when they went.[149]

After 1918, these anti-militarist campaigns went in different directions. Many of those involved in 'hands off Russia' campaigns turned to communist parties in their own countries. This applied, for instance, to Helen Crawfurd in Britain and to Anna Hornik-Strömer in Austria.[150] Others were drawn to communist front organizations like the League Against Imperialism, founded by Willi Münzenberg in 1927 and including socialist women activists from a variety of countries,

Figure 2.7 British delegation at the second international conference held by the Women's International League for Peace and Freedom, Zurich, May 1919. Helen Crawfurd is second on the left, middle row; Annot Robinson is fifth on left, back row; and Ellen Wilkinson is second on the left, front row. Source: Alamy.

among them – albeit briefly – the British Labour MP 'Red Ellen' Wilkinson.[151] However, not all accepted the communist line, and there were also ways in which anti-militarism brought pacifists and socialists closer together rather than driving them apart. The second WILPF congress in Zurich in May 1919 is an example of this, coinciding as it did with the men's peace conference in Paris. It was attended on the British side by Wilkinson, Annot Robinson and Crawfurd, among others, all of whom attempted to push WILPF's pacifism in a more pro-socialist direction.[152] The resolutions adopted by this conference included a demand for the 'establishment of full equal suffrage and the full equality of women with men politically, socially, and economically' as well as a call for the 'abolition of conscription' in all countries permitted to join the League of Nations.[153]

In respect to the west's 'military interventions' in Bolshevik Russia and Hungary, the congress added its voice to the

> protests against the warfare now being waged, without open declaration of war, upon peoples who are experimenting in a new social and economic order, which may prove to have a great contribution to make to the world, and which has not yet had a fair trial.

All aggression against the Lenin and Kun regimes, whether by armed force, by supply of munitions or money, or by blockade', should be immediately halted, it continued.[154]

Community-based and transnational campaigns organized by lesser-known women were equally important in developing the anti-militarist struggle at international level even after the First World War had officially come to an end. In April 1919, for instance, the wives of German POWs still being held in Britain and France staged rallies in Berlin with the goal of demanding that the new republican government make the prior release of all prisoners a precondition for signing any peace treaty. Peace while the Allies still held POWs would be no peace, but a continuation of militarism under another name.[155] Yet so too would be a peace that allowed the militarists in Germany to regain their power. This is why, for instance, during the counter-revolutionary Kapp-Lüttwitz Putsch in March 1920, unarmed working-class women in Frankfurt am Main supported the men in continuing a general strike 'until the army submitted and actually left the town',[156] and why in Leipzig and the Ruhr valley they 'participated in the fighting, helping to build barricades, supplying the [armed proletarian men] and even emerging from cover to halt *Freikorps* fire so that male comrades could scramble to better positions'.[157]

A second example comes from Sweden, a country which had never been *at war* during the 1914–18 period, but one which still felt itself to be *in war* in 1919, particularly as the victorious Allies continued their blockade of Germany – including restrictions on trade with neutral countries – after the signing of the November 1918 armistice.[158] On 28 January 1919, women's peace groups, including representatives from the Social Democratic Party, organized a mass meeting in Stockholm and collected 48,812 signatures in favour of a peace built on Wilsonian principles, especially arbitration between nations and freedom of the seas.[159] Again, the intention was that this action should coincide with the opening of the peace talks in Paris, the city in which the new battle lines between militarism and anti-militarism were now being drawn. It was, as Irene Andersson puts it, a call 'for universal peace' from Sweden's women's movement – socialist as well as bourgeois – in spite of that country's neutrality in the 1914–18 war and notwithstanding its subsequent position as a non-signatory of the Treaty of Versailles.[160]

Conclusion

This chapter has argued for a less hierarchized understanding of urban and suburban protest during the First World War, and for an approach that is also alert to the gender biases in the existing historiography of this period. Action that is emotion-based, community-focused or conducted by persons hitherto excluded from the bureaucracy and decision-making processes of established labour organizations is not in and of itself 'unpolitical', nor are crowds mindless and devoid of purpose. The war changed the parameters of protest and created new spaces for political action, both in the metaphorical sense – new ways of imagining citizenship at national and international levels – and in a literal sense – the urban/suburban landscape as a site of physical struggle and rival claims to legitimate ownership between militarists and anti-militarists. Above all, the war brought out the ability of working-class women to bring together the smaller world of the neighbourhood – increasingly female-dominated in the wake of the mobilization of young men – and the larger world of joined-up protests, strikes and anti-militarist activism.

Our focus on the urban and suburban has also led us to identify commonalities between cities *at war* and cities which, while they were not actively involved in armed hostilities, were still forced to live *in war*. Mary E. Cox's recent study, *Hunger in War and Peace*, while ostensibly focused on how women and children in Germany experienced food scarcity between 1914 and 1924, makes quite clear that the political and social impact of the Allied economic blockade extended to Switzerland and Sweden too (as indeed it did to the Netherlands, Denmark, Norway and Spain).[161] In response, governments in these neutral countries developed their own forms of (interior) militarism, mobilizing troops to defend their borders, and taking advantage of the all-round state of emergency to rearm, take control of streets and workplaces, and extend the reach of military justice into the civilian sphere. In so doing, they called forth opposition to militarism, voiced through spontaneous, grass-roots protest against the authorities at home and expressions of solidarity with blockaded and grieving populations in belligerent countries. Women and young people were at the forefront of these campaigns. But while, in contrast to activists from the middle-class women's movements, they were relatively new to battles against sex discrimination, for instance in the spheres of waged work, marital status, reproductive rights and voting rights, they were not inexperienced proletarians. Rather, as Sean Dobson has shown in the case of the German city of Leipzig, the chief target of women's and teenager's wartime street protests and wildcat strikes was the *Klassenstaat*, the state which protected the class privileges of landowners, factory owners, employers and male union bosses, and which failed to ensure a fair and even distribution of food and other necessities of life.[162] As such, they 'defin[ed] themselves as members of a working class [community], not as women per se'.[163]

Finally, the findings of this chapter support the call for a Europeanization of the Russian, German and Austrian Revolutions of 1917–18, in other words a recognition that the fight against militarism and for a just and lasting peace extended beyond national borders and beyond the dividing line separating belligerent from neutral countries.[164] Wartime protest, strikes and anti-militarism opened up unforeseen fissures within internationalist women's movements, especially between socialists and pacifists, as well as, by 1918–21, between anti-war Social Democrats and Communists. But they also created potential for new solidarities and new places for (re)imagining the social and the political. Socialist women who challenged the boundaries of citizenship and contested the state's monopoly claims on sovereignty within their own neighbourhoods, parties and movements also found themselves coming into contact with other outcast groups: conscientious objectors, deserters, prisoners of war, hungry mothers and underweight children, and above all teenagers whose lives and prospects had been turned upside down by the war. It was for their sake – and not just for abstract ideals such as 'world peace' or proletarian 'power' – that socialist women continued their campaigns after 1918 to prevent the Allied victory and the Central Powers' surrender from inaugurating a new age of militarism and social injustice in Europe. As a mark of their success in bargaining for an expanded notion of citizens' rights and normalizing the idea that the masses might have political claims on the state and employers rather than vice versa, conservative thinkers and counter-revolutionary jurists in the 1920s like Carl Schmitt were forced – in response – to adjust their own definition of sovereignty to exclude these very same forces of democracy and co-determination which threatened their understanding of an ordered, hierarchical world. 'Sovereign is he who decides on the state of exception', wrote Schmitt in his essay collection *Political Theology*, first published in March 1922,[165] thus underscoring just how much ferment had taken place at the level of gendered political imaginaries as well as routine, legally constituted forms of state and global governance since the beginning of the war in 1914.

3

Socialist Women and Revolutionary Violence, 1918–21

Veronika Helfert, Clotilde Faas, Tiina Lintunen and Mary McAuliffe

On 11 January 1919, towards the end of the Spartacist Uprising in Berlin, a group of men and women defended the so-called *Vorwärts*-Building, headquarters of the Social Democrat newspaper of the same name, against the counter-revolutionary *Freikorps*. Among them was Charlotte Steinbring,[1] a worker in the electronics company AEG in Henningsdorf. She was the last person still operating a machine-gun when she was disarmed and arrested in hand-to-hand combat.[2] Lotte Pulewka, a German socialist activist, described in 1958 how the former rebelled against the soldiers 'without fear and with fury in her eyes and mouth'.[3] Steinbring was a working mother of two, whose machine-gun antics attracted the attention of the leader of the conservative German National People's Party (DNVP), Count Westarp. Westarp was indeed later one of the main witnesses against her at the trial held in mid-1919 against Georg Ledebour arrested for his participation in the January uprising that saw the capture of the 'newspaper district', now in Kreuzberg, as well as the police headquarters.[4] Although three witnesses attested to her being in charge of a machine-gun, the version she gave to the judges was much more in line with the traditional female gender norms of the time.[5] She claimed not to have attacked government soldiers, but rather only to have tended to the Spartacists in the cellar of the building. Helene Behr, née Zirkel, also remembered the siege of the *Vorwärts*-Building in which she participated when she was only seventeen years old and the 'puzzled' look she received from the guard as she entered the building with the crowd. She was in charge of making and issuing passes so that the fighters could pass the guard posts easily and bear arms. It was only when her father, the Spartacist Max Zirkel, arrived that she was forced to return home.[6] In fact, Behr was the one who raised a red flag on the roof of the police headquarters on Berlin Alexanderplatz on 8 November 1918.[7] Even though Charlotte

Steinbring's and Helene Behr's actions in 1918–19 are among the better-known episodes of the German Revolution, they nevertheless stand out as exceptional – at least in popular accounts of the period.

Recent work on the violent aftermath of the First World War is still typically written with the male experience in mind, particularly when the violence is seen as political.[8] Only relatively few works on Germany and Austria published in the last years, for instance, reflect critically on the 'maleness' of earlier studies and incorporate gender historical perspectives.[9] In Ireland, while gender historians have published on the activities of socialist and revolutionary women for several decades now, newer aspects of women's experiences are still being researched and published. This is in spite of the fact that recent scholarship on war and gender emphasizes that everybody has a war experience, and that this experience is diverse, complex and manifold.[10] As we also note in Chapter 1 of this volume, women and children as victims of (gendered) wartime violence and of bodily violations as a consequence of food scarcity – in belligerent and in neutral countries – have long been a neglected aspect of First World War studies. Older publications still set the standard for narratives of revolutionary violence. In the Austrian case, for example, the studies of Gerhard Botz cast the political events of the November 1918 revolution as largely non-violent, thereby excluding social protests that occurred in the transformation phase like hunger riots in 1919–20, although they indeed ended in large numbers being injured or killed.[11] To exclude public protest in its diverse, sometimes seemingly unorganized forms, as well as the socio-economic demands of the masses, narrows the understanding of revolutionary social movements. It also misrepresents the character of some of those protest movements, as a number of the women participating in demonstrations were armed. This was the case, for instance, with the Germans Lucie Heimburger, Cläre Quast or Anna Erfurt, who carried pistols in their muffs.[12] Women as members of armed paramilitary groups also remain a marginalized topic. In Hungary during the period of the Councils' Republic, the participation of women in the Red Army was explicitly allowed, although the extent to which they joined the revolutionary armed forces remains unstudied.[13] In Finland, attention in the study of civil war history has for a long time been on men: only in the last two decades has research on women's participation, their histories as activists and not just passive bystanders, been published.[14] Research on women's participation in revolutionary movements in Ireland has seen a similar shift in focus in the last three decades. The official narrative has moved from simply seeing political and revolutionary women as passive auxiliaries of the male organizations, namely the Irish Volunteers during the 1916 Rising and the Irish Republican Army (IRA) during the War of Independence from 1919 to 1921, to seeing organized, political and militant women as central to the histories of the period.[15] The Decade of Centenaries in Ireland (2012–23) has led to a wealth of publications, including on socialist, militant and revolutionary women.[16]

Revolutionary women in violent times: four case studies

Women's actions in the revolutions presented here were characterized by their multiplicity. Based on a variety of sources we highlight the diverse activities of women socialists, including instances when they participated in violence themselves, when they engaged in non-violent actions in support of male fighting units, for instance through intelligence work, and when they became the target of counter-revolutionary and state violence. By using autobiographical writings, oral history interviews, political speeches and articles, police and court records, institutional material, pamphlets, photographs and press coverage, we aim to uncover the histories of revolutionary women. We are aware that different types of sources are accompanied by different sets of questions and therefore have to be interpreted accordingly. It is not only the memoirs that were written and preserved in the Socialist Unity Party (SED) archive in East Germany from the 1950s that must be subjected to the historical method of source criticism (see also Chapter 5 in this volume). From a gender-historical perspective, three things must be kept in mind when using sources in order not to reproduce the 'Narrative of a Soldiers' Revolution'[17] and what Brigitte Studer calls the 'gender-specific topography of relevance of the past'.[18] Firstly, women were often simply less visible than men in their revolutionary work, as they typically operated in areas that were less formalized and/or seemed less important. Secondly, the sources shed light on what actions or structural conditions appeared to contemporaries to be worthy of being labelled 'violence'. And thirdly, in the case of counter-revolutionary sources, misogyny (which was also present in the socialist camp) and anti-socialism must be taken into account, which either distort women and their political or militant activities into the monstrous or reduce them to the ridiculous. Coline Cardi and Geneviève Pruvost refer to this process as a 'double movement' that either turned female violence into a taboo or stigmatized it.[19]

Although we mainly focus in this chapter on violence as a form of doing, aimed at harming people's bodily and mental health and their integrity, often with the intent of furthering or preventing certain political causes, our underlying definition of violence goes beyond that limited understanding (including its nature as structural condition).[20] As outlined in Chapters 1 and 2, the experiences of wartime women workers included bodily harm caused by malnutrition, vulnerability to pathogens, lack of heating materials and increased risk of accidents in war industries, to name but a few. A gruesome accident in a munitions factory in Wöllersdorf near Vienna in September 1918 could also only have happened because of the war economy's disregard for life. To prevent the workers from starting their lunch break early, the gates of a large factory hall were kept locked. When a fire broke out, more than 400 female workers – 'soldiers of the hinterland'[21] as the Social Democrat Adelheid Popp, née Dwořak, called them – died, many of them young adults.[22]

Viewing revolutionary violence through a gender lens sheds light on spaces beyond formal politics and combat areas, and reveals gendered practices. Besides social protests or the effects of the supply crisis, especially in the empires of the Central Powers and Russia, it is sexualized violence that tends to be omitted from the major studies on political violence in the national contexts discussed in this chapter.[23] Such brutality ranged from physical assaults by men on women to symbolic practices of humiliation committed in places of institutionalized violence such as in prisons and internment camps or in the private sphere of households. Taking into account the presence of sexualized violence as a gendered weapon of revolutionary and (even more so) counter-revolutionary forces also helps to shed light on gendered spaces of revolution away from the combat zones of the post-war world. Feminist research in particular emphasizes the structural and symbolic aspects of violence, often based on the materialist or Marxist theoretical framework, which elaborates the relations of violence and power in capitalist society.[24] Moreover, in our exploration of the topic we take on board the concept of *Eigensinn*, theorized by Alf Lüdtke as 'wilfulness, a spontaneous self-will and a kind of self-affirmation' to combine one's own subjugation and personal dignity.[25] *Eigensinn* is not a direct resistance movement, but an attitude that allows the momentary creation of a space – both temporal and spatial – of one's own, and can help in reading various actions and interpreting them. Furthermore, violence is intrinsically linked to the emotions of those who commit it. Adding the emotional dimension to the political and economic ones allows us to reconsider the question of women's commitment to revolution in the years 1918–21.

In this chapter, we present texts of revolutionary violence authored by women socialists, explore re/presentations of revolutionary women in the (enemy) press,[26] examine the gendered performance and spaces of violence, show violence deployed by the state as well as counter-revolutionary forces against revolutionary women, and discuss sexualized violence as part of the revolutionary and counter-revolutionary terror used against women. Each sub-section puts case studies from different national contexts in the foreground (Austria, Finland, Germany and Ireland). The political situations of the countries in 1918 and after differed substantially from each other. The case studies reveal the impact of the First World War, the influence of the Russian Revolutions in 1917 and the specific contexts of four empires – the Russian Tsarist Empire, the Habsburg Monarchy, the British Empire and the German Kaiserreich. The revolutionary struggles and armed conflicts between 1918 and 1921 revolved around territorial and national independence, a democratic re/constitution of the state, and/or the building of a socialist society.

Finland is the case that was first and most directly affected by the impact of the Russian Revolutions. The Finnish civil war between the rebellious socialist Reds and the non-socialist Whites broke out in January 1918. There were several reasons for the war, both domestic and international. On the international level, the most important factors were the ongoing world war and the collapse of the Russian Empire, which had ruled Finland as a semi-autonomous Grand Duchy since 1809. The downfall of the Empire and the Bolshevik revolution enabled Finland to gain independence. However, it was in such political turbulence that civil war soon broke out.[27] The national turmoil had its roots in the previous year, 1917. Finland suffered from a severe shortage of food. That, combined with unemployment, made workers hungry and angry. Strikes, demonstrations and outbreaks of violence became more common, and working-class women were drawn into them as well. One key factor for the political unrest was the power vacuum that prevailed in the now independent, young country: there were no military or police forces to control the discontented and angry crowds. Both the workers and the owners established class-based local guards of their own during the strikes. From such local groups emerged the nationwide Red and White Guards, each with around 100,000 male soldiers. In addition, 2,600 female soldiers served on the Red side and roughly 10,000 women worked as auxiliaries to the Red forces. The Finnish civil war lasted for three and a half months, from late January to mid-May 1918, and ended in the defeat of the Reds. The war was short but brutal – 1 per cent of the whole Finnish population died due to the war.[28] Finland, which pioneered women's suffrage in Europe as discussed in Chapter 1 of this volume, is a notable case in our sample, with particularly strong integration of women into the fighting forces.

Similarly, the Irish case illustrates the diverse (organizational) forms of Irish women's participation in militant forms of socialism and feminism. The history of the Irish War of Independence (1919–21) reaches back into the nineteenth century, with phases of violent rebellion and constitutional campaigns for limited forms of self-government occurring with regularity, including campaigns for women's rights. Organizations such as the militant Irish Women's Franchise League (IWFL, founded in 1908) and the women's trade union, the Irish Women Workers' Union (IWWU, founded in 1911) included activists who were driven by the ideologies of women's and workers' rights, although the Irish situation was also complicated by the impact of militant nationalism. Militant feminism and the labour movement were deeply entwined, and from 1913, 'many of the more radical nationalist feminists were also socialists'.[29] As historian Mary Cullen writes, when considering Irishwomen's engagement with nationalism and socialism, 'an implicit feminist awareness appears to have informed almost all of the developments even when the objectives were not explicitly feminist'.[30] Politically active women, particularly those who supported nationalism, became more militant from 1914. *Cumann na mBan* (the Council of Women) had positioned itself, at its foundation, as an auxiliary of the armed male militia, the Irish Volunteers (founded in 1913 to defend Home Rule), something which brought forth tensions between suffrage and nationalist female activists. Militant and socialist women's activities were further influenced and advanced by the egalitarian promises contained in the Proclamation of Independence in 1916, which was deliberately addressed to 'Irishmen and Irish Women' and guaranteed equal rights for all in the new Republic: 'The Irish Republic is entitled to, and hereby claims, the allegiance of every Irishman and Irishwoman. The Republic guarantees religious and civil liberty, equal rights and equal opportunities to all its citizens.'[31] It was this promise of equality which motivated many middle-class and working-class feminist and socialist women to participate in the fight for Irish freedom during the War of Independence, 1919–21, and on whom violence was visited during this period.

The early post-war years in Germany were characterized if not by civil war on the same level as Finland, Russia and Ireland, then at least by a prolonged period of political unrest, the local establishment of workers' councils and even short-lived councils' republics, and battles between paramilitaries and units of the newly formed *Reichswehr* (the German armed forces during the Weimar Republic). In the German Kaiserreich, as in Finland and the Habsburg Monarchy, the turmoil created by the First World War and the dire shortage of food led to mass strike waves in April 1917 and January 1918, with women workers playing a prominent role.³² In October 1918, sailors' mutinies broke out in Wilhelmshaven and Kiel, as was already the case throughout the Habsburg Monarchy in the course of the summer of 1918. The sailors were quickly supported by the local working population. Soldiers' and workers' councils soon spread to the rest of the country. The empire collapsed and on 9 November 1918, the Social Democrat Philipp Scheidemann announced the foundation of the Republic from the balcony of the Reichstag. While the Kaiserreich expired without bloodshed or a sudden surge of violence, the battle over the city palace (*Berliner Schloss*) on Christmas Eve 1918, and further street fighting in the early months of 1919, nearly put Berlin in a state of civil war. Indeed, the left-wing forces of the Independent Social Democratic Party (USPD) and the newly formed Spartacists wanted to carry on with the revolution and called

Figure 3.1 Propaganda poster against the Munich Republic of Councils showing drunken revolutionaries indulging in orgiastic pleasures, 1919. Reproduced with permission of the Plakat- und Flugblattsammlung, Münchner Stadtbibliothek/ Monacensia.

for strikes and protests throughout the first half of 1919. In this troubled post-war context, the return home of thousands of armed soldiers led to further social instability and intense political unrest. Many of them joined the ranks of the Spartacists, who provided them with wages, shelter and food. Thus, most of the men arrested for revolutionary activities were demobilized soldiers or deserters. Nevertheless, male and female workers as well as housewives, (female) students and children were mobilized by calls shouted out in the working-class districts.[33]

In contrast to the civil war in Finland, the violent upheavals in the newly founded Weimar Republic or the Irish War of Independence, the situation in Austria looked rather peaceful. The transition from the Monarchy to the Republic was managed by the state council, composed of (male) representatives of all parties who had been elected to the *Reichsrat* (Imperial parliament) before the war. The territorial conflicts at the borders remained largely without bloodshed (with minor exceptions), and the same applied to revolutionary and counter-revolutionary activism in the Austrian interior. To some contemporaries, the creation of the Republic of (German) Austria might have looked like an afterthought, a reaction more to the dismantling of the old Empire, whose non-German nations declared independence one after the other at the end of October 1918. The Emperor abdicated and the Republic was proclaimed before thousands of people in front of the parliament in Vienna. On this day – 12 November 1918 – (communist) soldiers stormed the building, two people died and several were wounded. The offices of the conservative daily *Neue Freie Presse* were occupied by some 150 activists who printed issues of the communist newspaper *Weckruf*. This was not to be the last violent moment – in 1919, there were two more instances of unrest or attempted coups by the Austrian Communist Party (KPÖ) to establish a soviet republic. After workers' councils had already been founded during the January strike of 1918, in which probably half a million people in the Cisleithanian part of the Monarchy took part, they became relevant again in the first year after the war. Together with the soldiers' councils, they formed a parliament of the working class, and were only dissolved in 1924. In contrast, the tense political situation from the second half of the 1920s onwards led to increased violent clashes.[34] Despite its mostly peaceful character, the Austrian Revolution can serve as an instructive case for our discussions on the question of revolutionary violence and gender. Austrian socialist women, in their reflections on the implementation of a dictatorship of the proletariat, referred not only to Russia and Hungary, but also repeatedly to what happened in Germany and Finland – and to a lesser extent in Ireland. Some of them were actively engaged in armed political conflicts in neighbouring countries, like a group of women from Linz who had participated in building the two councils' republics in Munich in April 1919.[35]

Discussing revolutionary violence

'No one engaged in thought about history and politics can remain unaware of the enormous role violence has always played in human affairs', Hannah Arendt stated in 1970, during a period in which, in the face of worldwide social protest movements and a left activism that did not shy away from violence, the revolutions of fifty years earlier became topical.[36] And indeed, in the face of a four-year-long war that claimed millions of victims, the ongoing belligerent conflicts, and the disastrous consequences of the bloodshed for the lives of women, men and children, violence was a crucial factor for contemporaries in 1918 as well. We are interested in socialist women and their relationship to revolutionary violence in order to illustrate that it took on meaning in manifold ways. Physical and sexualized violence played an important role as a historical reality – whether for socialist women who were committed to the campaign against military violence as pacifists, or for female revolutionaries who understood the end of the Great War as the birth-moment of socialist societies. Sometimes they were drawn into the (civil) wars on their doorstep; and violence served as a means of empowerment and self-affirmation.[37] Violence implicitly and explicitly shaped socialist women's spheres of action and everyday life in 1918–21 – and many of them commented in their writings and memoirs on the role of violence in politics.

As we will show, socialist women's attitudes toward violence were less than uniform. In Finland, the Social Democratic women's movement was opposed to armed revolution. Their programme emphasized socio-political reforms and the extension of democracy by peaceful means. According to them, war was always a catastrophe for working-class women: they would lose their husbands and sons, the scarcity of food would get worse and the future would be filled with anxiety and worry. This had been seen throughout Europe during the First World War. In Austria, women Social Democrats took a similar line. Not always banned by the censors, they continued to publish pacifist texts during the war: a call for peace would unite 'the women of all peoples ... in their motherly spirit' (*in ihrer Mütterlichkeit*), it would turn into a 'battle cry against all warmongers',[38] their newspaper, the *Arbeiterinnen-Zeitung* (Women Workers' Paper), declared. In autumn 1918, they called for peaceful demonstrations and a parliamentary path, because 'as long as socialism does not have the majority ... we cannot force the others to recognise our colour as theirs as well'.[39] The pacifist stand – not uncontested in the context of their own belligerent states – was in line with the international socialist women's movement's opposition to war, as expressed at Bern in March 1915 (see Chapter 2), and with socialist women's campaigns in other countries such as Finland, where the Social Democratic women's movement arranged several anti-war demonstrations and published pro-peace articles in their newspapers.[40]

Notwithstanding this, women socialists in Finland were also strongly influenced by their Russian and German sisters. The leaders of the Finnish movement had close contacts to the Russian revolutionary Aleksandra Kollontai, who visited Finland several times prior to the Finnish civil war. Furthermore, Clara Zetkin was in contact with her Finnish colleague Hilja Pärssinen. Pärssinen was a member of the Finnish Parliament and a teacher, journalist and writer who was a linchpin in the labour movement. Kollontai encouraged Finns to join the revolution, but Pärssinen – although captivated by the spirit of internationalism and revolutionary uprising – never spoke in favour of an armed coup d'état.[41] True, after the Finnish Revolution started in January 1918 and turned into a civil war, the Social Democrat women's movement asked women to stand by their men. Nevertheless, they never encouraged women themselves to act as soldiers. Rather, they considered female combatants to be unnatural. According to the movement, women should act in the fields of nursing and maintenance and give only moral support to the armed forces.[42]

This was in contrast to communist women in Austria, who, admittedly, did not face a civil war in 1918. The call for revolutionary violence was justified, as Hilde Wertheim explained, by the fact that 'bourgeois' democracy itself is 'naked, brutal violence'.[43] She thus understood capitalist bourgeois relations as relations of economic violence, at times overt, at times veiled. In the newspaper supplement *Die revolutionäre Proletarierin* (The Revolutionary Proletarian Woman), women called for participation in violent struggles in favour of revolution and 'victory for humanity'. Even if violent confrontation should only be the last resort, communist-minded women were prepared to make this sacrifice. In doing so, women who 'as women would shy away from armed violence, need to replace their feminine sensibilities with class feelings'. To be revolutionaries, women workers must 'feel as proletarians'.[44] The opposite of bourgeois 'woman' in this case was therefore not simply 'man', but the proletarian revolutionary, a male-defined figure whose attributes women could also appropriate.[45] Or, as the

German theorist Bini Adamczak noted, the soviet 'New man [*Mensch*] was a universal drag king'.[46]

The events in Germany, Finland and Hungary were observed by all political camps in Austria and served as arguments for their own positions on possible military action. The left-wing Social Democrat Käthe Leichter, née Pick, for example, welcomed the establishment of workers' militias 'in view of the open arming of reaction in all places'.[47] Communists like Wertheim rejected the militias' defensive character. In her preface to an analysis of the Finnish civil war, published in German in 1920, she warned that the Finnish comrades had wanted to avoid the revolution with its battles and had only succeeded in being attacked unprepared:

> All this brought about the rapid victory of the counter-revolution, which now no longer asked for democracy and justice, but crowned its naked class rule with the bodies of the revolutionary fighters twitching in death.[48]

For left socialists and communists, support for political violence and civil war in the context of revolution was a way to participate on equal terms: 'A *tverdaia* revolutionary woman was tough, durable, and, if need be, merciless ... She was an equal member of an egalitarian movement',[49] as Barbara Evans Clements has put it in her work on Russian women. Matthew Stibbe observed in his research on German socialists that the question of violent militancy in the struggle for a better society was for many communist women an opportunity to demonstrate their party affiliation and a means of distinguishing themselves from Social Democrats.[50]

For militant Irish women, the difference lay elsewhere. Many of them theorized and wrote about the need for militancy, and a small minority wrote about the need to fight to establish a socialist republic. One of the main female organizations through which women made a militant contribution to revolution was *Cumann na mBan*. It was founded in April 1914 as an organization for women who espoused a nationalist ideology, and who would be a support to the Irish Volunteers, established in November 1913. The women adopted a green uniform with a slouch hat and a badge depicting a rifle with the initials of the organization intertwined. Their militarism was evident from their uniform, rhetoric and training. Almost all 300 women (other than the few in the Irish Citizen Army, ICA) who participated in the 1916 Easter Rising were members of *Cumann na mBan*, while thousands more joined after the Rising and were then involved in the War of Independence, 1919–21. Because of the perceived adjunct role of *Cumann na mBan*, many radical and socialist women chose to join the workers' militia, the ICA. This choice of ICA membership by the left-leaning middle-class women and younger radicalized working-class women reflects the combination of their political interests and their socialist activism through trade union politics. These women had been radicalized through involvement in militant suffrage activism and militant trade union activism particularly during 1913 when the Dublin lock-out strike occurred. This strike was met by violence on the part of the employers and the state, several strikers were killed, including one young female factory worker who died after being hit by a ricochet when workers protesting the use of 'scabs' (workers who broke the strike) were shot at. Despite their collaboration during the lock-out, tensions between the suffrage, socialist and militant nationalist women would remain throughout the revolutionary period – although by the outbreak of the War of Independence in 1919 friction between them was dissipating particularly as *Cumann na mBan* had altered the intent and tone of their manifesto in 1918 to one which was both militant and more avowedly feminist in intent. It pledged to 'follow the policy of the Republican Proclamation by seeing that women take up their proper position in the life of the nation'.[51]

With guns or kitchen knives in hand: women fighting for a different society

In August 1917, the Viennese illustrated magazine *Das interessante Blatt* published a report on revolutionary Russia and its war efforts in favour of the Entente. The author paid special attention to the women's battalion, a new fighting unit within the Russian armed forces. The paying public was also treated to two photographs: a caption drew special attention to the fact that the female recruits had their long hair cut. In addition to the practical aspect, the change from woman to soldier was thus also symbolically emphasized. But as the Finnish case in 1918 highlights, wearing men's breeches and short hair was also liberating, and young women were very proud of their outfits.

The newspaper of the Finnish Red Guards stated: 'Her new trouser suit looked pretty. It declared: I am free from old bourgeois skirts . . . I am a liberated woman of New Finland who does not take oppression anymore.'[52] Although the number of female soldiers and women deployed in armies in other functions was small, they occupied considerable space in the contemporary cultural representation of war and social disorder – as fearsome manifestations of the downfall of the known world, as symbols of sacrifice for the Socialist fatherland as well as bearers

Figure 3.2 Finnish Red female soldiers Tyyne Backman and Rauha Sinisalo, photographed in a studio on 20 April 1918. Rauha Sinisalo (on the right) was executed ten days later. Reproduced with permission of the Military Museum/Finnish Defence Forces.

of hope for a new age. In revolutionary Russia, women were involved in Red military organizations, for example, Rosaliya Samoilovna Salkind or Yevgeniya Bosch in Ukraine, both of whom had military leadership powers during the Russian civil war and Polish–Soviet war of 1917–21. As stated before, the Budapest Councils' Republic explicitly allowed women to join the Hungarian Red Army, but how many women made use of this right is unclear. In the emerging First Republic in Austria, the army played an important role in the deliberations of revolutionary actors – although women were not allowed to join the new *Volkswehr* (People's Defence Force). However, whether the paramilitary troops of the workers' councils made an exception is not known; there are only isolated references to women in the workers' armed forces (*Arbeiterwehren*).

Young women did take part, as in the case of Hanna Sturm, in skirmishes on the contested Austro-Hungarian border against White troops, as well as in demonstrations, some of which were bloodily repressed by the Austrian police. This can be seen time and again throughout the cases covered in our chapter. Women were involved in stirring up crowds, encouraging men to rebel and urging soldiers in front of the military barracks and workers in front of the factories to join the revolution.[53]

The cases discussed here show the extent to which women were mobilized for revolutionary movements and (civil) wars. They were involved in combat, in auxiliary forces, and in clandestine work. Historians encounter difficulties though, when researching the extent of their participation. As the example of Berlin Spartacist Charlotte Steinbring mentioned at the beginning of this chapter has shown, women often denied using or carrying weapons in order to receive a lighter sentence at court hearings and because of the misogynistic public attitudes. This is also documented in other instances, such as the Austrian *Schutzbund* uprising in February 1934.[54] In the case of the Spartacist Uprising, unlike men, women could not simply go to one of the Spartacist registration points scattered around the working-class neighbourhood to be registered and receive pay, ration cards, guns and food. Their commitment was rarely formally recorded and did not entitle them to any kind of financial benefit, as they were mainly described as volunteers. Paramilitary training for women was therefore often clandestine or poorly documented. The Berlin activist Cläre Quast nevertheless fought to be allowed to participate in the normally all-male shooting lessons at her local youth centre.[55] Little is known about the women involved in the fighting between revolutionary and government troops for control of the city, for instance, in January and March 1919 in the districts of Neukölln and Lichtenberg. The press rarely mentioned their presence beyond a few sentences, barring one or two exceptions, such as Steinbring.[56] They mostly only appear in the descriptions of attacks on food trucks supplying the city or the looting of shops, as they are the ones in charge of feeding their families.[57]

Also, the Finnish Red Guard did not seek to enlist women as combat soldiers. But girls and young women eager to fight for the Socialist Workers' Republic, who were not accepted in the auxiliaries, took matters into their own hands, and soon formed military troops of their own, which put the Red government under pressure to use the existing female companies for guard duties so that they could release more men for the front line. Later on, when the Reds were in retreat, women were also accepted for front-line duties and Red propaganda used these young women as role models. For once they were no longer seen as ridiculous but as 'the biggest and the most sacred gift that the proletariat has given or ever could give for the cause'.[58] Given the small number of female soldiers – at the end of the civil war, out of 100,000 Red troops, only 2,600 were women according to historian Tuomas Hoppu – their contribution to the battles was minor. Nevertheless, they played an important role in inspiring men to fight until the end. The common view seemed to be that if women were willing to take part in battle, men could not desert the ranks.[59]

After the defeat of the Red Guard in the civil war, many of the women faced trial. The relevant court records, held in the Finnish National Archive, are a rich source, with ten to twenty pages of information on each defendant consisting of the interrogation record and statements of all parties. From this and from oral history and memoirs stored in the People's Archive, voices of the female soldiers were recorded highlighting their motivations to enlist. They often joined the troops at a very young age: 85 per cent of them were under twenty-four years old, and 400 of them were girls aged between thirteen and sixteen years only.[60] Some of them joined the Red Guard seeking adventure; some of them were led by their idealism. If they were single and childless, the decision seemed to have been easier – those with family duties stayed behind the front and worked as auxiliaries supplying the troops. Since the Red Guard had taken possession of the Bank of Finland it was able to pay good salaries, so working-class women could easily double their earnings by serving as cooks, nurses or cleaners. Thus, these jobs were wanted and there were more applicants than places to fill. Women who had been already active in the labour movement and had shown political commitment to the cause were given preference in recruitment. Therefore, the women enlisted as auxiliaries were somewhat older and often already loyal party members. Approximately 10,000 women worked in the service troops fulfilling those tasks that were seen as proper for a woman.[61] Women at arms in the socialist or republican forces can be found repeatedly in the first half of the twentieth century. Research on other conflicts, such as the Spanish civil war from 1936–39, shows that their integration did not occur without problems. On the one hand, despite all the proclaimed equality, the everyday war life of female soldiers at war was more difficult and on the other hand, even left-wing governments and socialist women did not always approve of deployment at the front.[62]

Those who were not fighting with weapons in hand could still be at the centre of revolutionary socialist organizations, as the German example shows. Women thus ran the kitchens and infirmaries that were put in place during long sieges like the ones in Berlin at the *Vorwärts* headquarters or at the Silesian railway station in early 1919. They handed out pamphlets outside factories, wrote and carried messages around the city, stored guns in their apartments so that they could be given out later at the beginning of demonstrations[63] and brought food and ammunition when the conflict began to escalate.[64] Franz Beiersdorf, a sailor who joined the Spartacists in 1917, remembered in 1958 one of the women arrested with him, an ironing-woman who brought hot coffee to the men lined up at the machine-gun posts.[65]

Besides, women smuggled propaganda and ammunitions under their petticoats through the checkpoints between the different districts. The centrist *Vossische Zeitung* reported how women were sent to the Lichtenberg district of Berlin to track down the addresses of police officers so that the Spartacists could arrest them.[66] In Munich in May 1919, to give another example, women were the ones returning their husbands' or brothers' weapons to the authorities during the disarmament campaign after the crushing of the councils' republic. Unlike men who tried to give their rifles back, the women were less at risk of being immediately shot.[67] This inability of the authorities to consider women as revolutionary activists could allow many of them to go unnoticed. Clandestine activities of women disguised under the cloak of bourgeois gender relations like transporting weapons and inflammatory leaflets in baby carriages, opening their living rooms for secret meetings or acting as message carriers were a central part of illegal activities.

(Gendered) state violence against revolutionary women

But not all revolutionary socialist and feminist women could escape violence. In the Finnish civil war, for example, approximately sixty female combatants were killed in action. On some occasions, their corpses were violated by exposing their breasts and genitals. As a consequence of hate and revenge, some soldiers on both sides were killed after they had surrendered, among them also women. Tuomas Hoppu has identified 270 executed female combatants.[68] Yet it was not only women who served at arms who were subject to such treatment: female agitators and auxiliaries were also shot. Estimates of the total number of Red women killed are as high as 500, but as some of the corpses were disposed of secretly, the exact number is impossible to calculate. Prisoner-of-war camps proved to be especially dangerous for female detainees, some of whom were executed without trial. Court martials, where they were in operation, often sentenced women to death without fair legal proceedings. One of the worst places for a Red woman was the POW camp in Lahti. Approximately 200 women were executed there.[69] Nevertheless, most female soldiers survived the war and its aftermath. Many of the women who had served as soldiers were conspicuous since they wore trousers and sometimes had short hair, which was considered deviant and reprehensible by the counter-revolutionary side. These outfits were a sign of rebellion, and women who rebelled against both the social and gender system were regarded as double traitors. After the defeat, these outfits caused trouble. Women were easy targets since they were so distinguishable due to their clothing and attracted attention wherever they went.

While female fighters, like their male comrades in arms, not only risked their lives in battle but also had to fear reprisals after defeat, they were also often doubly targeted because of their sex and their transgression of ascribed gender roles. Yet, as the court records from Germany reveal, some, but by no means all, women revolutionaries were also able to strategically appropriate bourgeois gender roles for themselves in order to evade conviction. A study of trials conducted against those arrested following the revolutionary events in Berlin and Munich in the earlier months of 1919 shows how traditional gender norms influenced the way female and male defendants were treated by the authorities. Men and women experienced state violence differently which led ultimately to unequal sentencing in court. If one were to trace the path of women in the German justice system, one would notice that many women arrested by the police or the military troops never made it to court. They were often not taken directly to the police headquarters, as would have been the case in peacetime. Instead, they were tried directly by government troops on the spot, without leaving any paper trail. It was also possible for women to be released before trial, as was the case with Anna Erfurt, a thirty-two-year-old worker who had been involved in the strike movement since the beginning of the war and who joined the revolution in November 1918. In her memoirs, Erfurt recounts how she narrowly escaped the firing squad. But that does not mean that women evaded punishment all together. Many of them experienced sexualized violence or were heavily beaten. Indeed, although the state of war was lifted on 12 November 1918 following the abdication of Kaiser Wilhelm II, this decision did not reflect the reality experienced by the population, which had to get used to living under siege, even though peace had just been declared. Armed groups had free rein to restore order and the soldiers and officers were able to exercise justice as they saw fit, often in a summary manner. From February 1919, the new President, Friedrich Ebert, could also declare a state of emergency and suspend certain legal protections in particular states or provinces.[70]

The trial of the merchant Heinrich Sklarz provides an instructive example of the aforementioned fact that women were sometimes released before being charged and of the gendered and sexualized violence they nevertheless could endure. Prisoners, especially women, were taken during the night to Heinrich Sklarz's office in the police headquarters at Berlin's Alexanderplatz and were offered release in exchange for sexual favours, as some women defendants stated in court. All one had to do, they explained, was to 'be a little obedient with the man upstairs in order get the biggest charge dropped with impunity'.[71]

Research from Finland shows a similar pattern: here, living conditions at the POW camps were disastrous, with approximately 80,000 people waiting for their trials. The shortage of food was severe, dirt and vermin tormented prisoners, and infectious diseases reached epidemic proportions. More than 13,000 people died. In these circumstances, some of the female prisoners found themselves forced to trade sexual favours for food. Men were more likely to be prosecuted than women, who mainly appeared in the records because they were arrested alongside men. Subsequently, women were not the main defendants in their own trials and were instead tried in large group cases where their names turn up at the end of a long list of male defendants. This in itself suggested a hierarchical ranking of crimes according to gender. In the trial proceedings, women were usually not considered to be politically active, even when they were party members. Their involvement was typically explained by the negative influence of a close male figure, often a husband, meaning that they were not held accountable for their actions. Mothers, in particular, were often released from custody so as not to break up the family unit. This was one of the main arguments in the letters from lawyers asking for the release of their female clients, although in fact most of the women arrested in 1918–19 were not mothers, but single persons aged seventeen to twenty-five.

Despite this, many women can be found in German court records, albeit in much smaller numbers than men. They had a different experience of the judicial process than men. The case of Ida Bauer is typical in this respect. Bauer was a twenty-two-year-old woman in 1918 and the wife of the merchant Ernst Bauer, secretary to Rudolf Egelhofer, Ernst Toller's predecessor as commandant of the Red Army. The Bauer couple was politically active: both worked for the military police of the Bavarian councils' republic and were tasked with arresting counter-revolutionaries, one by conducting spying missions in cafés and the other by detaining suspects. Understanding the role she had to play, Ida Bauer claimed during the trial that she was not political; she had only followed her husband out of jealousy and to prevent him from seeing other women. Arrested at the same time, Ernst Bauer was accused of treason and sentenced to three and a half years' imprisonment, while his wife was only under indictment for assisting in a treasonous crime and was released. Ida Bauer had been as deeply involved politically as her husband; the only difference was that she had not carried a gun.[72] As an unarmed spy, she fitted the stereotype of female involvement by corresponding on the one hand to the stereotype of the false woman particularly suited to espionage and on the other hand to the woman who did not use physical violence, which was deemed unnatural.

This leniency towards female defendants also stems from the penal code of the time, which placed great importance on the intentionality of the crime. The defendants most at risk were those who were accused of being *Rädelsführer*, or rabble-rousing leaders. However, this accusation was not made against any of the women indicted in the eighty-four trials analysed. The male defendants all faced a list of charges that hardly changed from one to the other and that were centred on their conscious involvement in the overthrow of the government and their violent actions. In contrast, a constant in the accusations against women was the emphasis on their mere auxiliary role.

In Ireland too, the state authorities and the Crown Forces targeted militant women in a gendered manner – using both physical and sexualized violence, increasing in frequency and intensity as the war dragged on into 1920–21. Gemma Clark has stated that 'female republican sympathizers received humiliating, gendered punishments (such as haircutting) but nothing to match the violent retribution and "sexually charged torture" served on "politicized women" by paramilitaries in Central Europe in the same period'.[73] However, recent research has demonstrated that violence against women was widespread during the War of Independence, especially once the British authorities and the Crown Forces began to recognize the importance of militant women to the guerrilla war being waged by the IRA. They also recognized that political women were especially effective as creators and disseminators of anti-imperial, republican propaganda, in Ireland and further afield, in the UK, Europe and America. Some examples of the type of violence endured include an incident in County Kerry in 1920, when local schoolteacher and *Cumann na mBan* member Margaret Rohan was dragged out of her bed by the British Crown Forces and had her hair cropped as a punishment for her revolutionary activities. On the night of 18 September 1920, three *Cumann na mBan* women in Galway city were targeted when 'parties of men carrying revolvers and electric torches, wearing black and white masks, slouch hats and uniforms' visited the Madden, Broderick and Turke homes' and attacked and forcibly cropped the hair of Misses Madden, Broderick and Turke.[74]

As this was a guerrilla war where the enemy could be anywhere and everywhere, the Crown Forces focused their attentions on communities and homes. Violent home invasions, often accompanied by physical gendered and sexual assaults on women and girls, were the norm. However, it is only in the last two decades that the complexities of women's participation in the revolutionary period are no longer victim to selective and gendered remembering; while there is much more to research, analysed and written, their contributions and experiences, and particularly their very obvious roles as combatants, and the violence and traumas they suffered because of this, are no longer denied, downplayed, overlooked or indeed simply forgotten.

Maire Comerford, a militant republican, who after the War of Independence broke out in 1919, travelled the country, organizing *Cumann na mBan* branches, carrying dispatches for the IRA's Fourth Northern Division, and reporting for

Figure 3.3 Still image of Irish woman May Connelly after she was punished by the Republicans for associations with the British Crown Forces, by having her hair forcibly cropped, 25 November 1920. Reproduced with permission of British Pathé.

the White Cross on Black and Tan atrocities, was often targeted by the British Crown Forces. When in Dublin she lived with and was secretary to nationalist activist Alice Stopford Green and helped organize and distribute republican propaganda. Their house was often raided – one particular description in her memoir demonstrates the violence that political women endured. In late March 1921, the house was again targeted, and as Comerford writes,

> I opened the door. I was pushed back against the wall. He forced his revolver into my mouth ... my mouth was full of steel ... After those first few minutes this turned into an ordinary raid by men searching for papers.[75]

Many of the women who had been feminist, socialist and/or republican activists prior to the outbreak of war were similarly targeted, while some IRA men struggled with their inability to protect 'their' women. As IRA leader Ernie O'Malley wrote about the Crown Forces' reprisals on family homes and on women, 'there was silence for a time as we watched, helpless ... feeling cowardly and miserable'.[76] Lil Conlon, who had been a member of *Cumann na mBan* during the War of Independence, wrote in her memoir that by 1920,

> the going was tough on the female sex, they were unable to 'go on the run', so were constantly subjected to having their homes raided and precious possessions destroyed. To intensify the reign of terror, swoops were made at night, entries forced into their homes, and the women's hair cut off in a brutal fashion as well as suffering other indignities and insults.[77]

Another raid on the house of Dr Kathleen Lynn, a socialist and republican activist, was described in a newspaper report on 1 March 1920, where a 'half company of soldiers with glittering bayonets, and a dozen policemen' surrounded the house.[78] Kathleen Clarke and Kathleen McDonnell, both activists in *Cumann na mBan*, and well known, like Dr Lynn, to the Crown Forces, described 'houses occupied by women and children raided at night by armed men, the terror of the situation was underlined by the fact that the men were rude, insulting, threatening and undisciplined'.[79] Clarke described a terrifying raid by Crown Forces on her mother's home, conducted by 'seven men, all drunk ... [and] one never knew what drunken men could do'.[80] These raids, the *Irish Bulletin* (the republican propaganda newspaper) noted were a 'source of sleeplessness, nervous breakdowns, and in the case of expectant mothers, produce grave results for mothers and children'.[81]

The propaganda effect of these constant raids and the terror experienced by civilians, especially women, became a major issue for the Crown Forces and the

British government. As early as March 1920 Erskine Childers, writer and republican activist, described, in the English *Daily Mail*, to a horrified public, the awful effects these raids or home invasions had on the occupants, especially the women. A raid on the house of Una Brennan, wife of Robert Brennan, a senior republican, and herself a feminist and republican, was entitled a 'Young Mother's ordeal'. One night, roused by the knocking on her door and 'running down in her nightdress', she was met with voices shouting, 'Damn you open the door or we'll smash it in.' Worse still, 'one soldier came in drunk and used foul language, and in spite of her entreaties to be allowed to her children she was kept apart under guard while the rooms are searched and the search is conducted with the roughness and insolence worthy of veritable Huns'.[82] This, he concluded, at the end of the description of the Brennan raid, is 'not a civilised war'.[83]

But, as the aforementioned Lil Conlon acknowledged, just as *Cumann na mBan* women were being targeted by the British Crown Forces, so too were other women targeted by Irish republicans. As part of the boycott against the Royal Irish Constabulary (RIC), 'people were encouraged not to socialise with them or even speak to them. Girls who consorted with them were warned off or punished by having their hair cut off'.[84] During 1920–21, both *Cumann na mBan* members and women targeted by the IRA began to experience the worst of the raids and reprisals when 'masked raiders could come to threaten, bully and burn out their homes'.[85] Descriptions in many archives detail the escalation and intensity of violence perpetrated on women in their domestic space. The home became then, not a safe space, but a battlefront, a site of gendered and sexualized violation and terror. This violation of the intimate, feminine, domestic space reflected, as Louise Ryan notes, 'the intensely political work which was going on inside many Irish homes' in this period.[86] The Irish revolutionary war was 'intimate', a conflict in which the 'British security forces and the IRA routinely violated private spaces'.[87] A balanced account requires 'acknowledgement [that] women ... bore the brunt of the raids and interrogations ... [and] that some of the most vital contributions to the independence movement took place away from the ambush site'.[88]

Sexualized violence

Historian Ville Kivimäki has stated that in warfare a woman's body is an object of man's self-image, desire and psychic discrepancy. A fighting woman does not fit into the traditional arrangement where a man is a protector and a woman is protected. She is treated as an object of urges, abuse of power and sexualized violence.[89] Rape has been part of the conquerors' strategy for centuries, to humiliate the enemy on various levels. The first disgraced target is obviously the victim herself; the second object of humiliation is the men in the victim's family who were not able to protect her. The third and widest target is the defeated nation, as women often symbolize purity in the nationalist discourse.[90]

In Finland during the civil war, White propaganda described socialist women as sexually loose creatures without virtue. Due to this creation of 'otherness', some White soldiers saw Red women as whores who deserved neither protection nor respect. Quite the reverse: many Red women, especially soldiers, were raped and/or killed. The cases were hardly ever documented because the surviving victims did not trust the White authorities and did not want to make it official since a rape was a shameful taboo. Women dared not to reveal that they had lost their physical and moral integrity in a society that easily shifted the blame onto the victims. On the other hand, it was hardly in the interests of the perpetrator to document the deed either. However, knowledge of the rapes has been preserved in oral history instead.[91] In particular, stories of young women soldiers who were violated and killed after the fighting have been sustained within the labour movement. According to previous studies and known archival material there was sexual abuse in the POW camps after the Finnish civil war, even if it has not occurred systematically. On a few rare occasions women joined forces to launch a collective complaint after a guard had sexually harassed them. Sometimes they were believed, sometimes not. Nevertheless, in most cases women kept silent.[92]

The source problem is also reflected in the German example. While some women recounted sexual assaults in oral testimonies, the judicial and police sources remain vague or silent. As already mentioned in the previous subsection, contemporaries remembered assaults in prisons that happened in plain sight.[93] One of these testimonies is from the above-mentioned Franz Beiersdorf, who lived through the repression following the fighting in the Berlin district of Lichtenberg. In early March 1919, a general strike was declared, launching a bloody episode of street fighting between revolutionary forces and government troops in Berlin known as the 'March Days'.[94] Eventually, the revolutionaries were forced to retreat to the working-class district of Lichtenberg, which was subsequently reconquered, street by street, by the army. Once the district had been seized, the authorities turned their efforts to what was called in the newspapers the purge (*Säuberung*) of Lichtenberg, which meant the violent inspection of houses at gunpoint in search of the weapons and Spartacist hideouts. Beiersdorf recalls how, following his arrest, officers, with the agreement of their superiors, lined up prisoners against a wall and interrogated them immediately after their arrest, killing some, leaving others alive and raping women before releasing them.

> The next prisoner was a woman. I knew her. She was a worker in the laundry shop in the Gürtelstrasse by the railway bridge. She often brought hot coffee to us at the machine guns ... She was asked if she belonged to the Spartacus group. She said 'No ... I am not in any party'. 'You're lying quite nastily', roared the young lieutenant ... 'Turn around, there are still twenty of your fellow loyalists sitting there. To which of them did you bring the coffee?' The woman turned around. She was as pale as a sheet. Like all of us, she had been betrayed. She looked at us silently ... The woman shook her head, her whole-body trembling, and said to the officers: 'I don't know any of these men'. 'That's what I thought, you red bitch, you are about to experience something'. The lieutenant bent down and whispered something in the lieutenant's ear. The mercenaries dragged the woman to the back of the dance hall ... We heard the woman being whipped on the back. Then Godi (a friend of Beiersdorf who had been arrested with him) shouted in the officers' faces: 'You cowardly vermin ... You can beat and rape women, you're a real riffraff ...'. Four or five mercenaries attacked him and beat him.[95]

The officer's attitude here is one of revenge against a woman who, in his opinion, should not be among the combatants. The punishment he chose, the whipping and the rape, is intended to return the accused to her traditional position in the gender hierarchy. Women were subjected to sexualized and gendered violence, which aimed to re-establish the traditional and 'natural' paternal authority.[96]

In May 1921, the American Commission on Conditions in Ireland published the results of its research in Ireland on atrocities carried out by the British Crown forces. Statements were given by political women including veteran militant feminist Hanna Sheehy Skeffington who gave a statement to the Commission on the violence against women. While it detailed the horror of raids and reprisals on her home, her report included only one reference to an alleged rape, 'the rape of a girl in the presence of her father reported in Galway near Gort but not yet investigated fully'.[97] The Commission did report back that the sanctity of the home was often violated by the Crown Forces, and such was the terror of the population that 'in some places, those who were not "on the run", and the infirm and aged, the women and children, would appear to feel safer in the fields than in their homes'.[98]

However, Meg Connory, also of the militant feminist group, the IWFL, who reported on the assaults on women on behalf of the Irish White Cross Committee, wrote that 'women know that it is during curfew hours attempts of a sexual character have been made'. It was 'difficult to appreciate the effects which this continued strain is producing upon the health of women', but clearly many suffered from their nerves because of this.[99] Lil Conlon does distinguish in her writings between a woman having her 'hair cut off in a brutal fashion', during attacks on homes, and the fact that she might 'suffer other indignities and insults'.[100] It is through the euphemistic vagueness of other 'indignities and insults' that language may serve to obscure sexual assault in the sources. Lindsey Earner Byrne in her micro-study of sexualized violence during the Irish civil war (1922–23) notes that 'rape was a form of violence not easily accommodated in the script of the Irish revolution'.[101] However, deliberate gendered violence against women during the revolutionary period in Ireland can be uncovered, if we understand that, as Earner Byrne observed, the term 'outrage', and other terms such as 'insult' or 'indignity', were often used as euphemisms for both gendered and sexualized violence committed against women. Revisiting the use of language, the archives and other sources can and do re-balance the idea that gendered and sexualized violence was almost absent from the Irish revolutionary war and helps formulate a more nuanced and broader understanding of the trauma experiences of women and girls during this period. Something, that is also true of the other case studies.

The phantasma of the revolutionary women

As also noted in Chapter 1 of this volume, the German criminologist Hans von Hentig – who himself had been involved in the Bavarian councils' republic – published a misogynist essay, *The Revolutionary Woman*, in 1923. In it, he typified and pathologized women who became involved in the political upheavals of the post-war period and marched in the streets for their causes. He saw women above all as instigators: 'the insane woman places herself at the head of this leaping, overheated mass'.[102] The German press recounted stories of women participating in lynching, for instance:

> A captured soldier was … severely wounded by numerous stabs with pocket-knives. The scalp was hanging off his head in large shreds. A woman stabbed him in the neck with a knife so that the artery was torn open and the wounded man sank to the ground. He was now pushed aside like a log, but immediately a number of women threw themselves on him and trampled him. Another

captured soldier was literally stripped naked, put on the street in this state and pelted with hand grenades until his body was torn to pieces.[103]

Many of Hentig's theses, influenced by crowd psychology based on Gustave Le Bon and Scipio Sighele, can be found in different ways in the publications that dealt with women revolutionaries in the post-war period. For instance, the Austro-Marxist Otto Bauer spoke of female revolutionary activists as 'morbidly excited women whose husbands had been languishing in war captivity for years'.[104] The main themes that were used, especially by the conservative press in the cases discussed in our chapter, can be summed up as follows: women revolutionaries were pathologized, sexualized and their political action depoliticized – regardless of the fact that activism that affects daily life was understood by radical women as being related to social problems (and problems with the way society and the state were organized), and thus political. The women who joined the revolutions lived in a symbolic world influenced by the gender norms of the time, which governed relations between men and women.[105] Press articles, postcards and election posters allow us a glimpse into what Kathleen Canning describes as a gendered 'ideology'.[106] The press created stereotypical figures of violent or abused women for political purposes to show the fundamentally negative nature and ignominy of the revolutionary movements. In the German case it is additionally noticeable that women remained anonymous and the adjectives 'revolutionary' (*revolutionär*) or 'spartacist' were rarely attributed to them. Being only described by their gender identity, they are referred to pejoratively as *Frauenswesen, weibliche Wesen* or *Frauenspersonen*. Nevertheless, what is striking about the following examples is that revolutionary women could be simultaneously defined by their gender identity and portrayed as unfeminine. Although women were not at all rare in armed struggles and revolutionary conflicts throughout the long nineteenth century,[107] they nevertheless transgressed the bourgeois gender order. The apparent sexualization and pathologization of revolutionary women in the press can thus be read as a means of restoring women to their places. For political participation in revolutionary events was not only often dangerous, but also self-empowering and liberating. The freedom to lead a life of independence and partnership was a goal many women socialists shared as part of their revolutionary efforts.

In Finland, the White war propaganda addressed against all Red women was harsh. The right-wing press represented revolutionary women as violent beasts, amoral man-eaters or ridiculous wannabe soldiers. The aim was to create boundaries between 'us' and 'them'. The construction of 'otherness' was important

Figure 3.4 Cartoon mocking Red female soldiers in the Finnish satirical paper *Nya Fyren*, no. 5–7 (1918).

because the enemy in the civil war was a fellow citizen, possibly even one's neighbour or relative. The propagandists used stereotypes to create boundaries between the 'acceptable' and the 'detestable'. This dichotomy increased a sense of solidarity among 'normals' and eased the exclusion of 'abnormals'.[108] In White newspapers, four stereotypes were used to represent Red women. Nurses were called 'Sisters of free love', implying that they were on the front solely in order to indulge in sexual excesses. Finnish women who dated Russian soldiers were 'Russian brides' and were seen as traitors to the nation's purity. Red mothers were labelled as 'sources of evil' since they had raised sons who became rebels. They were even accused of being culpable for the whole war as a Red woman was 'the exact opposite to everything that she as a mother and as a wife should be. Such a woman should not be allowed to raise her children'.[109] The female soldiers were called tigresses as they were considered to have lost contact with their femininity and humanity and turned into beasts as they grabbed rifles. Immorality, be it sexual or otherwise, was common to all four stereotypes. Untrue rumours were spread, for instance, that Red nurses killed White patients in hospitals,[110] and female soldiers were disgraceful cowards and traitors:

> During the last few days the assassinations have shown us what a woman is able to do if she is captivated by malignity. Many assassinations, many bullets shot from behind in archways can be explained only this way.[111]

In one outstandingly aggressive text, all Red women were described as dangerous she-wolves who should be killed in order to prevent the birth of new harmful wolf cubs. They were also considered equivalent to prostitutes who should be eliminated from society.[112] These stereotypes had severe consequences as they influenced attitudes toward imprisoned women after the end of the civil war. They were seen as unwomanly creatures who were not worthy of gallant male protection.[113]

In Germany, a reading of the politically conservative press gives further insight into the different aspects of the phantasma of the revolutionary woman, denying the political nature of feminine involvement. Spartacist women were described as amoral and sexually depraved. They are for example often referred to as prostitutes storing weapons in their homes and participating in looting. Districts under the control of the revolutionary side, like Berlin's Lichtenberg in March 1919, were described as being infested with 'nests' of Spartacists,[114] forming a veritable 'Bolshevik menagerie'.[115] The left-liberal *Berliner Tageblatt* carried a report on its front page on 19 January 1919 about 'the hustle and bustle of Spartacists [who] celebrated real orgies with women from the surrounding area. [It] was so bad that hardly anyone dared to leave the house afterwards.'[116] On the same day, the *Tägliche Rundschau* reported how five women were killed at the Silesian railway station[117] because they dared to 'resist to the advances of the Spartacists',[118] hence portraying revolutionaries as sexual predators.[119] These

Figure 3.5 'Wen wähle ich?' ('Who do I vote for?'). German propaganda poster, 1919, promoting the Majority Social Democrats while warning against the dangers of the Spartacist movement represented by a dishevelled and armed woman in the front row. Reproduced with permission of the Plakat- und Flugblattsammlung, Münchner Stadtbibliothek/Monacensia.

abuses were a way to justify the call to 'liberate and purify' the Spartacist-occupied districts of Prenzlauer Berg, Neukölln and Lichtenberg from the 'Bolshevik dictatorship'. The description of pro-revolutionary women in the mainstream Berlin press was characterized by a preoccupation with their youth and their sexuality. On 8 March 1919, the *Tägliche Rundschau* portrayed people collecting merchandise and carrying it away in handcarts to sell to the numerous traders in the area near Hackescher Markt as prostitutes and prematurely sexualized (*frühreif*) boys and girls. The term 'frühreif' refers here to a sexual precocity linked to unbridled instincts that are supposedly uncontrollable and that revolutionaries allegedly share.[120]

Another omnipresent theme in these newspaper articles was the thirst for blood and the figure of 'Red Rosa'. During the 1919 trial of Georg Ledebour, a USPD politician arrested for the part he played in the Spartacist Uprising, soldiers described being haunted by the figure of Rosa Luxemburg. The revolutionary women fighting were all seen as 'Rosas', in other words as vampiric figures who drank the blood of soldiers. The trial records for Georg Ledebour contains a reference to such a vampiric figure: 'a female person with a pale face, dark hair and black eyes' known as 'Rosa' as she was in a leadership position during the storming of the Wolff's Telegraphic Bureau by the Spartacists.[121] This omnipresence of Luxemburg in the press and judicial discourse went beyond the borders of Berlin and was also found in Munich (and also outside of Germany, as is shown in Chapter 5). There, the activist Elma Klingelhöfer, wife of Gustav, one of the leaders of the Red Army, was described in her trial as the 'Rosa of the South'.[122] On small loose sheets, torn from little rectangular notebooks, which were added to the proceedings of her trial, she spoke of her decision to interpose herself alongside a whole group of women including Hildegard Menzi and Teckla Egl between the government troops and those of the Red Army in order to stop the fighting, re-enacting the Roman legend of the Sabine women, who ended the war between Romans and Sabines by stepping between the combatants.[123]

The Austrian press was also fascinated by women revolutionaries. In Catholic and right-wing newspapers, radical left groups were defamed in an anti-Semitic and sexist manner, and female activists were labelled 'hysterical ladies'.[124] But one of the most common themes seems to be the sexualization of revolutionary women as a means of devaluing their political concerns as well as their progressive alliances and social policies. The satirical magazine *Die Muskete*, for example, ran several drawings between March and July 1919 in which communism was portrayed as the sensual-erotic pastime of bored bourgeois ladies, and socialization – the taking of businesses into public ownership – as the moral equivalent of making all women sexually available. The personal lives of prominent women communists were discussed in the press. When Ruth Fischer, who had published a book entitled *Sexual Ethics of Communism* (*Sexualethik des Kommunismus*),[125] and advocated love freed from marriage, divorced her husband Paul Friedländer, the court case and her (alleged) promiscuity were extensively reported,[126] as well as her bourgeois upbringing and her German-Jewish family background.[127]

After the revolutions: closing remarks

The Social Democrat Hilja Pärssinen, a member of the Finnish Parliament since 1907, had to flee the country to Russia and then Estonia after the defeat of the

Figure 3.6 Cartoon '*Kommunismus*' in the Austrian satirical paper *Die Muskete*, 13 March 1919, equating the socialization of property with free sexuality and/or women with property.

socialist side in the civil war. After her forced return from Estonia to Finland, she was sentenced to twelve years in prison, but was released in 1923. When Pärssinen and other Finnish socialist women returned home after serving prison sentences, they faced a difficult socio-economic and political situation. In small rural communities, where everyone knew each other and where an elite sympathetic to the White side dominated the spiritual atmosphere of the village, life was probably harder than in the urban centres. In the cities, former Red women could hide among the masses. They could also rely more easily on networks of like-minded people, which helped them to endure the contempt that the White community exuded.[128] Negative attitudes became visible, for example, in job advertisements. Some of them directly stated that it was pointless for Reds to put themselves forward for the job in question, as the following example, from summer 1918, illustrates:

> A housemaid or a lady's maid is needed for work on a farm, preferably someone who has schooling in home economics (Reds and those with bastards need not apply). Answers should be sent to Perniö's post office and marked 'Housemaid'.[129]

There were so many unemployed that employers could afford to choose who they wanted to hire. Female unemployment doubled in 1918 compared to the previous year. If no jobs were available, working women had to seek municipal help or to rely on the goodwill of relatives or friends. After the war, the Reds were second-class citizens. The White widows were granted pensions but the Red widows were not entitled to such funds. Instead, they had to resort to poor relief, which was only a fraction of the amount of the pensions. In addition, those who relied on poor relief lost their voting rights. Red widows were offered unsolicited assistance in another form: they could place their children in foster homes. Most of the mothers were not ready to accept this help, as they did not want to give up their children, despite their dire financial situation. This may have been partly due to the lack of information on how children would be treated in an unfamiliar, alien White environment. The labour movement had also effectively disseminated the information that children in foster homes were educated to reject socialism in later life. Already during the war, Red mothers had been accused by the White propaganda writers of raising their children, especially their sons, in an atmosphere that nurtured socialism.[130] Even though the first year after the civil war brought with it much death, misery, unemployment and anger, the situation gradually eased after 1919. Even the anger gradually subsided into resentment and mutual distrust.

In Ireland, political women influenced by feminism, socialism and nationalism expected that a free and independent nation would guarantee them full and equal citizenship. However, for the new state the contribution of women would be most acceptable in the domestic sphere. The ideal Irishwoman was, above all, a wife and mother, the home and the hearth were to be her sphere of influence. Irishwomen's citizenship became 'rooted in their role in the family as wives and mothers ... Motherhood thus became a central mechanism through which women ... [were] incorporated into the modern political order.'[131] As motherhood within marriage and the home was the respectable and accepted feminine role, there were limited expectations and access to employment for women. The afterlives of many of the revolutionary women were impacted by poverty, trauma and marginalization. The politics of the new Irish Free State, founded in 1922, often revealed a real lack of acceptance of female participation in the public realm of politics and work. Public participation was seen as injurious both to women (it unsexed them) and to the political arena itself; it was felt by some that the presence of women brought a bitterness, hysteria and emotionalism which had no place in civilized, rational public (male) debate.[132] Many of the socialist and militant women rejected the Anglo-Irish treaty and new Irish Free State that it created. The attitude of the state to these anti-treaty militant women, its incarceration and mistreatment of hundreds of them during the civil war in 1922–3, and its construction of these women as dangerous 'die-hards', 'republican bitches', 'furies' and 'unmanageable, ungovernable' revolutionaries reflect what would be a deeply misogynistic attitude to women, generally, in the ensuing decades. Irish identity and Catholicism became enmeshed, with the state identifying itself as Catholic, governing a Catholic people and following Catholic social thinking and practices, and this state found the activities of women in the public realm problematic socially, culturally and politically.

One of the major sources for information about revolutionary women in Ireland are the military pension application files.[133] These reveal lives of quiet desperation, often denied support by male politicians who had been their comrades in the revolutionary struggle, making it 'difficult to avoid the conclusion that the female veteran was very much the poor relation among the old comrades of the Irish revolution'.[134] One example is Margaret Skinnider, a teacher, socialist, suffragist and militant nationalist, who was wounded in action in the 1916 Rising, fought in the War of Independence and civil war (on the anti-Treaty side, against the government), and was later a trade union activist with her teachers' union. When she first applied in 1925, she was denied her pension. While behind the scenes the government was determined that 'irregulars', those who had

Figure 3.7 Irish socialist and revolutionary Margaret Skinnider, 1915. Image courtesy of James Langton.

opposed the Treaty which led to the settling up of the Irish Free State, of which Skinnider was one, would not get pensions, it officially denied Skinnider the pension on the basis that 'the Army Pensions Act is only applicable to soldiers as generally understood in the masculine sense'.[135]

While many of the Irish revolutionary women did return to the domestic, marriage and motherhood, women like Skinnider continued to fight for women's and workers rights'. Skinnider, for example, was, by 1956, President of the Irish National Teachers' Organisation (INTO), the trade union for primary school teachers. One of her main campaigns throughout her career as a trade union activist was to get the marriage bar, under which any women working in teaching had to give up her job on getting married, repealed – this happened in 1958. Others such as Hanna Sheehy Skeffington, Kathleen Clarke or Kathleen Lynn campaigned against the gendered legislation passed between 1922 and 1936, which reaffirmed conservative views on women, traditional Catholic social thinking and the dominance of the discourse of domesticity for women.[136] Despite objections from feminists, the 1937 Constitution, containing articles which determined that the place of Irish women was in the home, was passed by popular vote. The social conservatism of the 1920s and 1930s found full force in the legislative actions against women, against the female worker, and in the constitutional definitions of women's life as within the home; this gendered ideology was to affect the lives of women and the position of the female worker in Ireland, legally and ideologically, until late into the twentieth century.

As we have been able to show with four very different national cases, women in Europe were very much present in the revolutionary movements and wars of the period 1918–21, participating in and finding themselves at the receiving end of revolutionary violence and the consequences of wars in multiple ways. Even though socialist women's attitudes toward violence were less than uniform, all cases showed that they were not only ready to take up arms and fight for a better future, but that by doing so some of them gained pride in their own role. Nevertheless, the cases also highlight the socio-economic conditions under which working women and men made their decisions to support revolutionary troops. All our cases make it clear that historical sources have to be read with analytical rigour, knowledge of codes and the toolbox of critical historical scholarship, in order to not adopt the 'gender-specific topography of relevance' identified and criticized by Brigitte Studer.[137] This is especially true for sexualized and gendered violence. As our case studies clearly demonstrate, revolutionary gender-based violence not only violated women's physical integrity, but also did not stop at the intimate sphere of their own households or the communities of neighbourly solidarity in their villages. The apparent sexualization and pathologization of revolutionary women in the press can thus be read as a means of restoring women to their places. For political participation in revolutionary events was not only often dangerous, but also self-empowering and liberating. The transgression of gender norms was countered in mainstream newspapers by the sexualization and pathologization of politically active women. This necessarily made the granting of female suffrage, where this took place, a less than whole-hearted victory for gender equality. Even so, many of the women discussed in this chapter remained committed to the socialist cause after 1921, as will also be demonstrated in Chapter 5 of this volume.

4

Suffrage, Democracy and Citizenship

Ingrid Sharp, Manca G. Renko, Ali Ronan and Judith Szapor

A major event after the post-1917 revolutionary upheavals was the introduction of universal adult suffrage in several European countries, leading to a strong association of women's suffrage with revolution. Post-revolutionary Germany in 1918 had the freest franchise in the world, giving all citizens over the age of twenty the right to vote and stand for election, regardless of gender, class or wealth, while the revolutions in Russia, Hungary and Austria also brought about female suffrage. In Britain, the franchise was more restricted: only women over thirty with particular property rights gained the vote in February 1918, while an Act of Parliament passed in November allowed women over twenty-one to stand as Members of Parliament. In other national contexts, however, the end of the war brought only limited suffrage for women, or none at all.

The case studies included in this chapter are Britain, Germany, Hungary and the Kingdom of Serbs, Croats and Slovenes (hereafter the Kingdom of Yugoslavia), a combination that prevents us from making any easy assumptions. The case of Hungary, which will be discussed in more detail below, clearly illustrates that the legal right to vote could be meaningless in practice: due to rapid regime changes between 1918 and 1920, most Hungarian women did not have the chance to exercise their rights to vote or to stand for election until January 1920, by which time the revolutionary period had ended. In the parliamentary elections held that month, Social Democratic women had to forfeit the chance to practice, for the first time, their right to vote, as the Social Democratic Party boycotted the election, held under a still raging White Terror. In Yugoslavia, where female suffrage was not gained until the Socialist Federal Republic was established in 1945, some of the most politically active women were sceptical about its value in the autocratic kingdom after 1921 where democracy and civil rights were limited and political culture unstable. Their ambivalence towards female suffrage was more closely connected to a distrust of 'liberal democracy' and capitalism than to reservations about women's capacity for political action. Looking at these diverse case studies reveals the complexities around suffrage and citizenship, and the political role socialist women were able to play after 1918 under different regimes as well as internationally.

Achieving suffrage is an event of extraordinary significance in the development of women as political subjects and as citizens, but the ability to vote and stand for election is neither a guarantor of democracy nor the only way for women to be politically active, as Rosa Luxemburg pointed out in 1912.[1] In the absence of suffrage, women's political cultures flourished in organizations within and beyond political parties and within trades unions. Whether or not they gained the vote in the aftermath of the war, women on the left were operating in national contexts that were a far cry from the principles of social, economic and gender justice they espoused and many were sceptical about the power of parliamentary democracy to bring about systemic change.

This chapter will centre the experiences, ideas and activities of socialist women who worked within national and international organizations for women's political rights during and after the war, exploring what suffrage and citizenship meant for them during a time of shifting allegiances and fluid political standpoints. There is no doubt that women's relationship with the state changed profoundly due to their achievement of political rights, and the award of suffrage, alongside other spaces for political activities, opened the possibility for women to develop new subjectivities. Citizenship is a fluid term that describes a legal framework, political rights and also a subjectivity – a feeling of belonging, a relationship to a nation-state. Kathleen Canning in her co-edited volume *Weimar Politics/Weimar Subjects* emphasizes the extent to which, regardless of how 'successful' or otherwise Weimar democracy was, and whether or not women were squeezed out of public life and political leadership roles, suffrage fundamentally and irreversibly changed women's relationship with the state.[2] Birgitta Bader-Zaar, Hedwig Richter and Kerstin Wolff also offer a more comprehensive view of women's political engagement and women's relationship with the state beyond the vote by focusing on rights at local level and women's political involvement beyond the national vote.[3]

Socialist women were active campaigners for suffrage within their own parties and within socialist women's organizations; their visions for a social order free of class and gender exploitation fuelled lives of activism in which internationalism, anti-militarism and equal rights for women were bound up with their socialist ideals. Their commitment to adult suffrage for men and women regardless of class, education, property or income put them at odds with many of the women's suffrage organizations, who often sought more limited rights. They worked within and beyond parties and groups, often marginalized and hampered by the attitudes of their male comrades, to create political spaces that recognized the priorities, aspirations and lived realities of women. In 1907, the Socialist Women's International (SWI) met for the first time, attended by at least sixty female delegates.[4] Socialist leaders Clara Zetkin and Rosa Luxemburg made sure that universal suffrage, regardless of sex, was adopted as the guiding policy for socialist parties in the Second International. The creation of an International Women's Day in 1910 was conceived as an annual day of action promoting awareness of the socialist commitment to women's suffrage by demanding the vote.[5] These annual days attracted huge numbers of women and were often opposed by male comrades who feared women's independence from party doctrine.[6]

Suffrage and the revolution in historical accounts and narratives

Although historiographies vary between national contexts, in Germany and Britain, much of the attention given to the campaign for, and award of, suffrage has focused more on middle-class feminists, 'as if it was only a concern for respectable bourgeois ladies'.[7] This has obscured the role played by working-class and socialist women working locally, nationally and internationally to argue the case for an expansion of democracy to include working-class men and women.[8] In *Socialist Women: Britain 1880s–1920s*, Karen Hunt and June Hannam examine in depth both the ideas and the political journeys of socialist women in Britain in the last years of the nineteenth century and the first decades of the twentieth century.[9] They explore some of the contested and contradictory ideas that socialist women in Britain held about the meaning of citizenship, women's emancipation and the relationship between feminism and socialism. They also explore in depth some of the themes that preoccupied women socialists, such as the suffrage and international politics. The standard British study of socialist women and suffrage is still *One Hand Tied Behind Us: The Rise of the Women's Suffrage Movement* by Jill Liddington and Jill Norris, which examines working-class women's relationship with the suffrage and the emergence of what Liddington and Norris call 'radical' suffragists because 'they shared considerable industrial experience and a political radicalism which set them apart from other non-militants'.[10]

In *Pacifists, Patriots and The Vote*, Jo Vellacott explores what happened to the British non-militant suffrage movement during the First World War, a movement which prided itself on its pre-war federal system of regional democracy.[11] She builds on Sandra Holton's *Feminism and Democracy: Women's Suffrage and Reform Politics in Britain, 1900–1918*,[12] which charts the emergence of a group of younger women who developed the links between women's political rights and anti-militarism. Vellacott investigates what she names as the 'erosion of democratic suffragism in Britain during [and immediately after] the First World War'. She reminds us that there was no effective attempt to win adult suffrage nor to widen the relatively narrow franchise granted to women in Britain in 1918, which meant that those omitted from the franchise included the bulk of women war workers, many of whom were under thirty, young widows and single women of any age except those few who met wealth and property requirements. Her work spotlights how the declaration of war in 1914 split the National Union of Women's Suffrage Societies (NUWSS) and how younger women activists, all of whom had been instrumental in developing work with the Labour Party before the war, became committed to the cause of peace. After the International Women's Congress at The Hague in 1915, local committees of the newly founded International Women's Committee for Permanent Peace, later Women's International League for Peace and Freedom (WILPF), were formed in all the major cities throughout England, Scotland and Wales and an Irish committee was formed in Dublin and soon renamed the Women's International League (WIL). Many of the women who left the NUWSS in 1915 became involved in the WIL. British socialist women like Margaret Bondfield and Ada Salter who had both attended the SWI Bern conference in 1915 (see Chapter 2), were involved in this new venture, as were socialist women like Ethel Snowden, Sylvia Pankhurst (briefly), Katherine Bruce Glasier and Eleanor Barton. Barton (1872–1960), who liked to describe herself as an anarchist communist, was also a member of the Women's Co-operative Guild. As a working woman herself, she was billed as 'a worker for the workers'; she stood for peace and for working women, co-operation and the labour movement. At the age of forty-eight, Barton stood as Labour candidate for Attercliffe in the 1920 council elections in Sheffield, a seat where women's suffrage was a prominent topic, and became the first woman to be elected to Sheffield Council.[13]

In Germany, women's suffrage has received steady scholarly attention by leading gender historians since the 1980s.[14] The centenary of women's suffrage in 2018 provoked academic as well as public interest, notably the large exhibition at the Historical Museum in Frankfurt, discussed below, leading to a number of publications important for an understanding of how socialist women have been commemorated within the suffrage narrative.[15] In her controversial monograph, *Demokratie: Eine deutsche Affäre* (Democracy: A German Affair), Richter argues that suffrage was a result of long-standing reform campaigns led by middle-class progressives and that revolutions rarely benefit the cause of women's emancipation.[16]

German histories of socialism tend to focus on the predominantly male leadership within official party structures and often overlook the role of women as organizers. This is especially true of histories of the November 1918 revolution, as many barriers kept women's representation in the *Räte* (Soldiers' and Workers' councils) very low (4 to 5 percent, according to Axel Weipert,[17] with similarly low rates for Hungary)[18] – and this has been misread as low participation rates in the revolution itself.[19] As William A. Pelz notes, 'Forgetting the importance of women to historical developments is more of a rule than an exception. The German Revolution is not one of the exceptions.'[20] Earlier publications on socialist women and suffrage in the German context include Werner Thönnessen's *The Emancipation of Women* (1973; German original 1969), which discusses in detail the prejudice against women as voters.[21] In her 1986 study, *Unsere Erwählten* (Our Elected Women), Christl Wickert outlines the suffrage campaigns, provides biographical details of those elected on the left and offers an insight into their parliamentary interventions.[22] Karen Hagemann's 1990 study on *Frauenalltag und Männerpolitik* (Women's Daily Lives and Men's Politics) contains in-depth analysis of Social Democratic politics and trade union activities, while Julia Sneeringer's 2002 study *Winning Women's Votes* analyses how the parties of the left, now divided into three separate parties, set out to appeal to the women voting for the first time.[23]

Suffrage accounts largely focus on the 'bourgeois' women whose vision was rejected by socialist women, or centre the research around the question whether the vote was won through campaigning or the revolution, as leading socialist women later claimed. SPD delegate Marie Juchacz's speech to the National Assembly on 19 February 1919, the first made by a women before any German parliament, began:

> Gentlemen and Ladies (laughter). It's the first time that a German women is able to address the people in parliament freely and as an equal and I want to make clear, as a matter of fact, that it was the revolution that swept away the old prejudices in Germany.[24]

Die Gleichheit, now under 'moderate' Social Democratic editorship, was also clear that the vote had been won by the revolution alone:

> The chains of millennia have burst. Overnight. Yesterday German women were unfree, an oppressed sex only able to prise minor concessions even from the growing democracy. Today German women are the freest in the world. They have complete equality with men, can elect and be elected to all political bodies. To whom or what do they owe their equality and freedom? To the powerful storm of the revolution which broke over Germany with monstrous and irresistible force on November 9th. Rejoice, German women, you have cause to do so![25]

This was echoed by Clara Zetkin, writing in the Spartacist *Rote Fahne* on 22 November 1918:

> One thing German women must never forget is that their political equality wasn't granted them as a victory prize for their struggle, but rather as a gift of the revolution. This was carried by the proletarian masses, which is why their demands had to include full democracy and citizens' rights for all ... It is now up to women to pay their debt of thanks to the revolution and to justify the trust placed in them.[26]

Sneeringer shows that that SPD (Social Democrat) strategy to appeal to women voters in elections to the National Assembly in January 1919 and the Reichstag in June 1920 was to remind them of their debt of gratitude to the party for supporting women's suffrage in their party programme from 1891 onwards.[27] Yet the more radical Independent Socialists (USPD) also claimed to be the true heirs of the 1891 programme, and its proletarian-revolutionary, as well as internationalist and democratic, spirit.[28]

Historians give different accounts of how suffrage was achieved: for Sneeringer, 'woman suffrage in Germany was the fruit not of a suffragist campaign but of the revolution' while for Helen Boak, 'the German women's suffrage movement ... had never been very strong'.[29] In contrast, German historians Gisela Bock and Sabine Hering argue that suffrage 'could never have come about without the many and diverse efforts by women since the nineteenth century'.[30] Far from being 'a gift of the revolution', suffrage was a long-standing aim towards which the organized women's movement had been painstakingly working at a national and international level, 'mosaic stone by mosaic stone', for over fifteen years.[31] However, these positions do not have to be a contradiction, as an event can happen suddenly after the ground has been thoroughly prepared over a longer period. Because it was debated and rejected in the national parliament as late as 8 November, the day before the Republic was declared, it is very clear in the German case that it was indeed the revolution that was the immediate reason for the extension of suffrage. However, the decision to include women in the suffrage was based on a number of factors, including to a large extent the agitation for female suffrage that had caused it to be successfully enshrined in socialist policy internationally, as well as being a major plank of feminist agitation. Women did not abandon their demands for suffrage during the war, although these were unlikely to be articulated due to press hostility and the pressure on the politicians continued.[32] During summer 1918, marches and petitions for suffrage in major cities confirmed women's commitment to political rights.[33] The demands of the first Russian revolution in 1917 were also a major factor in determining the shape of the revolutionary demands, but these in turn had been influenced by women's activism and political leadership in popularizing the demand for suffrage and triggering and sustaining the revolution.[34] The Russian revolution was covered extensively in the socialist, left-liberal and mainstream presses in Germany, Britain, Hungary and Yugoslavia.

In Hungary, there has been very little scholarly interest in women's suffrage to date, and to some degree socialist women contributed to their own marginalization, attacking liberal feminists for their narrow emphasis on the vote rather than claiming the issue as an important one for all women, a position which was for a long time reflected in the historiography. While the history of the liberal Feminist Association of Hungary, its efforts to gain the suffrage and its activities during the war are relatively well covered,[35] the first comprehensive study of the organization's history, activities, and press has been only recently completed.[36] Based on extensive research of the contemporary feminist press and Rosika Schwimmer's voluminous papers at the New York Public Library, the study by Dóra Czeferner also seems to correct some long-held views about the liberal feminists.[37] Czeferner argues that far from focusing solely on the central demand for the suffrage, the Hungarian feminist press covered a much broader spectrum. Relying on a comparative approach, she also shows a closer, mutual influence between Hungarian and Austrian suffragists than previously suspected. The only monograph on the history of female suffrage between 1848 and 1938 unfortunately fails to make a clear distinction between contemporary texts and the author's own interpretation.[38] A recent monograph by Judith Szapor offers a gendered history of the revolutionary and counter-revolutionary period between 1918 and 1922, but with its main focus on the paradigm change from liberal and left-wing to nationalistic and right-wing women's activism, it devotes less attention to socialist women than they perhaps deserve.[39]

When it comes to a basic history of socialist women's activism in Hungary from the beginnings to the Second World War, we still have to make do with

Mrs Peter Ágoston's slim but useful insider's account from 1947,[40] the orthodox communist account of Magda Aranyossi (1963),[41] or the more recent, scholarly but highly partisan accounts of Susan Zimmermann (1997, 1999).[42] The inter-war period's leading female MP, the Social Democrat Anna Kéthly, despite her impeccable anti-communist record and stellar international reputation, still awaits her biographer. Kéthly was one of the rare Social Democratic party leaders after 1945 who resisted the communist takeover and during the Stalinist period was jailed for four years. She was appointed as minister without portfolio in the 1956 revolutionary government, emigrated after its suppression by the Soviet Union, and subsequently represented the cause of the Hungarian revolution in the UN. Her contemporary, the socialist activist and poet Mariska Gádor was the subject of an unpublished inquiry by a literary historian but as yet not a historical study.

The 1989–90 regime change in Hungary resulted in the emergence of Western-type women's organizations and a rise in scholarly interest directed at the antecedents of late-twentieth-century women's rights activists. However, for a variety of reasons this momentum was not sustained and women's and gender history remained on the periphery of the historical profession.[43] In more recent years, the nationalistic, right-wing shift in Hungarian historical scholarship – in no small part due to the populist Fidesz government's efforts, since 2010, to shape domestic narratives of twentieth-century Hungarian history – rendered women's history an even more marginal, underfunded and undervalued field of research.[44]

Looking back, from a distance of three decades, we can see the historiographical trends more clearly and the ways in which the shifts in historical scholarship emerging after 1989 did no favours to the historiography of female activism, and especially of socialist women's movements. The first years following the fall of State Socialism brought unprecedented scholarly and popular interest in the political history of previously suppressed or distorted events, such as the post-1945 communist takeover, the oppressive measures and crimes of the Stalinist period, the history of 1956, and the long period of 'normalized' communist rule under János Kádár. This newly constructed narrative of communist oppression, popularly interpreted as continuous and relentless, that affected Hungarian society without distinction left little room for a consideration of the significant advances in women's economic and educational opportunities under State Socialism, or appreciation for the socialist and liberal feminist women who maintained a distinct women's rights agenda during the inter-war period.

This narrative does not apply to Yugoslavia, where women's suffrage was enacted in 1945 in the newly formed Socialist Federal Republic. As one of the flagship achievements of socialist Yugoslavia, female suffrage was always closely linked to socialism and historicized as a direct consequence of socialism and not as a dogma of liberal feminism. After 1991, many female historians have uncovered the life trajectories and activism of liberal feminists who campaigned for universal suffrage and whose names have, perhaps deliberately, been forgotten.[45] But at the same time, the State Socialist regime had a variety of reasons for deliberately erasing individual female socialist activists who campaigned for universal suffrage in the inter-war period. Although campaigning for women's suffrage in inter-war Yugoslavia was primarily the concern of prominent individuals and women's groups, these individual efforts were later erased and collectivized. In the mythology of women's suffrage in Yugoslavia, female enfranchisement was presented as a demand of the masses, the working class, and the new ruling political class, with agitation from below blending smoothly with the sense of a gift bestowed from above. The intellectual premise of justifying women's political activity relied significantly more on Bebel, Marx, Engels, Lenin and Tito than on the efforts of individual women (with the exception of Clara Zetkin), including socialists, who defended women's suffrage in the inter-war period. This means that histories of suffrage and histories of socialism have for a long time largely overlooked, marginalized or excluded women's crucial contributions.

The pioneering and key work for orientation on the issue of women's political rights and workers' organization in inter-war Yugoslavia is Jovanka Kecman's *Žene Jugoslavije u radničkom pokretu i ženskim organizacijama 1918–1941* (Yugoslav Women in the Labour Movement and Women's Organizations 1918–41), based mainly on primary archival sources relating to more than two decades of progressive women's movements.[46] The work captures, analyses and compares different women's movements within different national communities in Yugoslavia. This is one of the few integral studies that goes beyond individual national frameworks and treats the Yugoslav women's movement as a single whole with certain specifics, derivatives and peculiarities. Most of the other studies were written by female scholars in the post-1991 era and were more focused on the new post-Yugoslav national narratives. Of these, most were written in the last two decades, when several female historians, social scientists and anthropologists started focusing on gender studies and women's history in Yugoslavia. Feminist theorist, anthropologist and historian Lydia Sklevicky wrote several anthropological studies on this topic that were posthumously published in 1996 in *Konji, žene, ratovi* (Horses, Women, Wars – the title refers to her insight that horses were mentioned more often than women in the existing historiography) and shed light on women's movements in both the pre-1945 Kingdom of Yugoslavia and the post-1945 Socialist Federal Republic.[47] In 2013, Marta Verginella, a prominent Slovene gender historian, edited a special volume: *Dolga pot pravic žensk. Pravna in politična zgodovina žensk na Slovenskem* (The Long Road to Women's Rights: Legal and Political History of Women in Slovenia).[48] Two volumes were edited by sociologist Milica Antić Gaber: *Ženske na robovih politike* (Women on the Fringes of Politics, 2011) and *Naše žene volijo!* (Our Women Vote!, 1999).[49]

Understanding the role of gender in the Yugoslav context is one of the crucial points if we aim to understand women's access to political rights after the First World War. This is very well contextualized in Ida Ograjšek Gorenjak's book *Opasne iluzije: Rodni stereotipi u međuratnoj Jugoslaviji* (Dangerous Illusions: Gender Stereotypes in Inter-War Yugoslavia, 2014) that focuses primarily on the Croatian part of Yugoslavia, but also manages to make some comparisons with the Slovenian and Serbian cases.[50] There are several other researchers who have made important contributions to the question of women's political and social rights, as well as scholars who have for the past twenty years been uncovering other aspects of women's history of Yugoslavia.[51] They have been searching for lost women, rediscovering their life trajectories and activism in the archives, analysing the conditions in which these women lived and worked, and showing us how much is still there to uncover.

Complex histories, contested legacies

Because women's suffrage was not formally achieved in Yugoslavia until 1945, exploring the path to it differs from that of other countries discussed in this chapter. The 1920s and 1930s offered a fundamentally different historical framework from that in which suffrage was enacted just after the First World War. The struggle for women's suffrage thus met with the crisis of liberal democracy, the authoritarian constitution, the rise of fascism and the economic crisis. The conditions under which German, British or Hungarian women were given the right to vote already seemed like the *world of yesterday* for Yugoslav women in the 1920s and 1930s, and the global political crisis challenged those, especially socialists, who fought for their rights, to dedicate more time to rethinking the political system that seemed to be failing with each passing year.

Figure 4.1 Ive Šubic: 'Slovenian woman, you are free and you will vote for the first time', poster, 1944. Reproduced with permission of the National Museum of Contemporary History of Slovenia.

However, the period between 1918 and 1923 still held some kind of optimism, also political, that Yugoslav women tried to turn to their advantage. Yugoslav historiography does not yet have a clear, joint overview of the first generation of female socialists, i.e. those born around 1900, who were already politically active during and after the First World War. Such research is also somewhat lacking in individual post-Yugoslav national contexts. The obvious reason for this is that there were not many of these women; on top of that, traces of their activities, which were in fact illegal after 1921, are very difficult to find. That is why the fragments that have survived are all the more valuable, not only for understanding the struggle for women's suffrage but also as a contribution to the history of socialism, which still stirs spirits in post-Yugoslav countries.

The question of the legacy and memory of socialist women may be even more complicated in the case of Hungary. If their activism, in connection to and outside of the suffrage movement had been tied up with the failed liberal and radical socialist/communist revolutions in 1918–19, their memory was equally (but for different reasons) distorted and erased by the subsequent counter-revolution, the inter-war period's authoritarian political discourse, the short and lopsided democratic period of 1945–7, and the Stalinist and state socialist periods that followed, before the 1989–90 regime change. Neither can we call socialist women's position vis-à-vis the suffrage movement unambiguous. Until 1918, socialist and liberal feminist women frequently clashed over the priority of and strategies leading to women's suffrage, with the latter championing the fight for it, and the former obediently following (at least in public) the male party leadership's (and the SWI's) direction, which offered little practical support for women's rights. The introduction of universal (including female) suffrage in November 1918 and the overall trust in the new, democratic government brought some degree of unity into this previously fraught relationship between socialist and liberal activists. Both groups took full credit for the achievement of female suffrage; and while liberal feminists did so much more justifiably, the fact that socialist women also did underscores the almost mythical value – cutting across boundaries within the liberal Left – attached to the suffrage. At the same time, socialist women were vocal in their criticism of the electoral decree's gender inequality – the right to vote and stand for election applied to women over thirty, as opposed to men over twenty-one, along with a literacy requirement for women only. But with their campaign launched in November 1918 to educate rural women, they may have, tacitly, justified the decree's inherent gender discrimination. The political polarization, especially marked from January 1919, resulted in fracturing this temporary unity of female activists, with many of the socialists (and liberal feminists as well) joining the newly formed Communist Party. Many activists did so because they grew disenchanted with the government's failure to organize an election. Then, the hastily staged elections of Councils by the radical Left government, in power between 21 March and 1 August 1919, sealed the fate of any potential united front of left-liberal women's rights activists. The electorate included only registered trade union members and gainfully employed members of the working class, excluding the overwhelmingly middle-class liberal feminists, including such long-standing warriors for female suffrage as Rosika Schwimmer.

During the early years of the authoritarian, anti-Semitic and highly conservative post-1919 government, socialist women activists were exiled, with many prosecuted, jailed or interned. In this way, the wartime practice of political detention without charge or trial was extended into peacetime, and used by the right-wing Horthy regime against its political opponents, frequently including women.[52] The first post-war parliamentary elections, in January 1920, may have been based on the most democratic electoral rights – it included men and women over twenty-one, with a continuing literacy requirement for women only – but they took place amidst the ongoing White Terror and with a boycott by the Social Democratic Party in place. From 1922 on, electoral rights were gradually curtailed, disproportionally affecting women, and the return of the open (as opposed to secret) ballot in the countryside further hollowed out democratic procedures. The late 1930s and the war years brought a whole slew of authoritarian and anti-Semitic legislation, further pushing left-wing women activists underground and out of the public sphere.

Clara Zetkin's speech on suffrage at the International Socialist Congress in 1907

Despite the differences and complexities outlined above, there were also commonalities and shared influences. Clara Zetkin (1857–1933) was the outstanding theorist in the German women's socialist movement and had a huge influence on socialist women internationally. She was a passionate speaker and influential writer on women's issues, and she edited the socialist women's journal *Die Gleichheit* (Equality) from its founding in 1892 until she was removed in 1917 by the SPD Executive for her persistent anti-war stance.[53] She was the leader of the international women's group, the Socialist Women's International as well as the founder of International Women's Day in 1910. Although she is

Figure 4.2 Clara Zetkin (1857–1933) with Rosa Luxemburg (1871–1919), 1910.
Source: Getty Images, Universal Images Group.

perhaps best known for her outspoken anti-war stance and her refusal to work with middle-class feminists, her position on suffrage was adopted as policy at the Second International's Congress in 1907 and was highly influential within and beyond Germany.

In her speech to the 1907 Congress, Zetkin argued that the demand for suffrage must be conducted on socialist principles and included within the demand for universal suffrage for both men and women. Zetkin decisively rejected limited suffrage for women as a 'plural vote for the propertied classes' against the interests of the proletariat. Women had entered the workplace and 'emerged from the narrowness of family life to the forum of political activity' and they needed full political rights, symbolized by suffrage, to defend their interests in their battle against class exploitation and class rule. In contrast to liberal feminists organized separately from men, proletarian women needed to recognize that they could not achieve suffrage 'in a struggle of the female sex without class distinctions against the male sex' but only through a class struggle alongside proletarian men against their oppressors. Equally, socialist movements could not achieve their goals without mobilizing women politically. The success of mass strikes depended on women being willing to make the sacrifices these actions entailed: 'the proletariat has a vital stake in the political equality of the female sex and must fight for full civil rights for women'. Campaigning for female suffrage would ensure that women would join men in the revolutionary class struggle as well as using their votes 'correctly' when the time came.[54]

Zetkin's anti-war activism was gendered, but unlike the WILPF, where suffrage was at the heart of the feminist pacifism, as reflected in the resolutions of The Hague (1915) and Zurich (1919) Congresses,[55] it was linked with ideas of the internationalism of the working class, anti-imperialism and class solidarity. Her appeal to working-class women to oppose the war, for instance at the March 1915 SWI conference in Bern (see Chapter 2), was based on their role as mothers and wives of men sacrificed on the altar of capitalist greed. In the absence of a general strike, Zetkin's appeal stressed the common interests of mothers in all fighting nations to unite against the capitalist, militarist interests that pitted them against one another.

In Germany as elsewhere, class solidarity trumped feminist solidarity at all times. For Zetkin, the policy of a 'clean break' with middle-class campaigners remained central to her thinking and highly influential, shaping the approach of Alexandra Kollontai in Russia and Louise Saumoneau in France.[56] Despite this stance, there was considerable overlap between the groups during the final war years, partly due to Zetkin's loss of influence after 1917[57] but also due to the BDF

(*Bund deutscher Frauenvereine*, Federation of Women's Associations), the leading German middle-class umbrella organization, moving away from a limited suffrage towards a demand for universal suffrage without class privilege.[58] This shift culminated in socialist and liberal women's organizations marching together for the vote during summer 1918 and on 25 October submitting a joint petition to parliament demanding suffrage.[59]

German women's suffrage demands were roundly refused as late as 8 November 1918. The SPD proposed it and was voted down, only for it to be granted on 12 November by the new Council of People's Deputies.[60] This is why the vote was described by so many women as sudden and arriving like a bolt from the blue.

Suffrage and socialist women's priorities during and after the First World War

Suffrage was an important tool in women's quest for equality, but for socialist women it was closely linked to concepts of social justice which demanded universal adult suffrage for both men and women. As outlined above, Zetkin played a leading role in influencing socialist parties across Europe, and although many comrades argued against women's suffrage out of a conviction that women would be too conservative to vote for left-wing parties, the official position from 1907 onwards supported universal suffrage for all adult men and women. In some national contexts such as Germany and Britain there was limited overlap with feminist goals in the area of women's votes, especially as suffrage organizations moved towards a wider franchise that included more working-class men and women. Splits within socialist parties, especially over their support for the war and apparent abandonment of internationalism – a move supported by many socialist women as well as men –allowed different policies to emerge on the more marginalized left and new allegiances to form. There were also splits within the suffrage organizations, again over support for the war, that allowed a commitment to a wider and more equal franchise to emerge, for example within the WILPF, and made it possible for feminists and socialists in some national contexts to campaign together for female suffrage after 1917. This continued to some extent until the end of the war and into 1919. The states that emerged from the ruins of the former Habsburg Empire, however, were primarily concerned with their own political instability and attempts to establish new political and national contexts. In the Kingdom of Yugoslavia, they tried to achieve the impossible: to introduce the principles of democracy and modernize the legal system without at the same time shaking the traditionalism of the past value system.[61] Needless to say, women, marginalized groups and progressive movements did not prosper under such conditions. With the partial exception of Czechoslovakia, militant nationalist discourse carried the day in many of the Habsburg successor states, rendering emancipatory objectives – including women's rights and justice for minority nationalities – secondary, if not at odds with the (perceived) interests of the nation-state.

In Hungary, the official ideology after 1919 – which was militantly revanchist, nationalistic, anti-Semitic and Christian – succeeded in marginalizing any discussion of women's rights. Anti-Jewish and anti-emancipatory measures – such as the *numerus clausus*, introduced in 1920, that limited the ratio of Jewish students at universities to 6 per cent – were used to halt or reverse the pre-war and wartime gains in women's higher education. Using the *numerus clausus* decree as a pretext, overzealous university administrators banned women altogether from admission to the medical faculty of the University of Budapest until 1926.[62]

Women's rights activists often suffered from the combined effects of the inter-war era's prevailing anti-Semitic, anti-leftist and anti-woman rhetoric. Still, Hungarian Social Democratic women activists continued to represent the interests of working-class women in the trade unions, while a smaller number of younger, radical socialist women, often from middle-class backgrounds, used the cover of the moderate Social Democratic Party as a front to recruit members for the illegal Communist Party in exile. However, because of the 1921 agreement between the governing party coalition and the Social Democrats to limit their organizations to the capital and the largest cities, and because of the ban on the Communist Party, they operated in the shadows, outside of mainstream politics. In the same period, mainstream, public roles, ostensibly to represent Hungarian women, were reserved for a few high-profile conservative women intellectuals, who were allowed to demand the restoration of women's previous access to higher education, as long as they limited this right to women of the Christian middle class.

In Britain there was sustained, if muted, suffrage activity throughout the war which gathered pace after the establishing of the Speaker's Conference in 1916. By mid-1916, the House of Commons had been considering electoral reform for some time, without agreement. It was clear that some kind of franchise reform was necessary in order to allow men on military or naval service to vote at the next election. However, this localized suffrage activity was often not reported in the radical left-wing press. The *Labour Leader*, the *Daily Herald* and the *Call* tended to concentrate on anti-conscription, anti-war and socialist campaigns. However, the *Dreadnought*, *Votes for Women* and the WIL newsletters maintained a spotlight on the continuing suffrage campaign and kept activists informed about local and national events. What had begun for many women as a single-issue suffrage campaign then drew them into organizations that were specially focused on exposing gender inequality and class exploitation. The war experience heightened women's political consciousness. However, the granting of the vote to some women in 1918 did not mark the end of a fifty-year struggle for the vote; rather it marked the beginning of another set of struggles for social, political and economic equality that engaged political women during the inter-war years.[63] As the local constitutional suffrage group in Manchester declared in 1917, '[w]e are clear that, with the vote won, our work will be just begun.'[64] This sentiment will have been echoed throughout the country.

There was, however, a groundswell of grassroots support in the women's suffrage and labour movements for universal adult suffrage. Although as Karen Hunt notes:

> First there had long been divisions within the suffrage movement on how best to enfranchise working-class women within a franchise based on property qualifications. Secondly the one campaign that unequivocally sought to give the vote to all women irrespective of their social class was for Adult Suffrage.[65]

In October 1916, just as the Speaker's conference was being established, internationalist Kate Courtney (WIL), one of the women who managed to attend the Hague conference in 1915, and Jim Middleton (of the Workers' National Committee) wrote to a number of people from different suffrage and political organizations to generate support for a National Council for Adult Suffrage (NCAS). Courtney and Middleton reiterated in their letter that the wartime coalition government offered a rare non-party opportunity for the property-based franchise to be reformed. They argued that the war had 'revealed to many, what some sections recognised in peace time, that the strength of the nation lies in its men and women and not in the material property they may or may not possess'. They emphasized the way in which women's increased visibility in the war effort had 'won them the right, so long denied, to exercise a voice in national affairs'.[66]

For socialist women in Britain, class was seen as a fundamental in the debates over suffrage, although the question of class definitions and who was, in reality, a 'working woman' was always controversial. Even before the war the NUWSS had set up an informal alliance with the Labour Party, the Election Fighting

Fund (EFF), to work specifically in working-class constituencies to encourage local women to become involved in the suffrage campaigns. Many EFF workers were socialist women who created local networks which enabled women to be mobilized in anti-war protests after 1914. There were consistent attempts to recruit women to the WIL from the working-class districts in the cities, with the established strategies of house-to-house canvassing, distributing handbills and organizing factory gate meetings. The war offered further opportunities for women anti-war activists in industrial British cities to use their pre-war knowledge of local working-class women and their understanding of local organizational and municipal structures as a basis for their wartime organization, as also highlighted in Chapter 2 of this volume. This was particularly evident in the development of the WIL branch network, which unashamedly used the pre-existing NUWSS branch network on which to overlay the new WIL. Suffrage and socialist women in industrial cities like Glasgow, Bristol, Newcastle, Manchester and London were in regular contact, as speakers on anti-war platforms, through columns and via small advertisements in papers like the *Labour Leader*. The networks are extraordinary. The women took campaigning skills into anti-war arenas like the women-only spaces of the WIL and the Women's Peace Crusade (WPC) while still maintaining a concentration on preserving women's rights in the 'special circumstances' of the war and consistently arguing that 'social relations should be governed not by physical force but by the recognition of mutual rights'.[67]

These British examples show the fluidity of boundaries between women's rights, anti-war and revolutionary agendas. This is especially marked, too, in case studies of revolutionary activist women from Hungary, albeit here with the added dimension that they show the heightened scope and degree of political mobilization during the revolutionary months between October 1918 and August 1919. As outlined in Chapter 5 of this volume, they ranged from Jolán Kelen, who came from a Jewish, lower middle-class, educated family, to Ilona Duczynska, a woman of Hungarian and Polish gentry stock who was a member of the anti-militarist Galileo Circle. Not mentioned in Chapter 5, but considered here, is Gizella Berzeviczy, born into a lesser branch of an old Transylvanian aristocratic family, the socio-economic group whose members provided the traditional political elite before and after the First World War. A high-school teacher, she became politicized during the 1918 Aster Revolution. She organized a teachers' union, and kept it running during the Republic of Councils. During the counter-revolution, she was first interned, then put on trial and sentenced to a prison term. Her defence attorney, whose closing argument was preserved as a

Figure 4.3 Election of the Budapest Councils, April 1919. The second woman from the left in the back row is Jolán Kelen. Reproduced with permission of the Hungarian National Museum, Historical Photo Department.

rare document, used her noble origins, her misguided sense of public service, and the fact that she could not be labelled a 'Jewish Bolshevik' in her defence – thereby perhaps aggravating her sentence.[68] Eventually, Berzeviczy would be exchanged for Hungarian POWs in the deal that also included the leaders of the Republic of Councils. She lived in the Soviet Union until the end of the Second World War, experiencing the Stalinist terror but never speaking about it in public and, until her death in the late 1950s, enjoying an illustrious career in Hungary as a pedagogical authority.[69]

These examples highlight the organizational backgrounds and networks, whether they were parties, political organizations or grassroots, social-communal networks, of newly mobilized women. Moreover, they illustrate the specific Hungarian timeline of the rapid succession of war, armistice, continuing war with the surrounding, new or reconstituted countries emerging from the Austro-Hungarian Monarchy, the two revolutions and, lastly, counter-revolution and persecution.

Barriers to socialist women in male-dominated political places

Socialist women faced a number of barriers to political participation and influence during and after the First World War. A major barrier came from working within contexts hostile both to socialism and to women's influence extending beyond the domestic sphere. As well as lacking political and legal rights, women's opportunities for education, employment and reproductive rights were severely curtailed and their personal freedom limited by patriarchal laws that made them subordinate to men in every aspect of their lives. Socialist parties offered women opportunities for involvement, education and self-development unimaginable in any other mainstream parties, and this was reflected in the strength and broad appeal of socialist women's organizations as well as the international prominence of socialist women such as Rosa Luxemburg and Alexandra Kollontai. However, despite the commitment at policy level and by a number of leading socialist men to a programme of women's emancipation and gender equality, sexist, even misogynistic attitudes persisted, and traditional attitudes hampered women's advancement. Leading men within socialist parties also felt threatened by women's separate political organization and sought to bring these structures as well as events such as International Women's Day under party control.[70] In Germany, once adult suffrage had been achieved on 12 November 1918, male comrades used their entrenched positions of power to block women's political participation in the *Räte*, in parliament and in leading roles in the Party hierarchy.

There were considerable barriers to women's electoral success, too. Elections took place rapidly, giving women very little time to prepare for party selection and for their electoral campaigns. In Britain, the seventeen women who did stand in December 1918 were nearly all anti-war women, socialists and suffrage activists. The election was called very rapidly after the passing of the act enabling women to stand as MPs and many of the candidates were already exhausted. Marcy Macarthur was a socialist, a trade union activist and an Adult Suffragist. In contrast, Nora Dacre Fox was an ex-member of the WSPU and an incipient fascist. Standing for a Dublin constituency, Constance Markievicz won for Sinn Fein, although the other women candidates were not elected.[71] In Germany, with few exceptions, women candidates were given less prominence in electoral lists, meaning that they were less likely to be successful than male candidates, with only one in eight women candidates elected compared to one in three men.[72] As early as 1920, Anna Blos wrote in *Die Gleichheit* that 'there was only one woman high enough in Social Democratic lists to have good prospects.... Many a competent woman has had to stand down to make way for a man.'[73]

Of the forty-one women elected to the German National Assembly in January 1919, twenty-five were Independent Socialists or Social Democrats, and in 1920 this had dropped slightly to twenty-three, plus Clara Zetkin for the communists. Communist women boycotted the January 1919 elections to the National

Assembly and campaigned for workers' and soldiers' councils, where female representation was even lower at 4 to 5 per cent. Politically active women were acutely aware of the disadvantages and discrimination, and spoke out in very clear terms against male sabotage of women's political ambitions and education. Another source of tension was the SPD's and USPD's support for demobilization laws and processes that discriminated against women workers in favour of all male workers. Women were dismissed from their jobs to make space for men, regardless of whether they were returning soldiers or not, and whether or not women had dependents. Women veterans (nurses, auxiliaries, communications operatives) were given no ex-military status, financial support or recognition in reintegrating into the workplace or society.

In the German press, coverage of women as parliamentarians and voters, and reflections on the 'success' of enfranchising women were ambivalent, even hostile. Women were always seen as brakes on progress through their ignorance and apathy, and this was reported in the press as 'fact'.[74] Women's suffrage was presented as something achieved solely by the SPD, and women were expected to show gratitude by voting for the party. This did not happen as German women tended to vote within class interests, for the USPD, or more conservatively and disproportionately for centrist parties with strong religious affiliations. However, the claim that women voters cost the SPD the Reichstag elections in June 1920 seem to be based on prejudice rather than data. Men used their power to limit women's influence, and used their numbers to retain and reinforce that power. Once it became clear that women did not vote along sex but class lines socialist parties stopped wooing female voters and women's participation in their ranks declined steeply, both in terms of membership and elected representatives.[75]

With the end of the First World War, Yugoslav women were able to become members of political parties for the first time. There was no political tradition for women and this meant that politically active women were an absolute minority. Even the Yugoslav women's organization *Ženski pokret* (Women's Movement), which had women's political rights as one of its core goals, had a complicated attitude towards the role of women in politics.[76] After the war, when the Yugoslav women's newspaper *Ženski pokret* was published for the first time in Belgrade, it often reported on topics such as women's political rights.

However, women were encouraged to approach politics as 'neutral' actors rather than as campaigners.[77] Throughout the 1920s, only around 1 per cent of the membership of the Yugoslav Communist Party was female.[78] Women working within progressive parties were rare, but many of them were key players in both agitation and party ideology. In understanding the left's attitude towards women's suffrage, it should also be borne in mind that the majority of Yugoslav men who had previously lived in territories that were part of Austria-Hungary had only been able to participate in the general elections for the first time in 1907. This means that the democratic tradition of the Kingdom of Yugoslavia, which was politically, economically and socially a semi-colonial state, was different from Western European countries. Aljozija Štebi, born in 1883, a prominent Social Democrat who was also active within the party structures and worked as editor of various social democratic and progressive newspapers, wrote in her work *Demokratizem in ženstvo* (Democracy and Women) in 1918: 'In England, where parliamentarism educated the people very early, demands for political rights were soon awakened in women as well. In our country, where men had to fight fiercely for every right, the political demands of women were, of course, of very problematic value.'[79]

Štebi was a teacher, but her work was already impossible in the Austro-Hungarian Monarchy due to her advanced political beliefs. She therefore decided to devote herself entirely to party work, entering the JSDS, the Yugoslav Social Democratic Party, in 1912. This barely brought in enough money to survive: as she reported in a letter to Social Democratic politician Albin Prepeluh in 1918, her 'nerves [were] failing because I haven't had a quiet day in four years'.[80] She took part in many political controversies within the JSDS and advocated a more progressive line that would be closer to the communists. She recalled how hard it was for her to edit party newspapers, when her male comrades refused to let her be intellectually independent and were constantly trying to influence her work. She left the JSDS in 1919.[81] At the first Yugoslav Women's Conference (*Jugoslovanska ženska konferenca*), organized by the National Women's Alliance (*Narodna ženska zveza*) in 1919, she proposed a radical, feminist-oriented programme. There was also a demand for women's suffrage, but most of the societies that were members of this largest women's organization opposed it. Thus, after the plenary session in Split, the president of the National Women's Union, Danica Hrstić, even resigned due to the actions of the Belgrade Society for the Education of Women and the Protection of their Rights, which demanded votes for women. She claimed: '[t]he purpose of our Union, the largest women's organisation, is not to allow suffragettes to gain the right to vote. It is not and should not be a suffragette organisation. At least under my name and my leadership, it will never be'.[82] In 1923, Štebi was among a group of Yugoslav delegates, together with Leposlava Petković, Katarina Bogdanović, Adela Milčinović and Milena Atanacković, who attended the international congress on women's suffrage in Rome. This encouraged Yugoslav women to establish the

Feminist Alliance of the Kingdom of SHS, which was the initiator of almost all campaigns for women's suffrage.[83]

However, throughout her whole life after 1919, Aljozija Štebi tried to remain a moderate social feminist, who believed in the maternal power of women, although she herself never married or had children, and tried not to be too radical in her professional work. But knowing her history and her writings before 1920 makes one believe that this was a professional sacrifice, similar to the one that she attributed to her role model Jane Addams: 'She realised that all social work is a compromise between human will and the conditions in which [we have] to live.'[84]

In the same year that Štebi left the JSDS, Angela Vode, born in 1892 and the subject of further analysis in Chapter 5 of this volume, joined it, eventually rising to become Party secretary. Just like Štebi, Vode was a teacher whose career as a Habsburg civil servant was stymied due to her political convictions. This was the reason she started working in the private sector in 1917, but from 1919–21 she was also employed by the Social Democratic party. This employment paid hardly enough for her to survive; she got only one third of the salary that she would have had as a teacher. But she was not bothered by that as she believed in the greater cause and meaning of her political work. She believed she worked harder than all of her comrades, but she did not blame them, because she had 'time to sit down and they had families'.[85] She herself was at that time also left-leaning and closer to the Communists than to the 'moderate' Social Democrats. In contrast to Štebi, she considered herself a *suffragette*, despite the fact that the labour movement in general was against feminism and saw class struggle as the only proper and possible way to liberate the oppressed, including working-class women. This conviction was not foreign to her either: in 1920, she wrote that 'socialism liberates woman, and capitalism has trampled her' and that 'the liberation of woman became the task of socialism. The woman question has become part of the social question.' In the same article with the title *Socialism and Woman* (*Socializem in žena*)[86] she also pointed out that 'the solution to the woman question arises on the day when private ownership is abolished and replaced by a new social structure' which would move beyond 'bourgeois' defence of 'private property'. But she was also aware that the socialist discourse on the proletariat was primarily masculine: '[w]e are making a revolution in the world. We, the men, teamed up to tear down our dungeon, to kill injustice, to destroy violence … What about you, sisters? When will your First of May be?' She combined the proletarian cause with general gender injustice: '[h]ave you not been haunted by religion, morals, public opinion for centuries? … There is a large proletarian army, sisters, look, this is your place ... That our opinion will become public opinion, that our will shall be public will, that our constitutions will be the constitutions of the public.'[87] Within the party she had experienced herself what it was like not to be taken seriously. She described a certain 'Communist vanity' that made her male comrades act as if they were intellectually superior to her: 'If I asked about something that was not clear to me, ... they would never answer normally, but always somehow teasingly.'[88]

Although Vode was active as a socialist, communist and feminist, her attitude towards women's suffrage was multifaceted. For her, women's right to vote was not perceived as the most important goal for politically active women. She saw democracy as a broken system; a bourgeois political order that needed to be fixed, updated and changed, and not as the final and the finest political achievement. Politics had a 'dirty' connotation in the Kingdom of Yugoslavia and socialist/communist women and men often believed in the fundamental overthrow of the system through revolution, not in the modification of politics within the existing order. Economic independence seemed to be significantly more important than political equality or as Vode put it, with economic independence 'a woman can become an equal citizen even if there is not a single legal paragraph written about female equality. But if a woman believes she is worth just as much as her male counterpart, this is a far more lasting value than the law, written on a piece of paper, that can change daily.'[89] Women's suffrage was for her just 'a remnant from the history of parliamentary democracies'.[90] Vode not only problematized democracy within the authoritarian Kingdom of Yugoslavia, but also as part of a capitalist system that in her opinion would lead to fascism. 'Big capital is looking for a way out of the crisis. When it saw that all the paths along which profit had flowed were closed, it resorted to autarky ... The bearer of this movement is fascism.'[91]

This belief was not exceptional, but was widely shared among the inter-war Yugoslav socialists and communists. Leopoldina Kos was a teacher and socialist, and after 1923 a communist and anti-fascist. She was subjected to several disciplinary investigations, one for participating in a women's suffrage campaign that took place throughout Yugoslavia. Although she risked her job for the cause of suffrage in the early 1920s, later in life she was less sure about its importance. In her unpublished autobiography she wrote:

> [e]conomic exploitation cannot be abolished by political rights, as we see that men who have the right to vote are starving as well as women who do not. On top of that, however, the acquisition of political rights in bourgeois society cannot be final, because they last only as long as they do not threaten the ruling

class ... This is further illustrated by Germany, where women achieved full political equality with men, but once fascism started, everyone, men and women, all working people, became disenfranchised overnight.[92]

Internationalism and interdependence

Socialist women were at a theoretical level more committed to internationalism than to nation-states, seeing solidarity with workers as being more important than loyalty to one nation. For anti-war socialists, this was reinforced by their experience of persecution and imprisonment within their own country during the First World War era. In Germany and Britain, for example, socialist and working-class women were more likely to be prosecuted and imprisoned for expressing anti-war sentiment than middle-class campaigners.[93] However, as well as allowing transnational concepts of citizenship and belonging to emerge, the war years led to the collapse of the Second International and a rise in nationalist thinking that endured after the end of the war. Emerging and new nations in particular were heavily invested in creating and maintaining a national identity. In the case of the newly formed Kingdom of Yugoslavia, this was problematic, as it was made up of different nations, Slovenian, Croatian, Serbian, Montenegrin, Bosnian, Macedonian and Kosovo.[94] The women's movement also played an important role in building a unified Yugoslav identity.[95]

Although suffrage was very much a matter for domestic politics, there was a great deal of co-operation across borders, with all major international women's organizations – the IAW, WILPF and SWI – working to achieve enfranchisement of a kind for women everywhere. For example, the IAW held its ninth conference in Rome in 1923 to raise international awareness of the lack of women's rights in Italy under Mussolini. Among socialist women, too, there is strong evidence of transnational influence at individual and organizational level, and certainly events in one nation could have direct implications for others. At organizational level, the SWI set the political agenda for socialist women and Zetkin as leader was instrumental in establishing the direction it took.[96] In Russia, women agitators triggered the February revolution, which provided a script for revolutions elsewhere, and a major reason for inclusion of suffrage in the key demands and revolutionary decrees was women's activism over decades in which the local, national and international networks were inextricably interlinked.[97]

Although the local committees of the WILPF in Britain and Ireland were primarily concerned with the negotiation of peace, they were also involved in the continued campaigns for the vote, many becoming Adult Suffragists, and they were continuously highlighting the way in which the war affected women's rights. In 1917 and 1918, for example, they coordinated mass demonstrations against Regulation 40D of the Defence of the Realm Act (DORA), which threatened to reinstate the Contagious Diseases Acts, repealed in 1886. The short-lived regulation allowed the state to remand and imprison a woman for the transmission of venereal disease to a member of His Majesty's armed forces.[98] Their news sheets always contained reports from European branches of the WILPF, an organization that provided an international meeting point for some socialist women, who travelled to the congress in Zurich in 1919, influencing the organization's policies and attitudes to the revolutionary movements in many of the member states. The congress report shows several resolutions that mirrored socialist positions: although not all were adopted, they certainly fed into the wording and content of the final resolutions adopted by the congress.[99]

In April 1918, the WIL in Britain reported that German women members of the Committee for Permanent Peace had declared:

> We trust that the League that we formed at The Hague in 1915 has maintained its old strength, that we women, in spite of the hatred and enmity of our countries are faithful to each other and will build bridges between nations when at last the peace comes, which is dawning in the east.[100]

In the same news sheet, they quoted the 'minority Socialist' (sic) Clara Zetkin and reported that there had been immense mass meetings in January 1918 for equal and direct suffrage for men and women in Prussia.[101]

In 1919, the publication of the official summary of the Peace Terms coincided with the opening of the Women's Congress at Zurich and made it possible to use those terms as a basis on which to draft criticisms for submission to the Paris Peace Conference. In Zurich, there were delegates from fifteen countries, twenty-five each from Britain, Germany and United States, with smaller delegations from France, Austria, Italy, Hungary, Ireland, Australia, the Netherlands, Norway, Sweden, Denmark, Romania and Switzerland, while women from Poland, Argentina and Bulgaria unofficially sat in on the meetings.[102] An observer reported that:

> [t]he International Congress at Zurich differed from the Bern Socialist Conference in the perfect internationalism of its spirit. You could not tell by listening to a woman to what country she belonged. The war and its hate and national passions simply had not existed for these women: unknown to each other, they had been protesting against the same injustices and brutalities, united in a common humanity.[103]

The twenty-five women who formed the British delegation to Zurich in 1919 were all suffragists and socialists, and two of them, Charlotte Despard and Emmeline Pethick Lawrence, had stood unsuccessfully as Labour candidates in the General Election of 1918. All had been involved in the anti-war and peace movements in the United Kingdom during the war and most had been signatories to the Open Letter to German and Austrian Women in the winter of 1914–15 mentioned in Chapter 2 of this volume.[104] The *New York Times*, reporting on the Zurich conference, declared,

> Back in 1915, the International Congress at the Hague had voted to meet whenever the official Peace conference should be 'summoned'. Not even a long and bitter war had deterred them. It was the same group, yet it was quite different. Then the socialists among them could be counted on one hand: now they were not quite a majority … Many of the women from England and naturally the women from Central Europe occupied the extreme Socialist if not Communist left.[105]

The American trade unionist Florence Kelley noted:

> The English leaders amazed everybody by emphasising at every opportunity, that they were all Socialists. This included Mrs. Pethick Lawrence, Chrystal Macmillan, Mrs. Snowden (of course), and all the lesser lights. Hitherto I have found it hard to like Englishwomen, but this time I found myself their humble admirer.[106]

It is within this context that the Zurich congress 'sits': an immediate post-war context, where many of the delegates were suffering from the traumatic effects of war and the continued Allied blockade of food, which lasted until 12 July 1919. The resolutions regretted the unjust terms of peace, condemned the blockade and the inhumane starvation of women and children and warned of the dangers of militarization of the educational system. The session on 'Place of pacifists in a time of revolution' was chaired by Annot Robinson, and although many at the Congress recognized the fundamentally just demands underlying all revolutionary movements, the Congress voted down an amendment from that session which urged 'the possessing classes voluntarily to give up their special privileges and to consent to the reorganization of industry on a democratic basis so that a new order may be inaugurated without bloodshed'. The vote against was sixty-one to fifty-five.[107]

Kathleen Canning et al. note that the imaginary played an important role in revolutionary women's subjectivities – even where equality had not been achieved, women had entered into a new relationship with the state, one in which they were able to conceive of themselves as citizens and 'to reimagine the political'.[108] Canning argues that 'women's acquisition of citizenship rights opened possibilities for the emergence of new female subjectivities and self-representations'.[109] These subjectivities were at the heart of women's continued challenge to hierarchical gender norms and proved highly resistant to any attempts to restore these during the inter-war period. For internationally minded and connected socialist women active in the WILPF, their sense of citizenship and their development of political subjectivities was often more bound up with their membership of what Glenda Sluga has called an 'imagined international community' than restricted to their national contexts, and as Chapter 5 in this volume shows, these women often led nomadic lives. As well as creating a haven for women at odds with the post-war mindsets in their own national contexts, this imagined community offered women from defeated nations, especially those who did not have suffrage in their own countries, an opportunity to engage in political activity on an international stage.[110] After 1920, women were able to work in and with the League of Nations, which went a long way towards establishing international relations, disarmament, war and peace as key women's concerns and normalizing international political engagement by women at a time when this was still highly contested at national level.[111]

Suffrage commemoration

In Germany, the centenary of women's suffrage on 12 November 1918 was less commemorated than the revolution of 9 November, and the two were mostly kept separate. As will be described in Chapter 6 in this volume, major exhibitions in Kiel, Hamburg and Wilhelmshaven as well as national events such as *Die Revolution rollt* (The Rolling Revolution) presented the revolution as the cornerstone of German democracy. The account left women's voices out almost entirely, and female suffrage was presented out of context as a gain of the revolution, reinforcing the impression that revolutionary men had granted women this gift without their own efforts and that women had been spectators to the birth of the new democratic order, hence the gratitude expected of women voters. In the unfortunately named 'Damenwahl' (Ladies' vote – a play on words of ladies' choice) exhibition in Frankfurt in 2018, women's agency in bringing about the vote was clear and socialist women was certainly included. The last pre-war International Women's Day, on 8 March 1914, for instance, was presented as a major socialist rally for women's suffrage and Clara Zetkin as leader of socialist women's struggles for political rights was given space alongside liberal progressive suffrage campaigns.[112] Coverage of the revolution and the political system of *Räte* or councils made clear that despite their marginalization in revolutionary histories and memory, 'women were revolutionaries, they were not in fact just onlookers and certainly didn't stay peacefully at home'.[113] Key socialist women were featured prominently – Toni Sender, Luise Zietz, Marie Juchacz and an excellent image of Clara Zetkin (who was not elected to the National Assembly in 1919 but strode triumphantly into the Reichstag in 1920 as a representative of the KPD, and remained there until the final parliament before the National Socialist dictatorship in 1933).[114]

In Austria, the exhibition *'Sie meinen es politisch' 100 Jahre Frauenwahlrecht in Österreich* (They Mean it Politically: 100 Years of Women's Votes in Austria) and accompanying book also stressed the agency of women, feminists and socialists alike, in achieving suffrage and included the women revolutionaries within the tradition of women's political activism.[115] It is notable that these exhibitions were curated in consultation with feminist scholars, including Kerstin Wolff (Archive of the German Women's Movement, Germany) in Frankfurt, and a team of leading labour and suffrage historians including Gabriella Hauch and Birgitta Bader-Zaar in Vienna.

Figure 4.4 Clara Zetkin (1857–1933) with Lore Agnes (1876–1953) (left) and Mathilde Wurm (1874–1935) (right). Source: Ullstein Bild via Getty Images.

In Hungary, there was no official or scholarly commemoration of the centennial of universal or female suffrage in 2018. A small-scale event in 2013 was organized by the National Library on the centenary of the 1913 IWSA congress that was held in Budapest, with the focus on liberal feminists. A further, telling example of the erasure of socialist women from historical memory has been provided by the recent centennial of the 1918–19 revolutions and the 1920 Trianon Peace Treaty. Among the dozens of monographs, edited collections and documents published to mark the centennials of these political events, not one included even a basic appreciation of the introduction of female suffrage. Similarly, no existing historical account of the 1918–19 revolutionary events has mentioned the liberal and socialist women activists elected to the governing National Council in the early days of the 1918 Aster Revolution. They were Rosika Schwimmer and a Mrs Groák, representing the liberal feminists, as well as Ernő Müller, a leading Social Democratic activist also discussed in Chapter 5 of this volume[116] – women who would be rightly celebrated in any country that expresses even a token appreciation for its female pioneers.

As outlined above, in both historical and public discourse, women's suffrage has always been closely linked to socialism and was understood as one of the key and first achievements of socialism in post-1945 Yugoslavia. Inter-war efforts for women's political and other rights were thus forgotten in public discourse and not commemorated during the period of State Socialism. The nation-states that emerged from Yugoslavia after 1991 are similar in this respect. There is no systematic commemoration of inter-war efforts for women's suffrage in any of the countries, which is logical, given that the efforts were unsuccessful, and the attitude towards the emancipatory achievements of socialist Yugoslavia is conflicted in similar ways. During the transition in the 1990s, the belief prevailed that gender inequality had been eliminated by the socialist revolution, but at the same time the political emancipation of women was understood as a socialist legacy and was therefore viewed negatively. The commemoration and remembrance in public discourse thus depends more on contemporary attitudes towards socialism or socialist Yugoslavia than on women's own campaigning efforts in the First World War and inter-war periods.

In Britain, there was a great deal of commemorative activity around the century of suffrage in January 1918. The focus was on the pro-war Pankhursts (Emmeline and Christabel) and figures who supported the war effort such as Millicent Fawcett, whose statue was unveiled in Parliament Square in April 2018 – the first and so far only statue of a woman in this central position. Suffrage commemoration fitted into a narrative of patriotic war service and hardly made mention of women-led anti-war, anti-militarist demonstrations and the increasing influence of socialist

Figure 4.5 Ellen Wilkinson (1891–1947), MP, speaking at Labour's London May Day Celebration in Hyde Park, 1939. Wilkinson was Labour Party MP for Middlesbrough East (1924–31) and Jarrow (1935–47) and Minister of Education (1945–7). Source: Daily Herald Archive/National Science & Media Museum/SSPL via Getty Images.

ideas. In Manchester there was a competition for a 'womanchester' statue which was won outright by a public vote for Emmeline Pankhurst whose move to London in 1906 and pro-war stance were hardly mentioned. At the time of writing, there is a small but vocal campaign to get recognition for the other five shortlisted women: Margaret Ashton, 1856–1937, who was the first woman councillor, suffragist and pacifist; Elizabeth Gaskell, 1810–65, novelist and champion of the poor; Louise Da-Cacodia, 1934–2008, anti-racist campaigner and activist; Labour politician and suffragist Ellen Wilkinson, 1891–1947; and eighteenth-century entrepreneur Elizabeth Raffald, 1733–81.

Conclusions

Approaching the question of suffrage within different national and international contexts reveals the complexities around suffrage, citizenship and the roles socialist women were able to play after 1918. It also shows how fluid and changeable the women's self-understanding and identities as socialists became after 1917, and how this was reflected in support for or rejection of the systems of parliamentary democracy that emerged from war and revolution, which for many seemed to be unable to deliver their vision of fundamental social reform. In Germany, we see communists, including Clara Zetkin, initially boycotting parliamentary elections and championing the Soviet system. In Hungary rapid regime change meant that women were unable to exercise their right to vote, while in the Kingdom of Yugoslavia socialist women did not see female suffrage as a priority for political engagement within a broken system.

Political activity and a sense of citizenship were neither dependent on nor defined by suffrage – many socialist women were sceptical about suffrage and their experiences in Hungary in particular showed that they were right to be sceptical. In other contexts, women were excluded from influence within parties, trade unions and workers' councils, and suffrage did not prevent this. Even where suffrage was awarded, socialist women faced additional barriers because of the actions and attitudes of socialist men, who cast them as 'undisciplined' or politically immature. Socialist women committed to female suffrage often had to overcome barriers within their own parties – male comrades often blocked their progress and side-lined their achievements.

There was a great deal of transnational exchange among socialist women at a policy level, as well as through personal influence and friendships that guided development within nation states. The newly formed Kingdom of Yugoslavia had roots in Austria-Hungary, and this was reflected in its women's movements. International journals such as *Jus Suffragii* and *Die Gleichheit* were widely distributed and read. In addition, press coverage of the revolutions and their consequences for the left acted as both encouragement and deterrent for parties in non-revolutionary nations.

A study by Daniel Hicks has found a significant correlation between war, revolution and the expansion of democracy, and this is borne out by the experiences in some of the nations under consideration in this chapter.[117] Whatever the subsequent limitations and disappointments, the revolutions in Russia, Germany and Hungary undoubtedly brought about a much freer adult franchise without the class and property qualifications for women found in the non-revolutionary British case. In many belligerent nations, too, the war changed attitudes to social equality and political rights, leading to demands for an expanded male franchise and arguments for universal adult suffrage on the basis of citizenship and contribution to the national community rather than through property, wealth and social status. This move from limited to inclusive suffrage within a discourse of social equity made cooperation between socialist and non-socialist suffrage campaigners easier, at least on a short-term basis, as the example of the 1919 WILPF Congress as well as numerous cases of joint marches and campaigns in Germany and Britain demonstrate.

In stressing the role of war and revolution in the timing and nature of suffrage in post-revolutionary national contexts, it is therefore important not to lose sight of the agency of working-class women in the suffrage story. Our examples have shown that suffrage was a central demand of socialist women, and it was their agitation during the war – in food riots, strikes and other forms of protest – that created the revolutionary context among the civilian population and placed women's political rights high on the agenda of revolutionary demands.

5

Life Trajectories: Making Revolution and Breaking Boundaries

Corinne Painter, Veronika Helfert, Manca G. Renko and Judith Szapor

'There was no "last battle" on the horizon, but a long succession of battles, campaigns, activities, efforts and sacrifices. The struggle would be on many issues and on many fronts,'[1] wrote German revolutionary and journalist Mary (Maria) Saran (1897–1976) in her 1976 memoir about the slow pace of progress after the 1918 revolution in Germany. For her, even though the revolution had not brought on the socialist society based on true equality that she had envisioned, she had no intention of quitting the fight. Eighteen-year-old Vladimira Jelovšek (1901–20), who wrote from Zagreb (the capital of modern Croatia) to Tomaj (annexed to the Kingdom of Italy after the First World War, today in Slovenia) to her former classmate Karmela Kosovel not long after the proclamation of Kingdom of Serbs, Croats and Slovenes, demonstrated a full awareness of what this struggle meant:

> And at the birth of freedom the whole nation will bleed. It's gruesome, but the spectre will come to us too. And maybe we too will perish in the blood and in the flames. But our children will lead a beautiful and sunny life. This is only human, revolution is passion. And it devours its own children. But we still hope for a better, far future. Many have already forfeited themselves for freedom and these sacrifices will not be in vain![2]

Research on the lives of revolutionary women must keep in mind the complex conditions that shaped their political and professional activities. We therefore not only focus on those socialist women who achieved top positions in their respective parties, we also follow the trajectories of those women whose activism was forgotten or overlooked because of their gender. The biographies discussed in this chapter show that for many of them the revolutionary years after 1917 were an integral part of their lives, even shaping their course. Many of them were young – students and young workers – when thousands of women took to the streets in Petrograd on 8 March 1917 and the world of empires and monarchies began to crumble. The activists we have assembled crossed numerous borders in the course of their lives: in their private lives, in their political activities, but also national borders, sometimes voluntarily, often forced, and carried along epochal thresholds. By changing the focus, from the male revolutionaries to women, and widening the frame to look beyond the immediate revolutionary years, this chapter challenges the erasure and silencing of women and highlights their role – not merely a part of transnational movements, but integral to them. Most of the women discussed here, with a few notable exceptions, remained in Europe, but through the journeys they made and the intellectual spaces they occupied, they were operating in a transnational context, one in which definitions of nation-states, national borders and the concept of the centre versus the periphery were destabilized.

For female revolutionaries, their political activities often do not feature in the historiography and, where they are recognized as having participated, their actions are often dismissed as fleeting and spontaneous responses rather than lengthy, political agitation.[3] There were many specific barriers to women's participation, unique to each context in which the revolution occurred, but in more general terms, women's assumed traditional roles as caregivers and their perceived restriction to the private, domestic sphere meant that they were less likely to be in a position to take on leadership roles or to be identified as suitable for nomination to a leadership role. The inequality in society that prevented women from becoming public political figures was also often reproduced in revolutionary groups, further contributing to deterring women from revolutionary activity.[4] When women were arrested or interrogated for revolutionary activity, male officials dismissed their activities on the grounds of their youth or made assumptions that the women had been drawn into revolutionary roles through misguided romances (see, for example, eighteen-year-old Hilde Kramer's experiences with the Munich police in 1919 or the examples in Chapter 3). Conversely, female revolutionaries themselves also exploited gender stereotypes to evade detection or escape punishment. The assumption that women were caregivers and therefore predisposed to avoid revolutionary activity has, ultimately, also affected how female revolutionaries have been perceived by historians. Women's political activism was depoliticized both at the time and later in the historiography.[5] As Emmeline Pankhurst put it: 'Window-breaking, when English men do it, is regarded as an honest expression of political opinion. Window-breaking, when English women do it, is treated as a crime.'[6]

To live under such conditions demanded that women constantly opted for revolutionary resistance, even if only on a personal level and even if resistance did not lead to revolution. Sometimes women could not be officially active in political structures, since it was forbidden for women to join political parties (for instance, in the Cisleithanian part of the Habsburg Monarchy until the autumn of 1918 or in Germany prior to 1908). It also often meant that the whole family was involved in this activism; divisions such as the personal and the political become meaningless. Often politically active married women would not enter the party formally in order to protect the family: at least one parent could then have a guaranteed permanent job.[7] In the case of the husband's revolutionary activity, the wife had to agree to the lifestyle dictated by that activity. It was often up to the wife to take care of her husband's or the family's economic survival, and she also had to agree to live in unenviable conditions of deprivation, fear and frequent migration. Often a woman agreed to such a role because she herself followed radical political beliefs, yet her work – the maintenance of her husband and family – was not seen in historiography as a revolutionary role, but at most as a caring one. Behind closed doors married women socialists performed domestic, economic, intellectual and emotional labour that supported the revolution: some of the lives that we will therefore highlight here depict the life of a revolutionary wife as a case study of hidden labour. According to Maria Todorova,[8] many socialist women became socialist wives, rather than socialist wives becoming socialists. But what is often overlooked is that although many wives were not politically active at first glance, their husbands would not have been able to perform their revolutionary tasks without their wives' hidden work. Some women left their children in the care of family members, (divorced) husbands or state institutions to spare them the unsteady and often dangerous life with their revolutionary mothers. For example, Isa Strasser (1891–1970), born von Schwartzkoppen into a Prussian noble family and married to Viennese Josef Strasser, sent her young children to her parents in Germany when emigrating to Moscow in the 1920s.[9] Ruth Fischer (aka Elfriede Eisler-Friedländer 1895–1961) initially left her son with her soon-to-be-divorced husband Paul Friedländer and his parents in Vienna while moving in 1919 to Germany to pursue her career in the German Communist Party (KPD).[10] Female revolutionaries made huge sacrifices to join the revolution because they had to resist a myriad of societal expectations before they could even join a movement, and public scrutiny and condemnation of their decisions afterwards was often greater.

This chapter repositions the revolutions across Europe as an integral part of the female revolutionaries' lives. They did not risk their reputations and lives to join the revolution on a whim and neither did they retreat from the political sphere after the initial phases of the revolutions had passed. We also shed light on the hidden labour of revolutions that was also performed by women. Women could indeed be found in armed conflict but equally as often as administrative or first aid workers, ensuring vital supplies were delivered and lines of communication were maintained, as writers who spread the revolutionary message, and as community organizers who rallied recruits. In the Austrian Reich Conference of Workers' Councils, to which very few women were officially delegated, they were, however, certainly permitted as reporters, such as Hilde Wertheim (1891–?) and Anna Hornik-Strömer (1891–1966) for the Austrian communist newspaper *Rote Fahne*.[11] Brigitte Studer cites as an example the German Hilde Kramer, who worked as an assistant during the 2nd World Congress of the Communist International, undertaking the vital tasks of typing, translating documents and taking minutes.[12] In this chapter, we examine work that presents itself in its multiplicity in the lives of women activists, as waged labour as well as invisible reproductive work, as revolutionary care work. As a result of their activities, female revolutionaries were able to use the skills and networks that they had developed in their later careers as fascism and violence swept across Europe and then as the Cold War polarized the continent. By looking at the legacy of the revolution on their lives, the nature of women's activism and their understanding of themselves as political actors is highlighted.

Positioning women at the centre of our study also changes the interpretation of the revolution within the historiography. As this chapter demonstrates, women on the home fronts across Europe were at the heart of revolutionary organizing and preparing the ground for the dramatic political revolution at the end of the First World War. It also highlights the importance of the revolution in the lives of socialists and allows an insight into their motivations and the decisions they made afterwards. Overlooking socialist women and the role the revolution played in their lives results at best in a partial understanding of the twentieth century, at worst in inaccurate conclusions about how and why events happened. This chapter alone cannot correct the current gender imbalance but provides examples and paths for further research.

Dedicating one's life to the pursuit of a better world leads to a precarious existence and many of the women discussed in this chapter led lives that traversed Europe as they were hounded out of one country or they chose to join the fight in another. In this chapter, we will mainly focus on women from Germany and the former Austro-Hungarian Empire, with a particular focus on the regions that became Austria, Hungary and the Kingdom of Yugoslavia. We take a thematic approach in order to find the commonalities in the revolutionaries' experience and to highlight how women continued, or attempted, to live out their revolutionary goals after the initial revolutionary phase. We begin with an examination of the theme 'making revolution' to uncover how socialist women were involved in the initial revolutionary moments at the end of the First World War. But we also look beyond these few months or years to see how these women carried the revolution with them in their later work. For them, revolution was a process that did not have a clear beginning or end and that inspired and sustained them and their comrades. As revolutionaries, even after the revolution was deemed to be over, they were in an almost perpetual state of rebellion and frequently became members of opposition movements. In this chapter, we examine their involvement in resisting fascism, resisting Stalinist terror, resisting capitalism and resisting the Cold War. In these movements, women were frequently facing persecution, but these movements could offer the means of escape too. Resistance also became part of women's personal lives as they fought against societal expectations and relationship norms. Through this thematic approach, the lasting effects of the revolution become visible but also the ways in which revolutionary activities brought the women into different movements and networks that in some cases put them in danger and in others were their salvation.

Revolutionary contexts

As discussed in Chapter 1, there were a range of revolutionary events during this period and the states that emerged also followed different paths. The revolutionary period after the First World War was experienced differently in each region and the inter-war and post-Second World War periods also presented different opportunities and barriers to left-wing women. This chapter cannot comprehensively cover all female socialists for all European nations; it serves as an introduction to some key women, draws connections and distinctions between their lives, and indicates further women who can add to our understanding. It highlights the connections and the trans-European networks that grew from this revolutionary era and the injustice that so often the male members of networks are well-known whereas the women involved are not. Where possible and relevant, examples from other European nations are introduced and suggestions for further research appear. To aid understanding, a brief overview of the women whose life trajectories are at the heart of this chapter and the revolutionary context in which they operated is provided below.

In Germany, the immediate post-revolutionary period presented opportunities for socialist women to enact their vision of a new world. For German socialists, the Weimar Republic provided a new political system to which women had equal access, at least theoretically. Countering the rise of fascism presented a challenge that occupied much of their time and energies in the latter part of the 1920s and they were then faced with the inconceivably tough choice of joining an underground resistance or fleeing during the Third Reich. Here, as elsewhere, gender also played a key role, allowing some women to use gendered expectations of the lack of political interest by women to hide in plain sight or to navigate international border crossings. In this chapter, we focus on Hilde Kramer (1900–74), the teenager who became the secretary to the Bavarian Soviet before travelling to Moscow to work on building a new nation, Maria Saran (1897–1976), a university student who joined an international militant socialist organization, and Cläre Jung (1892–1981), a left-wing author who was involved in the Workers' International Relief.

Prior to the transition from monarchy to republic in Austria by the (male) deputies of all parties elected to the Reichsrat before the war, there had been social unrest. During the second half of the First World War, in a phase characterized by hunger riots and strike movements that can be identified as proto-revolutionary, anti-war activities had mixed with social discontent and revolutionary slogans. The territorial conflicts at the new borders with Slovenia and Italy, the revolutionary toppling of the old order, and subsequent counter-revolutionary activism, played out largely (with minor exceptions) without bloodshed. Before the Republic of (German) Austria was proclaimed to thousands of people in front of the Parliament in Vienna on 12 November 1918, the non-German nations declared independence from the Habsburg Monarchy one after the other at the end of October 1918. Women socialists participated in the several violent clashes between communists and police, and organized together with – and often against – social democrats in the workers' councils, an alternative Parliament of the working class, founded during the January 1918 mass strike and dissolved in 1924.

The First Republic was marked by domestic (and international) tensions, especially between the Austro-fascist *Heimwehr* and the Social Democratic paramilitary organization *Republikanischer Schutzbund* – and the National Socialists were also involved. In 1933, the Christian Social Chancellor Engelbert Dollfuß took advantage of an abandoned National Council session to de facto abolish parliament and transform the state into an Italian-style dictatorship, known as the *Ständestaat*. Parties as well as democratic institutions and principles

Figure 5.1. A woman addresses a communist demonstration in Vienna, 1929. Reproduced with permission of the Österreichische Nationalbibliothek.

were gradually abolished, Social Democrats and Communists were persecuted after the failed uprising in February 1934, as were the National Socialists, who assassinated Dollfuß in July of the same year. However, under the leadership of Arthur Seiß-Inquart, the National Socialists were included in Kurt Schuschnigg's Austro-fascist regime in 1937. As is well known, Austria became part of the National Socialist German Reich in 1938. Political opponents, and especially Jews, Roma/ni and Sinti/zza, and other groups considered 'unworthy of life', were exiled and murdered. After the end of the Second World War, some of the exiled socialists returned and helped build the Second Austrian Republic. After ten years of occupation, the country regained independence in 1955. Even though it positioned itself as a neutral state in the Cold War, it was a relevant political context for the women revolutionaries of 1918. In this context, this chapter reflects on the lives of Ruth Fischer, a founding member of the Austrian Communist Party (KPÖ), Käthe Leichter (1895–1942), a member of a radical youth organization and a prominent social democratic activist during the First World War, Anna Hornik-Strömer (also spelled Hornik-Ströhmer), a journalist and member of the KPÖ, and Berta Pölz (1894–?), an anti-war activist and agitator, who joined the Communist Party after being organized in the syndicalist Federation of Revolutionary Socialists International (Föderation Revolutionärer Sozialisten 'Internationale', FRSI). Both Hornik-Strömer and Pölz had been organized in the social democratic workers' youth movement before the end of the war.

In Hungary, like elsewhere in the Austro-Hungarian Monarchy, military collapse on the fronts resulted in the formation of a National Council, reuniting old and new liberal parties and the extra-parliamentary Social Democrats and Bourgeois Radicals. Backed by the organized workers and initially even enjoying the support of the old political elite, Count Mihály Károlyi formed the government of newly independent Hungary, and on 31 October 1918 the so-called 'Aster' revolution (named after the flower tucked into the returning soldiers' caps) triumphed. The new government was fervently committed to peace, as well as democratic electoral and land reform. A few days into the liberal revolution, a People's Republic was declared, and universal suffrage, including women – albeit with additional age and literacy requirements – was introduced. As described in Chapter 4, suffrage remained on paper, as it was repeatedly postponed under conditions of ongoing war with the neighbouring successor states of Romania and Czechoslovakia who were eager to create a *fait accompli* and gain a territorial advantage ahead of the Paris Peace Treaties.

As became clear very quickly, Károlyi's genuine democratic and anti-war credentials, as well as his personal connections with the political leaders of the Entente powers, could not stave off the dismemberment of the old multi-ethnic Kingdom of Hungary. The old elite turned against Károlyi and organized a counter-revolution, while former POWs returning from Lenin's Russia agitated for a Bolshevik revolution. In March 1919, Károlyi resigned and the newly formed Communist Party, with the Social Democrats as junior partners, was handed over the reins of government. Hungary's radical socialist experiment, Europe's second Councils' Republic, lasted 133 days. It was a feverish period of large-scale nationalization, collectivization of only-just-distributed land, cultural revolution, messianic communism and ad hoc application of freshly learned Leninist policies. Overthrown in August 1919, it was followed by a full-fledged White Terror and counter-revolution that dwarfed the atrocities committed during the Red Terror. Physical and judicial, paramilitary and official violence against communists and socialists, as well as anti-Semitic violence against Jews, continued until 1922.[13]

Born out of paramilitary violence, the inter-war era's authoritarian system, based on a desire for the revision of the harsh Treaty of Trianon, illiberal and anti-Semitic ideology, limited parliamentarism, and repression of the extreme left and right, remained in place for the duration of the inter-war period. The counter-revolution and White Terror also led to the exile of many thousands of Hungarians, ranging from liberal politicians to communist and socialist activists, artists and intellectuals.[14] During the entire inter-war period, until the end of the Second World War, the Communist Party was forced underground, and the Social Democrats and their unions faced severe limitations on their activities. From March 1944, the country's German occupation resulted in the last chapter of the Holocaust, the deportation of 450,000 Hungarian Jews to Auschwitz-Birkenau, an operation carried out with the collaboration of Hungarian authorities. In October 1944, a Hungarian Fascist regime came to power and served the Nazi cause until the end. The trajectories of Hungarian women in this chapter highlight this oft-changing, complex history.[15] They include the revolutionary socialist Ilona Duczynska (1897–1978), whose upbringing and frequent forced moves to escape persecution took her across Europe and North America, Magda Aranyossi (1896–1977), a journalist and communist activist, Jolán Kelen (1891–1979), a founding member of the Hungarian Communist Party, and Irén Müller (née Singer 1890–1964), a Social Democrat turned Communist activist. All of them, at some point or multiple times in their lives, became émigrés, lending an important transnational dimension to their activism and personal biographies.

The Kingdom of Serbs, Croats and Slovenes presents an interesting case for the work of revolutionary women as, in contrast to Germany, Austria and Hungary, there was no widespread outbreak of revolutionary activity at the end of the First World War. However, the absence of a revolutionary uprising or coup does not mean the absence of resistance or even the absence of revolutionary work itself. After the Yugoslav Communists became the third strongest party in the country (with sixty MPs) in the 1920 elections, they were banned by the end of the year, and in 1921 all activities and actions of the Communist Party of Yugoslavia went underground. Moreover, following the Treaty of Rapallo (1920) between the Kingdom of Italy and the Kingdom of Serbs, Croats and Slovenes, certain territories of the former Austro-Hungarian Empire in which the vast majority of the population was Slovene were annexed to Italy. In the case of non-Italians (mainly Slovenes and Croats) living on the border, Fascism was a real danger, and many women became radicalized. For the next two decades, all communist and progressive action was achieved secretly, illegally and in an increasingly repressive authoritarian kingdom. Communists were persecuted, denied work (and any means of economic survival), and often found themselves in prison, undergoing harsh interrogations. Their human and civil rights were violated, and some of them spent their entire lives without citizenship papers. The women whom this chapter highlights include Anica Lokar (1897–1976) and Pavla Hočevar (1889–1972), who were influenced by the Italian border and the experience of *fascismo di confine* (border fascism) that violently shaped the lives of the non-Italian population from 1919 onwards. The chapter also sheds light on Angela Vode (1892–1985), a teacher and member of the (illegal) Communist Party of Yugoslavia, who found herself in opposition to the new communist regime of the Socialist Federal Republic of Yugoslavia after the Second World War.

Finding voices in and beyond archives

Some women turned to other activities after 1918–21 and disappear from the historical sources. Others, however, remained politically active. For Jewish women, revolutionary work was hampered by anti-Semites in both the opposition forces and in socialist circles.[16] In this chapter, we understand involvement in revolutionary movements as a component of life biographies with varying importance for the respective actors. Archival practices prioritize official documents that, due to the long history of women's exclusion from the realm of political decision making, are usually written by men and/or are about men. The archival documentation is also made more difficult by the fact that more was published about top functionaries than about ordinary party members, and that articles in newspapers often do not have an author's name. The imponderables of the twentieth century also complicate the historical work: Austrian Käthe Leichter's unfinished autobiography was smuggled out of Gestapo imprisonment and it is a matter of luck that it has survived, while personal papers such as those of the Hungarian Ilona Duczynska are scattered across several continents or have only been preserved in fragments, as is the case with the Austrian German Ruth Fischer. For many revolutionary women, there is no extant documentation about them and their activities, meaning that any attempt to understand their revolutionary activity can only ever be partial.

However, there are sources written by women that can be used to uncover how female revolutionaries saw themselves and their world. Autobiographical writing, interviews and articles can all be analysed to find women's perspectives on revolutionary events and their understanding of how these events shaped their lives. On their own, these sources cannot tell us the 'truth' about an event, even if such a 'truth' existed, but they can tell us about the author or interview subject, how she constructed her identity from events that she witnessed and how she understood the role these events played in her life.[17] For both interviews and written autobiographical texts, the events are being narrated for an audience and the subject or writer is likely to narrate these events in a way that is comprehensible but also puts forward a version of the self that the subject or writer feels makes sense. They are inevitably influenced by public discourse that has expectations of women and women's lives.[18] In cases where material is available that covers a large period of time – perhaps even a whole life – it can be seen that the writers themselves are highly active in the construction of their biography. They give it meaning and omit, overemphasize or even change certain aspects.[19] Autobiographical writers are also readers themselves and adjust their narratives to conform to patterns of how life memoirs are supposed to function properly. Writing is therefore by its very nature always creative and always fictionalizing.[20]

In the cases of Hungary and Yugoslavia in the post-1945 period, we encounter the memoirs of communist women activists who survived the repressive inter-war years and, often, exile from Nazi-ruled Europe or the terror in the Soviet Union. They left testimonies and some of them even published memoirs at a time when the political narrative of the events they had witnessed (or participated in) was strictly controlled by the ruling Communist parties. Read against the grain, however, or even with a fine-tooth comb, they might reveal alternative narratives or hint at the authors' internal struggle to make their personal experiences conform to the official version. For women such as these female revolutionaries, their lives and the autobiographical documents they have created are an intervention in pre-existing narratives about historical events and provide insight into women's involvement in making history.[21]

Making revolution

As also shown in Chapter 1 of this volume, opposition to the First World War and the suffering it inflicted on the civilian populations was often a motivating factor for women's participation in proto-revolutionary organizing and action. They found ways to work inside and outside of traditional party structures to educate others, promote their cause, improve the lives of their communities and ultimately fight for the world that they wanted to create. This activism, what we refer to as 'making revolution', did not end once reactionary forces pushed back against the tide of revolution across Europe. Instead, we find socialist women continuing their work, often enduring periods of imprisonment, frequently crossing Europe to join new struggles, escape persecution or continue the fight for social justice in a new land. In this analysis, it is important that revolution is understood as something that socialist women made, or tried to make, rather than something that happened to them or was imagined by them. This chapter, therefore, focuses on the actions of socialist women to highlight their roles and the role of revolution in their lives, but in so doing, it also uncovers the strategies by which women were dismissed or ignored by both their contemporaries and later historiography.[22]

In Hungary, like in other regions in Central Europe, the roots of radicalization reached back into the early war years, with socialist women leading the first attempt to reorganize in early 1915 following the breakdown of the original, anti-militaristic principles of the Second International in 1914. One of the leading socialist women activists, Irén Müller, described the regrouping of pre-war Hungarian Social Democratic women's organizations in her memoir, published in 1964. Supported by the socialist (male) leadership, they set out to reorganize women along three axes: protecting and improving the living and working conditions of women working in the militarized industry where pre-war gains had been erased by the war; agitating for peace; and taking control of the increasing, spontaneous protests staged by unorganized working-class women.[23] Her account of successive International Women's Days showed the celebrations mirroring, to a degree, the resurgence of women workers' activism, the parallel rise of spontaneous, sometimes violent popular resistance of working-class women to wartime shortages, and the Social Democratic leadership's efforts to channel the latter into the party's highly centralized women's organizations. The celebration of International Women's Day throughout the war in itself represented socialist women's defiance of wartime emergency measures (which included the suspension of freedom of assembly), and Müller's emphasis on its significance in helping socialist men and women to 'find their voice' echoes the motif mentioned earlier in our chapter. In March 1916, International Women's Day was celebrated in several Hungarian cities and *Woman Worker* (*Munkásnő*), the Social Democrat women's magazine, published Clara Zetkin's letter to her Hungarian comrades on its front page.[24] In 1917, the celebration – advertised as a commemorative event – turned into a street demonstration for peace. Müller implicitly hinted at comparisons with the legendary women's demonstration that heralded the February 1917 revolution in Russia, which highlighted the event's significance as not only the first in a series of large-scale street demonstrations that followed but also the trigger for them.

Another sign of the radicalization brought on by the war was the emergence of an opposition – of socialist women activists – within the ranks of the official Social Democratic women's organization. In her account, Müller described the attacks on the moderate, centrist Social Democrat leaders (including herself) as an attempted coup by a disgruntled minority, and the leadership's response, the formation of a Women's Secretariat with her at the helm, as an appropriate move to give voice to previously under-represented women workers.[25] This detail, among many others, helps to lend credence to her memoir as a genuine historical source, even if (or exactly because of the fact that) it was published in Hungary in 1964 at a time when in Hungarian historical scholarship moderate Social Democrat leaders would be routinely characterized as traitors of the working class. Soon after the episode described above, following the fall of the Councils' Republic, in exile and in a process she ascribed to her husband's (an activist of the underground Communist Party) influence, Müller became a member of the Communist Party, an affiliation that would last for the rest of her life. But this fact, along with her long exile in the Soviet Union, apparently failed to erase her loyalty to the Social Democratic Party and trade union movement to which she had traced her long activist past.

The wartime situation also spurred pre-war organizations to take an anti-militarist path. One example is the Galileo Circle, an organization founded in 1908 by Hungarian Karl Polanyi and liberal socialist students. Defying wartime emergency laws – anti-war agitation carried the prospect of a long prison term, possibly even the capital charge of treason –, they distributed anti-war leaflets and looked to establish links with radicalized workers in the munitions factories, as well as soldiers. Eventually they were caught in early 1918 and sentenced to long prison terms. Newspapers sensationalized the unusual presence among the otherwise exclusively male and mainly Jewish, middle-class defendants of one Ilona Duczynska (1897–1978), a young woman of aristocratic background: in typical fashion, they explained her political involvement with reference to the pernicious influence of her fiancé and later husband, a young Jewish fellow student. In fact, it was Duczynska who initiated the small student group's highly ambitious and risky endeavour: a year earlier, in April 1917 as a student at Zurich's *Eidgenössische Technische Hochschule* (ETH), she had met Russian revolutionary Angelica Balabanova who gave her a copy of the Zimmerwald Manifesto. This manifesto, produced by the French and German delegations to the socialist 1915 Zimmerwald Conference, denounced German aggression and criticized socialist parties for not opposing the war more strongly. Duczynska carried the manifesto to

Budapest, and in the following year she mobilized a small group of radicalized Galileo students. She also built the illegal printing machine on which the students printed hundreds of anti-militarist flyers.[26] On the night of 31 October 1918, as the National Council and Károlyi took power, organized workers liberated the imprisoned students and carried them to the headquarters of the National Council.

The months of revolutionary upheaval between October 1918 and August 1919 in Hungary opened up an unprecedentedly broad range of political activities – it mobilized previously apolitical women and turned some liberal and moderate socialist women into radical socialists and communists. The liberal democratic revolution led to the realization of long-fought political goals, such as suffrage and the promise of political representation, discussed in more detail in Chapter 4. The National Council's invitation to feminist and socialist women to join its executive offered a significant, if symbolic down-payment on this promise. Suffrage was the long-standing mantra of the Social Democrats to which organized socialist women had long sacrificed their distinct interests. Now it had been achieved, ever the good little soldiers, they doubled down on their efforts to educate rural and unorganized working-class women. Yet as the weeks turned into months and the suffrage remained on paper, they increasingly grew disenchanted with the slow pace of the revolution and welcomed the Councils' Republic programme of all-encompassing, radical change.

Other examples of radicalization reinforce a more characteristic trend of revolutionary mobilization in the period leading up to the Republic of Councils, which was especially marked from January 1919. Apart from the disappointment over the repeated postponement of the election, the murder of Rosa Luxemburg in Berlin and the growing influence of the newly formed Hungarian Communist Party seem to have prompted many women activists – including formerly liberal feminists or liberal intellectuals – to join the party of radical change. During the Republic of Councils' rule between March and August 1919 many of them took on token or genuine leadership roles and functions deemed suitable for women in fields such as education, public health, and child welfare, and many more engaged in local educational or social welfare initiatives on a small scale but with world revolution in their sights. The decision to participate in political life during both revolutions but especially during the Republic of Councils also meant a rough bargain: the experience of a short-lived utopian period of little more than four months was traded for an extended period of persecution, internment and/ or imprisonment in the revolution's immediate aftermath, often followed by decades of exile.

Seasoned socialist activists, such as Müller were given leading roles – she was even nominated by the Social Democrats to head the Commissariat of Public Welfare, although in her memoir, she expressed relief when, in the end, she was not appointed. Still, looking back in 1964, she obligingly confessed that at the time, her thinking was still limited by 'the yoke of Social Democratic illusions'.[27] She resigned from the leadership of the Women's Secretariat of the Social Democratic Party and held local, municipal positions during the Councils' Republic – but that did not save her from arrest, internment and prison during the White Terror. Following her arrest, Müller was supported by and maintained close ties to the moderate Social Democratic leadership; and she even represented the Hungarian Social Democratic women at the Austrian Party's 1920 women's congress. In 1921, she left Hungary and the Social Democratic Party to join her husband, back from Russian captivity, in exile – first in Vienna, then, due to her husband's role in the underground Hungarian Communist party – in the Soviet Union. She left behind her decade-long, and in many ways fulfilling, Social Democratic activism, and her long-standing, high-profile position in the party for a life in exile and virtual anonymity on her husband's account – much like the stereotypical picture of the 'wife of an activist'.

The process of 'making revolution' enabled socialist women to create networks of like-minded thinkers that both sustained their activities and inspired them to continue. New democratic systems brought women into contact with each other and gave them a new platform from which to protest and disseminate ideas. In Austria, while women's suffrage at the municipal level had already been a slogan – albeit a controversial one – during the great January strike in the Habsburg Monarchy in early 1918, the Republic of (German) Austria then brought political equality into effect. Even before the first parliamentary elections, women from all walks of life were sitting on municipal councils throughout the Republic. Many of them had previously been active in trade unions, the youth movement or the women's movements. Left-wing socialists, who organized themselves in the KPÖ, founded on 3 November 1918, or in the FRSI, did not think parliamentary democracy went far enough. It is true that Ruth Fischer – in contrast to her male party comrades – emphasized that 'women's suffrage [was] certainly a political advance, because for the first time it establishes equality in political life and because the granting of this right can precisely be the impulse for every woman to reflect'. However, like the Austrian teacher Hilde Wertheim or the worker Berta Pölz, she demanded: 'Exploited, poor people must only be represented by exploited people; for the others will always forget the interests of those they represent.'[28]

However, soon, radical socialists in Austria saw the workers' councils as an instrument of social democracy to keep social revolutionary sentiment under control. In any case, activists from nearly all socialist camps were represented there. One of them was Käthe Leichter, née Pick.[29] Born in Vienna in 1895 as the daughter of a lawyer, she came from a Jewish bourgeois family. She graduated from high school in 1914 and studied political science at the University of Vienna. In order to complete her studies officially – which was not possible for her in Vienna as a woman – she moved to Heidelberg, Germany, in autumn 1917 and earned her doctorate under the renowned sociologist Max Weber. While still studying in Vienna, she became an educator for children in the working-class neighbourhood of 'Die Krim' in the otherwise rather bourgeois district of Döbling. She had been interested in social issues since childhood, made curious by the works of social criticism that she found in the library in her parents' house. Leichter seems to have shared this with other socialists who came from the middle class or bourgeoisie, like Ilona Duczynska. Both in Vienna and in Heidelberg, she was active against the war and formed strong relationships with German radicals like Ernst Toller. A published anti-war appeal earned her a charge of high treason in the German Empire – she was expelled. Leichter, who was on the left wing of the Austrian Social Democratic Party (SDAP), saw the councils movement as 'a common fighting ground for the entire proletariat'.[30] She was one of the few women who held official positions in the workers' councils. She was active primarily in the Vienna District Workers' Council, but also in the Reich Workers' Council (Economic Commission and others). There, Leichter worked alongside the Social Democrat Emmy Freundlich (1878–1948), who was, among other things, the president of the International Cooperative Women's Guild for more than twenty years and combined the activity in the revolutionary organization with participation in the Socialization Commission of the Austrian Parliament, tasked with translating various economic measures into a draft law. Leichter also served as an advisor in the Ministry of Finance. In 1921, she married the social democratic journalist Otto Leichter and became the mother of two sons in the course of the 1920s. After the end of the councils movement, she built up the women's department of the Chamber of Labour (*Arbeiterkammer*) in Vienna from 1925. The Chamber of Labour was criticized by the Communists – in their opinion, it was only a toothless alternative to the workers' councils. The influential social science studies that Leichter carried out within the framework of the Chamber of Labour became famous: she researched the working and living conditions of female home workers, domestic helpers and factory workers, and cooperated with female trade unionists to use the findings for concrete demands.

Figure 5.2. Käthe Leichter (1895–1942). Reproduced with permission of the Institut für Historische Sozialforschung, Vienna.

Even though a councils' republic had not been established in Austria, many socialists in Red Vienna saw a society in the making according to their ideas. For many it was a piece of 'revolutionary reality in its own right', as Ilona Duczynska had called it.[31] And this had to be defended in the increasingly polarized society of the First Republic. In 1931, Leichter warned readers in a pamphlet of the dangers of fascism: women would lose their political rights in a clerical-fascist or National Socialist state and be reduced to childbearing machines who had to bring forth children for the fighting fronts and factories of a coming war.[32]

For the young worker Anna Hornik-Strömer, one of the principal organizers of the January 1918 strike, the revolution brought her into a network of international revolutionary-minded women. Originally active in the Social Democratic girls' organization, she joined social revolutionary circles during the war and the newly founded KPÖ in 1918–19. In the 1920s, she took on the task of leading the party's women's work and was responsible for the women's newspaper *Die Arbeiterin*. As a delegate of the KPÖ at Comintern congresses, she also established contacts with Clara Zetkin and was a delegate to the International Conference of Communist Women in 1921. There she stressed the important role of women workers in the strike movements before and after the First World War in support of Soviet Russia.[33] Before the National Socialists took power in Austria, Hornik-Strömer worked in the Austrian cooperative movement, alongside the aforementioned social democrat Emmy Freundlich. Little is known about her time in Britain, where she lived in emigration after 1938. In any case, she participated in the activities of other exiled Social Democratic and Communist Austrians who were building up an anti-Nazi public. In 1942, she published a pamphlet entitled 'This is Austria: The story of a beautiful country'.[34] Hornik-Strömer was placed under surveillance by the British Intelligence Service MI5 and briefly interned together with her husband Leopold Hornik as suspected leaders of the Communist group inside the London-based anti-fascist refugee organization, the Austrian Centre.[35]

In 1946, Hornik-Strömer returned to Austria and continued her party political and women's political work. Among other things, she was the president of the Federation of Democratic Women (BDFÖ) – a women's organization that was linked to the KPÖ in terms of personnel and organization. The issues put forward by the BDFÖ were not only the all-dominant question of peace, but also women's political demands for a reform of marriage and family law, equal pay for equal work, a reduction in working hours and a lowering of the retirement age for women, as well as the so-called Economy Day and campaigns for cheap housing, the replacement of glass destroyed in the war and mitigations against inflationary measures and insufficient food rationing. This 'politics in the saucepan' campaign, as it was called in the organization's magazine *Stimme der Frau* (Voice of Women), brought together unorganized women and activists of the *Bund demokratischer Frauen* (Federation of Democratic Women, BDFÖ) at the local level, often as action committees or women's activists. In 1948, the BDFÖ joined the Women's International Democratic Federation (WIDF) – the largest international women's organization after the Second World War, in which anti-colonial, anti-racist and anti-fascist women's politics were made while keeping the interests of the Soviet Union in mind. Many of the BDFÖ's policies, especially its peace activities, were in line with campaigns launched by the international organisation. International cooperation represented a thread stretching back to the First World War, as Hornik-Strömer's articles on the history of International Women's Day, peace activism and the founding of the First Republic show.[36] She herself continued to network internationally, attending and then reporting on international congresses, such as the International Co-operative Alliance Congress in 1948. But she was also a tireless chronicler of the proletarian women's movement – a rare female voice commemorating the history of the communist workers movement in the country. In various publications, she repeatedly recalled the January 1918 strike, the days of the Austrian Revolution, women's struggles for political rights and campaigns for better working and living conditions. She was not only honoured by her own party as a pioneer. In 1950, she took part in the jubilee meeting on the occasion of the fiftieth anniversary of International Women's Day in Copenhagen. Communist Irma Schwager, also a participant in the rally in 1950, recalled: 'I experienced there the high regard in which she was held by women from all over the world.'[37]

Many socialist women struggled to make their voices heard within traditional party structures after 1918–19. In Germany, some became politicians, either taking a chance with the Social Democrats, the party that had campaigned for female suffrage before the war (Toni Pfülf, for example, who was a member of the Reichstag between 1920 and 1933) or maintaining their allegiance to the Independent Socialists who had opposed the war (see Toni Sender) or joining the Communist KPD (as was the case with Martha Arendsee and Clara Zetkin). As Chapter 4 discusses, left-wing parties were more supportive of their female members and candidates, but significant barriers to women's participation remained and standing for election was no guarantee of winning a seat. Due to the party list system, female candidates' success depended on party goodwill to put their names high enough on the list to enable them a realistic chance of being elected. Moreover, for the women who did become politicians, many struggled to make their voices heard. Female politicians were active in welfare and education policy but not a single woman took a cabinet position during the Weimar Republic and economics and foreign affairs remained dominated by men.[38] Instead, many women remained active in trades unions and as social workers or journalists to try to campaign and bring about change. For example, Hilde Kramer, a key figure in the Bavarian revolution, and Maria Saran both worked for the Berlin Electricity Works that ran classes and had dedicated social workers for their employees.

As in the Austrian case, the process of making revolution brought German women into an international network of radicals and this network became a lifeline. Maria Saran and her dissident Communist group the ISK (*Internationaler Sozialistischer Kampfbund*, Militant International Socialist League) supported a united left front against the fascists but saw this collapse in the 1932 presidential election. In this election, the SPD supported Hindenburg's candidacy for president instead of the KPD candidate Ernst Thälmann, who was explicitly anti-Hitler. Hindenburg, as the KPD and ISK had warned, appointed Hitler as Chancellor in January 1933. Saran, like many German anti-fascists, decided to flee after the Reichstag fire in February 1933 and was supported by like-minded women in Britain who provided her with a home and helped her establish a new life.[39] Being outside Germany offered different opportunities to work towards building the socialist state. Saran and Kramer both joined the Labour Party and campaigned for the Labour victory in 1945. Saran described refusing to allow the bombs falling on London to deter their branch meetings and referred to the 1945 electoral campaign as 'a happy and exciting period for me. The nightmares of Hitler and the war were over. An era of peace was beginning which seemed to hold out prospects of progress.'[40] Kramer wrote documents for the 1948 National Health Service (NHS) Act, a cornerstone in the goal of bringing equality as it ensured free universal health care.[41]

As the Second World War wore on towards the bitter end, there were also opportunities in Germany to begin to dream and then to campaign to realize a new socialist state. Saran wrote articles and pamphlets from Britain demanding investment and education to create a Germany that was a bulwark against fascism and a bastion of human rights.[42] Others joined or re-joined German politics to enact socialist policies. Kiel revolutionary and trade unionist Gertrud Völcker (1896–1979) became an active and visible local Social Democrat politician after the war, particularly working to improve the lives of children from poor families. Just like for the women in the Kingdom of Yugoslavia, gendered expectations of women's work continued to be a burden for those seeking to change the world. Both Saran and Kramer divorced their husbands and struggled to reconcile society's demands of motherhood with the realities of their political activism.

Through the process of making revolution, the distinction between the personal and the political, between the private and the public, became meaningless. Marriage to another socialist meant that the revolution was a part of socialist wives' daily existence. As shown in the case of Irén Müller, this could provide shelter, but it could also lead women into further hardship, while at the same time, hiding their revolutionary actions. In what was to become Yugoslavia, Anica Lokar (1897–1976), a political and public worker and wife from the rural

Slovenian town Ajdovščina, saw herself and her generation as living in a 'revolutionary era'[43] that shaped their worldview with the help of the Austrian Socialist newspaper, the *Arbeiter-Zeitung*. She became more radicalized with the news about the October Revolution in Russia and through her readings, especially of August Bebel's *Die Frau und der Sozialismus* (see Chapter 4). She soon upgraded the urge for a national uprising against Habsburg autocratic rule to the class struggle: 'We underwent political persecution under Austria and Italy because of our national consciousness, but now it was about another, to me completely new thing, class struggle. I met a new circle of people who earned my greatest respect for their belief in a great world revolution.'[44] She met her future husband, Dragotin Gustinčič (1882–1974), in 1920 and her bourgeois family opposed their relationship. But she chose to resist family values, another political and personal act of resistance. Already in the first months of her relationship, as she recalled, she became familiar with all the prisons in Ljubljana, at the time a brutal police town, as other women also report in their memoirs.[45] In fact, the whole of Yugoslavia was 'in the wake of a terror like no other in Europe'.[46] Due to her husband's political activity, the couple were forced to move several times, none of the family members could gain Yugoslav citizenship, and they could only travel and work illegally. She and Gustinčič lived a perilous life crossing many different countries and frequently torn apart by national borders. They separated in 1941.

During the Second World War, she worked as a radio announcer in Moscow, and after the war she initially lived in Belgrade, which seemed like paradise to her on her return. She could not become an editor, because she was not a member of the Yugoslav League of Communists:

> Everyone who knew me from 1920 onwards was amazed that I was not a member of the Communist Party because I had been active in the Party all this time ... When I was called upon to join the Party in 1927, I asked Gustinčič for advice, but he strongly opposed the idea, asking, who would take care of the children if I were arrested.[47]

To her husband, her role at home clearly seemed more important than her role in politics. But given the course of her life, we can also argue that her role as a wife and mother in the conditions she lived was in fact political.

She first got her Yugoslav citizenship in 1945, in the new Socialist Federal Republic.[48] She lived a varied and active life in socialist Yugoslavia. She was hard working (as she wrote in one of her letters about her son Jurij Gustinčič: 'I found my real child in him when he said that he also works permanently and that he cannot live without work. I'm like that too.'49 She remained preoccupied with politics or as she wrote to her brother in 1952: 'I do nothing but worry about political problems. They are infinite as life is infinite.'50 What especially interested her was the global position of socialism during the crisis year 1956: 'I think a lot about the political positions. The events in Hungary and Suez brought socialism to the fore. I wonder how free, progressive people are seeing this question now. And all my efforts go into searching for such answers. I know a lot of interesting things.'51

Her former husband Dragotin Gustinčič found himself in disgrace after the Tito-Stalin split (1948) and was sent to the Goli Otok island prison camp. Despite being one of the key inter-war communist activists who devoted most of his and his family's life to the idea of revolution, he was erased from public life and forgotten. He was bitter and his diaries are full of political reckonings and historical explanations. His family and the wife are hardly ever mentioned.[52] Here, too, we can see the difference between a revolutionary husband and a revolutionary wife: for him, the revolution was something external, while she deliberately narrated her own revolutionary experience through the perspective of the family, as her internal experience. But what they had in common after 1945 and in separate lives was the disappointment with the course of the communist revolution for which they had sacrificed so much. As Anica Lokar put it: 'I may belong to the Communist movement of the future, but I no longer belong to the one I experienced after 1920.'53 Despite disappointments over the revolution of the past and present, she had not lost hope in the revolution of the future.

Resistance

Following the social and political upheavals at the end of the First World War, many socialist women in Hungary and Yugoslavia found themselves in a new battle for social justice as repressive forces took control. Many of the Austrian women who had participated in the revolutionary period of upheaval at and after the end of the First World War, while celebrating the enactment of equal suffrage, also discovered that resistance to right-wing and authoritarian forces had to continue. In the process, different political and personal circumstances took effect. It was also not uncommon for anti-fascist women to have to continue their political work and resistance against National Socialism and fascism from a place of exile, for example Berta Pölz in France or Käthe Leichter in Switzerland.

In the context of the turbulent European history of the first half of the twentieth century, the boundaries between political activity and resistance, between forced flight and exile or migration for personal and political reasons became fluid. Ilona Duczynska, for example, changed her place of residence and political action (at least) seven times between 1916 and 1945, as did Ruth Fischer. The causes ranged from the opportunity to pursue a university education, to involvement in the Comintern, to family reasons, to flight and exile due to possible political persecution. They shared their transnational lives and their spheres of political activism spanning from Soviet Russia to North America with many other European émigrés forced to leave and rebuild lives and careers.

The life of Berta Pölz, who was born in Vienna in 1894 and came to prominence on the eve of the First World War as a youth functionary in the SDAP, demonstrates how women trod a path through revolutionary activity to antifascist resistance. She was chairwoman of the party's section for young girls in the Vienna working-class district of Favoriten. Female students held numerous demonstrations, especially toward the end of the First World War, such as on the occasion of the conviction of Friedrich Adler, who had shot the Austrian prime minister in protest against the war. Pölz was arrested during one of these demonstrations in 1917. By then, a part of the young workers had already separated from the Social Democratic majority. They were close to radical left-wing actors who, among other things, founded the first Bolshevik party outside Russia, the KPÖ, in November 1918. Like other socialists who later joined the KPÖ, Pölz was active in the January 1918 strike, during which 750,000 people throughout the Habsburg monarchy ceased work and went on strike for peace and better working and living conditions. Many of them also wanted a socialist soviet republic. Here, too, Pölz was among those who became involved in the Federation of Revolutionary Socialists, and in July 1919 sought (but failed to achieve) the proclamation of a soviet republic in the small industrial town of Vöslau to the south of Vienna.

In 1922, she married the Czernowitz lawyer David Pollak, but then, as is the case in the traces of many women's lives, her trail is lost until she reemerged in public with a spectacular appearance in 1936. In March 1936, the so-called Socialist Trial (*Sozialistenprozess*) took place in Austria, in which twenty-eight members of the Revolutionary Socialists were accused of high treason. The Revolutionary Socialists consisted of Communists and Social Democrats who worked together to carry out underground activities against the clerical-fascist regime. Berta Pölz – now Pollak – was among the spectators and disrupted the trial to protest against press censorship and restrictions on freedom of assembly.

She was sentenced to two weeks' imprisonment. Finally, in 1938, she and her Jewish husband fled to France via Luxembourg and Belgium and Pölz continued her agitation for a better world. They lived as submarines in Paris and Montauban and were active in the *Résistance* – allegedly together with their son. In April 1945, she broke with the group of Austrian socialist resistance fighters in France for political reasons; no further details are known. A year later the couple returned to Austria, soon afterwards they filed for divorce. This disruptive and disrupted life is shared by many of the revolutionary women who became involved in resistance movements. Germans Hilde Kramer, Maria Saran and Cläre Jung experienced relationship breakdowns and Kramer and Saran also had fractured relationships with their children, but this had not deterred them from pursuing their cause. Peter Haumer, who researched Berta Pölz's biography, found a last sign of life from her in the mid-1970s: she was awarded compensation as a victim of National Socialist persecution by the Republic of Austria.[54]

Käthe Leichter also joined the anti-fascist resistance movement and after 1934, when the Chambers of Labour were dissolved under Austro-fascism and class politics was highly restricted, fled to Switzerland for a few months with her family. After her return, she continued her political activities for the Revolutionary Socialists under assumed names, now in illegality. Among other things, the group printed leaflets addressed to 'proletarian women' and often met at the Leichters' home in their garden on the outskirts of the city. After the National Socialists seized power, Otto Leichter went into exile again with his sons, while Käthe Leichter stayed in Vienna – also to help her mother escape. She was betrayed to the Gestapo; during her imprisonment, she wrote an autobiographical text that somehow survived – unlike herself. In 1940, she was deported to the Ravensbrück concentration camp. Her fellow prisoners remembered that she had continued to try to give hope for a better life with plays and lectures during her imprisonment.[55] She had apparently also been working on a study on female murderers, thieves and other criminal women. In 1942, Käthe Leichter was killed at the Bernburg Euthanasia Centre.

For many socialist women, resistance to fascism and authoritarianism did not end in 1945. For Ilona Duczynska, the experiences of the revolution in 1918 and what followed had given her a strong belief in autonomy, resulting in her exclusion from the Hungarian Communist Party, the SDAP and then the KPÖ. She worked in the Commissariat of Foreign Affairs during the Councils' Republic in Hungary. Sent abroad on a diplomatic mission, the news of the fall of the revolution found her in Switzerland. She travelled on to Soviet Russia where for four months, at a critical point in the Russian civil war, she worked at the newly formed Comintern as secretary to Karl Radek. In 1920, the exiled leaders of the Hungarian Communist Party sent her to Vienna; shortly afterwards she was expelled from the party, consumed by the internal divisions so typical of defeated revolutionaries in exile. Her marriage to Karl Polanyi, founder of the Galileo circle, was certainly also a reason for her estrangement from the Hungarian Communist Party in the early 1920s, which she criticized in her publications. In 1970, she characterized this as a 'critique of Stalinism, so to speak, before it even existed'.[56] With linguistic wit and a sharp tongue, she described the internal party power struggles and diagnosed an undesirable development. The leading party functionaries would rely on a 'dialectic of evil': the crimes and moral sacrifices committed in the name of the revolution would be glorified and reinterpreted into something good.[57] Duczynska, who herself did not fundamentally reject political violence, nonetheless insisted that inner-party democracy and pluralism were the only possible paths to a socialist future.

Duczynska was committed to revolutionary activities throughout her life.[58] She operated an illegal radio station during the *Schutzbund* uprising, about which she later wrote a highly regarded historical study. She followed her husband the economist Karl Polanyi to Britain in 1936, and learned to fly during the Blitz.[59] Duczynska's journalistic activities in the 1960s and 1970s perhaps also can be seen as an attempt to create a critical public sphere in Hungary, a continuation of her aspirations for a democratic socialist society. Remarkably, this was after she had urged her daughter to go to Hungary – a country basically unknown to her – after the Second World War and help build a socialist society there. In the 1960s and 1970s, Duczynska sought contact with the generation of young people in Europe who placed themselves in the tradition of the freedom struggles in the decolonized countries. In her 1975 study on the Austrian civil war in February 1934, she also made two points: in the face of the fascist threat, violence was sometimes a politically permissible, even necessary means. However, the exercise of violence had to be combined with a pluralistic, democratic, indeed, anti-hierarchical mode of organization. Only with such a model could the sphere of power be linked to that of humanity. 'For power is inevitable', as she wrote, but 'humanity is indispensable'.[60] For the last decades of her life, she lived in Canada, outside of Toronto.

For those in exile, continuing resistance in their new country was a difficult tightrope to walk. Maria Saran, who fled to Britain from Nazi Germany in 1933, had been critical of British imperialism in the 1920s and maintained this position, but her autobiography is somewhat vague on her opinions on this matter, despite being very clear on her German socialist standpoint. She met

Irish trade unionists in 1924, whose accounts of the Irish struggle for independence fascinated her: 'How revealing to see Britain for the first time through Irish eyes!' she wrote, although she did not elaborate on what exactly it was that she had learnt about Britain.[61] Her descriptions of meeting individuals fighting for Indian independence in London in the 1930s are even more vague: 'I gradually became familiar with the problems of India, Ceylon and other parts of the British Empire.'[62] Nonetheless, she credited these discussions with inspiring her post-1945 work of touring the world and promoting socialist causes. British socialist women, moving in similar circles to Saran, were more vocal in their support for Indian independence and Saran may have shared many of their ideas.[63] However, for Saran, even meeting supporters of Indian independence could have resulted in her deportation to Germany. Even when she wrote her autobiography in the 1970s, this legacy of caution remains, but it was not enough to deter her from her activism in the 1930s or from writing about it later.

Angela Vode's life trajectory in the Kingdom of Yugoslavia demonstrates how the revolution could lead socialist women to champion unpopular causes, placing them in a position of resistance that became anti-fascist.[64] Born and raised in a working-class family, Vode's worldview was shaped by her railway

Figure 5.3. Angela Vode (1892–1985). Reproduced with permission of Narodna in univerzitetna knjižnica.

worker and social democrat father and his subscription to the Austrian socialist publication the *Arbeiter-Zeitung* (see also Anica Lokar). From 1911, she worked as a teacher in several primary schools around the Slovenian capital Ljubljana, but she lost her job in 1917 due to her political activism, especially her anti-Austrian propaganda (including irreligious views, Slovene nationalism and socialism). She then held several white-collar jobs in a bank (the *Jadranska banka*) and later in a foundry factory. In 1919, she became a member and secretary of the Social Democratic Party. She was among the more radical members, who in April 1920 established the Slovenian Communist Party. At the same time, she was studying teaching methods for disabled children in Prague, Berlin and Vienna. After her training, she began teaching at the Special School for the Disabled in Ljubljana. She did not see her work in the party as a paid vocation (her salary from the party could have hardly covered any living expenses), but more as a calling and moral stand in the increasingly authoritarian Kingdom of Serbs, Croats and Slovenes. At the same time, she was a leading member of various Slovene and Yugoslav women's organizations that fought for women's and workers' rights.

As a devoted anti-fascist, she did not accept Stalin's pact with Hitler (1939) and was therefore expelled from the Party. This was a crucial turning point in her political activism that had a huge impact on her life after the Second World War. During the war, she organized humanitarian aid for refugees and their families until she was sent to Ravensbrück concentration camp in 1944, where she was imprisoned for six months, until she was released due to a fortunate turn of events. This was not her only imprisonment. In 1947, she was accused of treason against the new Communist regime and sentenced to twenty years in prison and deprivation of civic rights for five years in a show trial called the 'Nagode Trial'. She was held in prison for more than five years, until she was sixty-one years old, but even after she had been 'pardoned', she was not allowed to do any public work. Her name was deliberately airbrushed from official publications, and her books were unavailable.

Moscow was frequently imagined as a left-wing haven by women across Europe. German revolutionaries Hilde Kramer and Cläre Jung both travelled to Moscow in the 1920s to help build the new nation.[65] Although a convinced communist at the time, the Austrian/German Isa Strasser already brought 'a good portion of scepticism' to Moscow. Referring to Angelica Balabanova's experiences, she called such scepticism 'contraband'.[66] Nevertheless, she spent several years with her husband there, before leaving Russia in 1927. The October Revolution was a shared imaginary for many Yugoslavs, since the idea of Russia was, especially in the former Austrian Littoral, where Slavic populations often felt caught between nationalistic persecution by Italian elites and German-speaking governors, often present as an idea of a big Slavic brother, a saviour or at least a bright example. Progressive teacher, editor and inter-war socialist Pavla Hočevar (1889–1972) from Trieste, who, because of her Russophilia, even had to defend herself before the authorities, saw the October Bolshevik Revolution as 'a social democratic coup in a Slavic state that was for us of particular importance'.[67] However, this enthusiasm was not matched by the reality of the experience. Jung, as part of her participation in the Workers' International Relief organization, witnessed the devastating and overwhelming poverty in the Volga region of Russia in the 1920s. Kramer, working as a translator and secretary to the Comintern, saw how the linguistic and, in particular, cultural divides between the Communists of Central Europe and the Russian Bolsheviks could not be bridged. Both Germans returned to Berlin in the mid-1920s.

Anica Lokar's experience crossed from anti-fascist resistance to anti-Stalinist resistance as she traversed southern and eastern Europe, occasionally finding solidarity that crossed political boundaries and frequently escaping persecution. In the early 1920s, in the mining town of Idrija, where national and class consciousness intertwined amongst mostly Slovene miners in the Italian-run mines, Lokar's then husband Dragotin Gustinčič was a target of a planned fascist liquidation. They lived in difficult conditions that became next to impossible after the stillbirth of twins.[68] Neither Yugoslavia nor Italy were safe places, so she moved in 1922 with her husband to Vienna, where the most active part of the Yugoslav Communist Party lived in emigration. After a tiring process of looking for an apartment, she started helping Yugoslav Communists by typing party material, despite the fact she was not a member of the Party. Vienna was not only a city where Yugoslav Communists of different nationalities could work together, but it was also a temporary, transitional home for other communist emigrants. Lokar fondly remembered visiting a theatre with Italian communist Antonio Gramsci.[69]

After two years, she and her husband returned to Yugoslavia and he was immediately imprisoned. She was forced to live with her mother in her hometown Ajdovščina, where she 'developed the biggest political activity of her life'.[70] She was working full time in an office to support her family, taking care of her three-year-old son, attending trade union meetings with spinning mill workers, acting as a treasurer for Willi Münzenberg's International Red Aid organization, participating in working women's organizations, and was typing up Party material as well as rewriting her imprisoned husband's political writings. When

Figure 5.4. Idrija in 1934. Source: Alamy.

her husband was freed, they lived in Ljubljana for a while until he was arrested again and sent to pre-trial detention in Belgrade for two years. In 1931, as soon as he was free again, he fled to Vienna and from there to Moscow. Lokar, after several years of living on her own, decided to follow him: in bad health, and with their two little sons, she undertook a long journey from Ljubljana to Moscow. At the time, it was impossible in Yugoslavia to get permission to travel to the Soviet Union and she needed almost a year just to get as far as Austria. However, Lokar soon realized on her arrival in Moscow that she was not to witness a communist fairy tale; the letters she had received from her friend Malka Regent, another forgotten wife of a communist politician and his close co-worker, who migrated to the Soviet Union, about how amazing it was to live in Moscow, did not reflect reality. The first person to tell her that, immediately after her arrival, was no other than Malka's husband Ivan, who had already been sensitized to the tense atmosphere of Moscow in the 1930s.[71]

The neighbourhood they lived in was mostly German and they enrolled their son Jurij in the German-language school (the *Karl-Liebknecht-Schule*), because her husband was convinced that the revolution in Germany was close at hand. In 1934, she started working for KUNMZ (the Communist University of the National Minorities of the West), where she worked as a typist for Slovenian and Serbo-Croat-language publications. She did not find this job intellectually stimulating enough and was unhappy but Ivan Regent claimed she was much needed there and therefore she stayed. Branislava Marković, the wife of another famous Yugoslav communist Sima Marković, who devoted her life to the idea of communism, but is rarely even remembered as a wife, suggested that they enrol on a course to become German teachers, because this seemed like a better professional opportunity.

Life in Moscow was hard: the commute to and from work was long, and there were endless queues in the shops. Lokar worked long hours and took care of the children herself. When the whole family went to bed, she started re-writing and editing her husband's communist manuscripts. Her husband dedicated his life entirely to revolutionary work. Once, when she was with their sick son in a health resort outside of Moscow for a month, she noticed on her return that her husband and his comrade had not changed the bed linen for a whole month because they were so passionately discussing revolution that they forgot about the world around them. She could never allow herself to be that passionate nor did she have the same opportunities as her husband did. Some other women describe similar experiences in the exile community in 1930s Moscow. Gusti Jirku Stridsberg (1892–1978), for instance, wrote in her memoirs: 'No one has time for emotions. They work, sleep, coincidentally make babies, and throw themselves onto cabbage soup. And in the heart burns the fire of ideals.'[72]

In the 1930s, she changed jobs frequently. When she worked at the Censorship Bureau for Foreign Media, she first came into contact with Western media coverage of the Soviet Union. She became increasingly frightened, the people she knew began to disappear in the Stalinist purges and, as she wrote, 'we were all in a psychopathic state'.[73] She then began working as a translator and control officer for translations of Marxist texts into Slovene. She met many people from all over Europe; among others she was especially close to Imre Nagy and György Lukács and some other Hungarians, as she shared an office with two Hungarian comrades. Her circle of friends was very international, but she was afraid of purges and started asking herself: 'By what right do our people die here in the Soviet Union? Maybe because of internationalism?'[74] At the time of the Nazi attack on the Soviet Union in 1941, she separated from Gustinčič. Ever since they were in Moscow, they have lived separate lives and even earlier, in the 1920s, they had spent as many as seven out of ten years apart. Most of the time, the material care for the family was entirely dependent on her. Marriage to a revolutionary required too much self-renunciation and devotion, perhaps even more than the revolution itself.[75]

For many, the Stalinist purges and the terror resulted in a fragmentation and, for some, a total destruction of their revolutionary networks, their families and intimate relationships. Ruth Fischer, who went into exile in France in 1933 and then to the USA in 1941, is known today for her opposition to Stalin and her testimony against her own brothers Gerhart and Hanns Eisler before the House Committee on Un-American Activities (HUAC) in 1947. In addition, she was also a publicist in the post-war period (when she returned to France). Of more importance here is that the correspondence in her papers painfully shows the torn networks: companions disappeared in the Gulag system, were murdered in Nazi concentration camps or were politically alienated.[76]

In Hungary, the inter-war Horthy regime was able effectively to silence resistance from socialist women, especially those who had been in exile. Magda Aranyossi (1896–1977) was born into an upper-middle-class, assimilated Jewish family, trained as a teacher and married a leading illegal Communist Party member, also from a bourgeois family background. Escaping looming arrest in Hungary, the couple moved to and spent the inter-war years in France and participated in the *Résistance*, first in France and then Hungary. After the war, they became communist functionaries, with Aranyossi appointed in 1945 as the first general secretary of the Democratic Alliance of Hungarian Women; this

Soviet-style organization supplanted all grassroots women's organizations. Aranyossi had no previous ties to any of the genuine women's organizations that had existed before the war, but as a faithful party member, she took to the task with relish. And to all appearances, at least publicly, she remained a loyal member of the Stalinist and then the State Socialist *nomenklatura*. Her memoir appeared twice: first in the mid-1980s, after the author's death, then in 2018, annotated – often tongue in cheek – by the author's nephew, the leading Hungarian writer Péter Nádas.[77] It is more than likely that Aranyossi, highly intelligent, well-educated, with an upper-middle-class education, family background and decade-long exposure to French culture, harboured serious doubts about the post-war communist regime, especially when her husband fell out of favour with the Party. But in public, she kept her silence and was rewarded with the privileges accorded to 'old comrades' to the end.

Jolán Kelen (1891–1979), in contrast, came from an impoverished middle-class Jewish family but also trained as a teacher. She originally joined the Hungarian Social Democratic Party and was a member of the Galileo Circle. Together with her husband, she was arrested and tried – but not convicted – in the famous 1918 Galileo-trial in which Duczynska was one of the accused. Kelen, along with her husband and brother-in-law, became founding members of the Hungarian Communist Party in November 1918. It was a family of leading communists – her brother-in-law was Ottó Korvin, the chief of the political section of the Commissariat of Internal Affairs, executed in August 1919. Her husband was also a high-ranking official of the Republic of Councils. Husband and wife were both arrested during the counter-revolution, but she was allowed to emigrate while her husband was exchanged for Hungarian POWs – in this prisoner swap, the leaders of the Councils' Republic were exchanged for Hungarian POWs captured in Russia. Unlike the Aranyossis, the Kelens went into exile first in Vienna, then in Moscow, and were trusted enough by the Soviet Party to be sent to serve at the Soviet Embassy in Berlin before the Nazi takeover. But it was back in the Soviet Union that Kelen and her two children experienced the build-up to the Second World War. Her husband and her younger brother were executed during the Stalinist terror, while she was arrested and spent years in the Gulag. She was allowed to return to Hungary after 1956 and worked as a researcher and historian at the Party Institute.[78] In appearance and in her public roles, Kelen remained the picture of the puritanical old comrade, and a hardliner to the end.

Kelen's memoir, published in the late 1970s in Hungary, gives very little away. Most of all, it does not contain any reflection on the fate of her husband, killed in the Stalinist terror, apart from a brief description of the event.[79] Neither does she linger on her own terrible experiences in the Gulag. The silence over the tragedies of her own life and closest family, as well as a cliché-filled passage at the end about a short visit to the Soviet Union in 1958 which extols the wonderful achievements of the Soviet Union, speak eloquently of the psychological need to maintain her unbroken loyalty to the Party.[80] Aranyossi and Kelen differed somewhat in terms of their socio-economic origins but had much more in common when it came to cultural background, education, marriage, the beginnings of political engagement, and major life events. Most of all, they both dedicated their entire lives to the cause, serving Hungary's Communist and State Socialist regimes. Despite their differences, their respective memoirs illustrate the various ways in which activist women grappled with – or refused to reflect on, at least in public – the sacrifices and the tremendous personal cost they had paid for a life in the service of a cause.

In Yugoslavia, socialist women who did not fit within the inter-war model of gender relations and behaviour were marginalized, treated with suspicion and frequently forgotten. In the inter-war period, Angela Vode showcased how the woman question was an integral part of the social (and economic and cultural) questions.[81] In that period, she self-identified as a socialist and a feminist, a combination regarded with great suspicion in socialist Yugoslavia after 1945. The ruling party ideology denied the legitimacy of a separate woman's question and foregrounded the social question instead, with the claim that the liberation of the proletariat would lead to the liberation of women. Feminism was condemned as a movement of the liberal bourgeoisie and therefore erased from the public discourse, together with the works of Angela Vode. Vode died in 1985, only occasionally and privately remembered. Her work was rediscovered in the late 1980s and her life and publications received feminist attention in the 1990s. Today her most important works, as well as her memoirs, are reprinted, contextualized and extensively used as a historical source.

All of the resistance discussed so far has been clearly political resistance in a multitude of forms, but we can also see personal resistance running throughout these lives, once again rendering the distinction between personal and political meaningless. By becoming revolutionaries, socialist women defied expectations of their gender but also used this to evade detection. Cläre Jung smuggled guns in Berlin in 1919, knowing that she was far less likely to be stopped than her male comrades. She also helped deserters cross Berlin by playing the role of lovers, pretending that she was wrapped up in a romance rather than engaging in a political act.[82] Some women resisted bourgeois expectations of marriage, choosing equal partnerships or a single life. Strategic marriages could also protect women by giving them access to a different citizenship or condemn them when they became stateless or subject to deportation.[83] Women's relationships can erase them from the historiography as their motivations become ascribed to their romantic attachment and deemed less worthy of study than their husbands, and their change of name can also make them harder to follow in the archives. However, these relationships also brought the revolution into the home as women made difficult choices about raising children, visiting their husbands in prison, and propagated revolutionary ideas. The many examples that have come to the fore in this chapter of socialist women's personal relationships as resistance and as a hindrance to revolutionary participation indicate the importance of reading against the grain, of understanding women in their own right, and of challenging the erasure of women from the history of revolution.

Conclusions

Enzo Traverso once called revolutions 'factories of utopia'.[84] Even if the revolutionary years were not always the central site of utopia for the women actors gathered here, it is clear that they had a profound impact on their remaining political and personal lives. Focusing on the life trajectories of female revolutionaries allows us to see the revolution in more detail. By looking beyond the (male) revolutionary leadership, we can learn how the revolution was organized, administered and spread. The interplay between the political ideas of the revolution and how these ideas could be translated into action is visible. The lives of the revolutionaries discussed in this chapter provide insights into the significance they placed on making revolution, something which is especially important to understand for female revolutionaries who had so much to lose. This chapter has also reflected on how the desire to bring about social justice led the women to try to build a new state from exile or move into resistance against fascist (and Stalinist) regimes. Wherever they had experienced the revolution at the end of the First World War, the revolution often became a transnational phenomenon.

Undoubtedly, the revolution caused problems for the female revolutionaries. They often led precarious lives, struggling to find stable employment, and facing arrest, harassment and even death for their beliefs. However, the dedication to the revolutionary cause also sustained these women. It gave them a raison d'être and also methods to escape danger. They had relationships with other revolutionaries or witnessed the breakdown of marriages as their dedication to the cause pulled them apart. We can see the tensions between the loyalty to family or friends, the loyalty to a party and the loyalty to an ideal. Occasionally, this loyalty led to silence, particularly during the Cold War, or led to arrest: but loyalty between comrades also helped to provide safe haven for those needing to flee one or more oppressive regimes.

Examining the life trajectories of the revolutionaries destabilizes the notion that the revolution had a clearly defined starting point and finishing point. Many of these women had been involved in activism to prepare the groundwork long before the close of the First World War, and the termination of their revolutionary work frequently only came with the end of their lives. The category of revolutionary is also expanded by including these women. The women who provided ration cards for revolutionary soldiers or worked as interpreters in Moscow and beyond were cornerstones of the revolution. Without their labour, there would be no revolution. They were also transgressive; refusing to accept national borders as the limits of their work and transecting Europe, through Vienna and Moscow to Britain and beyond, to foment the revolution. At the same time, they transgressed societal norms and expectations of their gender, destabilizing gender categories. Understanding their lives also changes our perception of the geography of revolution. For instance, socialist women in the Kingdom of Yugoslavia were not at the periphery of Europe, they were at the heart of a trans-European revolutionary movement. By considering the revolution in the context of their entire lives, frameworks of power become upended and our categories of what is a revolution and who is a revolutionary fall apart.

6

Commemorating Revolution, Commemorating Women

Mary McAuliffe, Ingrid Sharp, Clotilde Faas, Tiina Lintunen and Ali Ronan

The centenary commemorative landscape of the first two decades of the twenty-first century, in many parts of Europe, has been dominated by two main themes: war and revolution. Within those themes, the memories, legacies and commemorations of two major episodes of European history eclipse much else; these are the First World War, 1914–18, and the Russian Revolution, 1917. While both had far-reaching impacts on the nations involved, and even on those not directly involved, the concentration on the commemorative events surrounding these histories tends to obscure and marginalize other important European histories, in particular the impact of feminist and socialist politics on smaller but no less important revolutions, both within the countries impacted by the war, and others not directly impacted. The challenge for memory scholars and, more especially, historians of gender in the twenty-first century is to understand what is included and excluded within commemorations of war and revolution, because, as noted by Lucy Noakes, the study of women in wartime (and revolution) can be a 'particularly potent method of analysing the means by which memories are constructed'.[1] In commemorations of the First World War, the remembrance of male sacrifice and trauma is imbued with different meanings for diverse groups. For example, for the Irish Ulster Unionists (those loyal to the Union with Britain) the losses of the 36th (Ulster) Division at the Somme are often 'relayed as containing the essence of what it means to be an Ulsterman', while for the French it is Verdun, rather than the Somme, 'which encapsulates' the French experience of the war.[2] As Alan Kramer has written, for Germany, Verdun is also the 'great historic battle' even if the Somme caused more casualties.[3] A collection of essays on the Somme explained why it does not feature as a German 'site of memory'; it was a defensive battle and 'in 1917 the German forces retreated from it, leaving behind no significant memorials, only a deliberately devastated region'.[4] It had no value as a 'site of memory', unlike Gallipoli, also a lost battle, which for the ANZAC troops of Australia and New Zealand, fighting within the British Imperial army, served as 'a foundational 'militaristic, masculinist, and mono-cultural' imagining of what it means to be Australian'.[5] As John Horne has also noted, the First World War, although often ignored in Irish revolutionary historiography, was a transformative event as it 'defined and polarised four competing kinds of Irish statehood: unionism, northern unionism, Home Rule nationalism, and separatist nationalism, and those conflicting mobilisations determined Ireland's post-war development'.[6]

These few examples demonstrate that, as Maggie Andrews puts it, 'commemoration, memories and narratives of past wars and conflicts are utilised to construct a sense of nationhood, but the appeal of any specific version of the nation constructed in this way will not be universal'.[7] It is, however, the case that the issue of gender exclusion, to a greater or lesser degree, from national commemoration events, has been universal.[8] With many of these myth-making memorials and commemorations continuing to be male-centric, it is incumbent on historians, especially feminist historians, to challenge these foundational narratives and 'to ensure this story is inclusive or that its exclusions are at least noted'.[9] It is important therefore to note that the development of the discipline of women's and gender history over the last half-century, and the embedding of feminism as a political ideology in most European states, has meant that recent commemorations will inevitably be viewed, and critiqued, through a gendered and feminist lens. In this chapter, the centenary commemorations of several chosen countries will be studied from a gendered perspective. The revolutionary decade in Ireland provides the opportunity to review the transformation of what were initially male-centred commemorations of politics and the road to war and revolution to more gender-inclusive commemorations as the decade continued, and how and why that happened. Commemorations of suffrage activism, socialist politics and/or female participation in revolution in Britain, Germany and Finland will also be critiqued. What this chapter seeks to challenge is 'gendered' forgetting in commemorative practices, and question what we are missing if we marginalize or neglect to include gender.

The chapter centres on centenaries of suffrage and female revolutionary activism in Ireland, Britain, Finland and Germany, and the key concepts under discussion here are historical politics, memory politics, historical culture and historical consciousness. Historical politics uses history in order to achieve a particular goal. It is an intentional activity in which history is interpreted according to the interests of a particular political group. The groups in power have their own important narratives that embody their identities and values, influencing how historical knowledge is used. At its most eloquent, history is mobilized in the service of issues of war and peace. In building a national identity, those in power make choices about what is included in the national story and what is left out of it, who are given a voice and who are silenced. When certain people or groups decide what to include in the national story, it always is a matter of memory politics.[10] Many governments set up advisory boards on commemoration and often exert pressure, overt or covert, on what should be commemorated. Memory politics, whether local, national or European was, and continues to be, important to state funders. For instance, in Ireland, the Decade of Centenaries was from the beginning (2012) to be 'measured and reflective ... inclusive and non-partisan', although it did also acknowledge that the state (that is, the Irish Republic) should not be 'expected to be neutral about its own existence'.[11] However, in the early years of the Decade, anxieties about the impact of revolutionary commemorations on the relationships with the Northern Irish unionist communities and with Great Britain were evident. Meanwhile, in the context of post-Brexit politics, many in Northern Ireland were anxious about the commemoration of the 1921 foundation of that state, especially as it included the centenary of the creation of the still contentious border on the island of Ireland. Likewise, there was a strong steer from the German Foreign Office that the commemoration of the First World War at home and abroad should emphasize European integration.[12]

This applies also to gender in history. In this chapter, we understand historical culture as the numerous ways and means which produce images and information about the past. These include, for example, history research, schooling, music, fiction, memoirs, plays, performances, games, movies, museum exhibitions, visual arts and monuments. These are the tools that help one to remember. According to James Wertsch, remembrance is tied to a cultural and social context. In order to preserve certain memories in the community, the above-mentioned cultural tools are needed to connect individuals to their social environment.[13] Jenny Edkins points out that people cannot control the formation of their memories themselves but remember things as social individuals.[14] An individual's historical awareness is built on many levels, including history teaching, research and writing, oral tradition, generational memory, social discourse, and popular culture. Thus, the perception of past events is never merely informational, but builds on past values and ways of thinking.[15] Historical research alone does not affect people's historical consciousness, but it is a complex and continuous process of interaction, which Jorma Kalela, a political historian, calls the process of social construction of history.[16] In this process, the study of history is of equal value to other sources in historical culture. The commemorative case studies we use in this chapter will include: the Irish Decade of Centenaries, 1912–23; the commemorative campaigns to remember socialists and pacifists in Manchester and the North-West, focusing on Selina Cooper (1864–1946) from Nelson in Lancashire; the 'male-centric' commemorations of the 1918 revolution in Germany; and, in Finland, the 2018 commemoration of the 1918 civil war.

One hundred years of male historiography

The first two decades of the twentieth century were witness to political and revolutionary upheavals across Europe. Driven by the momentum of revolutionary ideologies, particularly the rise of the nation-state, as well as the forces of feminism and socialism, violent revolutions were not unusual, before and after the First World War. Coming to the terms with these violent pasts was, as Aleida Assmann and Sebastian Conrad write, 'largely a national project',[17] involving processes of historicizing the 'nation'. Where cultural memory is closely linked to the development of these nation-states, narratives emanate most often, as Cynthia Enloe notes, from 'masculinized memory, masculinized humiliation and masculinized hope', where heritage and commemorative sites focus on the experiences, contributions and histories of men.[18] Women, as actors and as contributors, are most often marginalized, overlooked or represented in narrowly focused, and passively domestic, ways which do not challenge the dominant male-centric histories. Finland's history writing works as a good example of a national project. Following independence from Russia, the country ended up in a civil war in early 1918. Several stages can be outlined in research on the events of 1918. The first phase started immediately after the war and was written from the perspective of the victors. The agenda of historical politics was clear, and the winners wanted to justify their own wartime activities and penal policy. At this point, it can be seen how the drive to build a new young nation strongly guided official historical research. Historians were tasked with creating a robust, solid national story. It was important to justify what had happened and to keep quiet about difficult and controversial issues, such as rapes and illegal executions. The historiography was very male-centric; men were writing about men. Slowly, during the intervening 100 years, the perspectives have changed and become more unbiased. In the twenty-first century, research has been largely influenced by the new war history. Many civil war researchers have now studied such phenomena as violence, experiences, feelings and everyday life. At this stage, previously marginalized groups, such as women and children, have also become key research topics. Taking a broad view of the research literature over the entire period since 1918, it can be said that while winners, men and battles were at the centre of research 100 years ago, in the twenty-first century, losers, women and the experiences of the individuals have come to the fore.[19] This change has also impacted on other areas of historical culture in Finland. Indeed, the same trend as in research is clearly visible in fiction, so that women have become actors in civil war literature and cinema in the twenty-first century. The survival of Red women, especially Red widows, has been the theme of several novels and films. According to historian Tiina Kinnunen, fiction is especially necessary when people want to understand a difficult past. Emotion management is also needed, and fiction can help more than academic research. The power of fiction lies in the fact that it can open up new horizons to the reader and help them understand how anger and bitterness may have led to violent acts.[20]

Conversely, in 2018 commemorations of the 1914–18 war in Manchester and more generally across the United Kingdom, focused on patriotic efforts on the home front and the memorialization of the dead. Local groups in towns and cities were encouraged and often funded to research names on the local war memorials, and to honour those men who had been killed on the fighting fronts. In that year, there were, almost simultaneously, national and local commemorations for the partial granting of the vote to women in early 1918, often praising the patriotic commitment to war shown by the majority of suffragettes. Various relatively unknown suffrage campaigners like Elizabeth Wolstenholme Elmy from Congleton, Lydia Becker from Altham in Lancashire and Alice Hawkins from Leicester have been memorialized with statues and blue plaques while a national mapping project of suffrage activity was untaken. There was, however, very little acknowledgement of the socialist and suffragist women who campaigned against the war and maintained international links with their 'sisters in sorrow' across the Channel. Women who were nurses or munitions workers during the war were included in the story and the possibility of female heroism and courage was acknowledged, but the exclusion of female war-resistors, a radical minority who actively opposed the war in highly political ways, has reinforced the tendency to expect an undifferentiated account of 'women's' experience in support of the war effort that in no way challenges contemporary gender assumptions. So, although there was some willingness during the centenary to broaden the scope and understanding of the war beyond the battlefield and to include the experiences of women in the narrative, this only went so far.

This century-long valorization of war, even glorious defeat in war, is evident in the masculinist underpinning of most commemorative events prior to the twenty-first century, ensuring that the politics of memory is often bound to the politics of identity. According to John R. Gillis, commemorative activity is by definition 'social and political', as it involves 'the co-ordination of individual and group memories, whose results may seem consensual when they are in fact the product of processes of intense contest, struggle and in some instances, annihilation'.[21] As Gillis also notes, the role of women in national commemoration was, and in many ways, continues to be 'largely allegorical'.[22] The creation of national days such as Mother's Day in Europe and America in the early twentieth century reflects the acceptable, domestic, maternal position of women within most national foundational myths. Women, Gillis writes, just like racial minorities, repressed social classes or the young, can serve as symbols of a 'lost' or 'glorious' past but 'their actual lives are more readily forgotten'.[23] However, memories are now breaking out of the 'container of the nation-state', although the process of European 'historical transactional memory' proved 'more difficult to construct than its anticipated'.[24] The problem is the existence in Europe of 'multifarious cultural traditions and histories' that need to be 'translated, transformed or boiled down' into a shared legacy.[25] However, despite these challenges, cultural history replaces the frame of the nation with the frame of the transnational, and, as Assmann writes, challenges 'bounded views on national belonging and open[s] up new perspectives for internal differences and relational connectedness between nations'.[26]

One aspect of this transnational 'relational connectedness' is the 'gender issue', and, in particular for this volume, gendered and trans-European national commemorations of revolution in the early decades of the twenty-first century. However, we have to question if a pan-European 'shared sense of memory' is possible or even desirable. Is what happened in Ireland between 1912 and 1923 in any way similar to the revolutions that occurred post-1918 in other European countries such as Germany, Hungary and Finland, which also experienced violence and the trauma of war during the years 1914–19? Similarities are to be found. For example, the brutal suppression of the Irish uprising in 1921 was compared in the Finnish Social Democrat newspaper to the White terror in Finland in 1918. One year later, in 1922, a similar parallel was drawn in that newspaper between the Finnish civil war and the terror and brutalities of Miklós Horthy's Hungary.[27] However, despite these few examples, Edgar Wolfrum et al.

argue that 'a uniform European memory, in the sense of a shared narrative of the First World War, is undesirable and maybe even impossible'.[28] In fact, they continue, the goal should not be a 'uniform European memory' but rather 'the sharing and subsequent recognition of divergent memories'.[29] Indeed, 'the commemorations of 2014 have shown different perspectives of the war across Europe and in other parts of the world'.[30] The difference between content, presence, narratives and, indeed, context in different regions and areas makes a 'shared narrative' of war impossible. As argued, in Eastern Europe 'the First World War does not even form part of an active cultural memory', while in Ireland, for example, commemoration of the First World War happens in an extraordinary number of ways because of complicated political divisions.[31] With the outbreak of the Troubles in Northern Ireland in the late 1960s, First World War memorials to Irish men who fought in the British Army became 'legitimate targets of attack' and a marginalization of commemorations of that war occurred in the Irish Republic.[32] In Northern Ireland, however, commemoration and in particular the remembering of the sacrifice of the Ulster Division at the Somme was central to Unionist memory. Commemoration can also be dangerous, and it was at a commemoration at the Enniskillen War memorial in Northern Ireland on 8 November 1987 that one of the worst atrocities of the Troubles occurred, when eleven people were killed in an IRA bomb attack.

As asked by Wolfrum et al., 'given these differences, what does it mean to establish a European perspective?'.[33] We would suggest that looking to gender history and appreciating the universality of involvement in 'transnational movements such as socialism, the women's movement or peace activism' can perhaps allow us to develop a shared experience of inclusion and exclusion, and shared critiques of gendered commemoration. In her introduction to her edited collection *Women and the Decade of Commemorations*, which deals with the commemorations of the Irish revolutionary period, 1912–23, Oona Frawley notes that 'memory in the present is determinedly transnational'.[34] The 'environment' of the Irish Decade of Commemorations, particularly commemoration of the First World War, has been influenced by events both inside and outside Ireland, and in the case of women, 'wide, even global, questions concerning women's rights has had an impact on our commemorative agenda'.[35] Against the background of contemporary reproductive rights campaigns and campaigns such as #MeToo and #TimesUp, as well as broader gender equality campaigns, who and what we commemorate is informed by contemporary politics, as is how aware we have become of gendered absences in commemorative events. A shared feature of commemorative events for the centenary is the determined and confident intervention of feminist scholars who have been willing to challenge the male-centric, military-heavy and often nationalistic narratives within and beyond specific national contexts – for example, uncovering and trying to centre transnational female anti-war activism as well as the involvement of women, including militant women and socialist women, in revolutionary activism. As outlined in the 2018 special issue of *L'Homme, Zeitschrift für europäische Geschlechtergeschichte*, on '1914/18 revisited', this has had varying degrees of success in influencing public history and commemorative practices, but, if archived and shared, might offer a model for organized transnational feminist intervention in public commemoration that could be effectively mobilized in future.[36]

Frawley echoes Jenny Edkins in explicitly stating that 'performed commemorations and sites of memorials must not just evoke symbols', but rather recognize how contemporary commemorative work being done by 'activists, artists, scholars and critics' continues to 'inform strands of the women's movement in Ireland'.[37] Indeed, according to Rebecca Graff McRae, 'commemoration is not merely an event...it is not an act or a word...commemoration is itself constantly under negotiation'.[38] 'Commemoration,' she writes, '(re)produces a relationship between memory, history and identity, past, present and future, which is itself inherently political.'[39] For instance, in the context of the First World War, during the Decade of Commemorations in the Republic of Ireland there was a renewed interest in the notion that 'shared military experience and the shared human costs of that experience might transcend local Irish political and sectarian differences'.[40] This was constructed in the context of a new maturity in the relationship between Ireland and Britain, beginning in November 1998, at Messines in France, when the Queen of England and the President of Ireland stood together at the new 'Island of Ireland Peace Park'. Here the 'ghosts of the 36th ["Unionist" Ulster Division] were joined there by those of "Nationalist" 16th (Irish) Division – whose war record had previously been "forgotten" – to tell a new reconciliatory parable about shared sacrifice'.[41] This 1998 commemoration was followed by the installation of a new 'Cross of Sacrifice' in Dublin's Glasnevin Cemetery in 2014. The fact that this Cross stands in the same cemetery where many of the men and women who fought to free Ireland from British rule during the revolutionary war of 1919–21 were laid to rest makes it explicitly political.

The question then is, how, in divergent circumstances, and given its explicitly political nature, do we come to terms with the contemporary challenges of commemoration? Returning to Wolfrum et al., they note that the 'role that politics played and still plays in commemoration remains vital'. This is mainly because it defines the scope of the relationship between societal commemoration and the politics of memory: ranging from developments at grassroots or communal level, as well as everyday experiences and family memories, to top-down decisions made by politicians and their interests.[42]

Owning commemoration and public space

Two questions of importance occur here, particularly in relation to the issue of gender and commemoration, namely who has ownership over commemorations and what are the political implications of how the commemorations are performed in public spaces? In most countries commemorations are funded and driven by the state, combined with academic, cultural, local and community initiatives, which are often also financed through the state or its agencies – arts councils, lottery funds, community funds, university seed funding and so on. In Ireland, the government established seed funding for several capital projects and expansion of national and local museum exhibitions on the revolutionary period 1912–23. These commemorations range from the passing of the 1912 Third Home Rule Bill, the 1913 Dublin lock-out strike, the 1916 Easter Rising, the 1919–21 War of Independence, the 1921 Anglo-Irish Treaty and the creation of the Northern Irish State, the 1922 setting up of the Irish Free State and, finally, the 1922–3 civil war.[43] Within these events, issues of nationalism, unionism, trade unionism, feminism and socialism were present, and women were integral to all of these histories, however much it was not reflected in the mainstream narratives until the influences of second-wave feminism and a generation of feminist historians changed this. It is useful to see how, over the course of the Decade of Centenaries, the inclusion of women's histories and contributions has transformed both the commemorative landscape and how we write histories of the Irish revolutionary period. The Irish government provided funding for arts, cultural and local communities to develop centenary programmes. Most recently, as the Decade of Centenaries draws to a close, the government decided that in order to promote an 'inclusive, respectful, authentic, measured and consultative approach to commemorations ... recognising the differing perspectives on our shared history and seeking to strengthen peace and reconciliation on the island of Ireland', it would provide funding for 'sensitive' commemorations for the years 1921–3 – years regarded as the most divisive and contested in the commemorative decade.[44] Included in the guidelines for the Arts Awards were 'the experiences of women ... during the revolutionary period and their changing role in society'.[45]

Along with this mainstream seed funding the government also created a major, well-funded, specialist Arts award, the Markievicz Award, which was set up to provide 'support for artists … [and to] develop new work that reflects on the role of women in the period covered by the decade of centenaries 2012–23 and beyond'.[46] The award was named after the socialist, feminist and militant revolutionary, Countess Constance Markievicz. Coming from an aristocratic Anglo-Irish Protestant background, Markievicz, in rejecting her class privilege, became involved in militant suffrage, socialist and revolutionary activism. She was imprisoned for her part in the Easter Rising 1916, became the first woman MP elected to the House of Commons in 1918 (although, as an Irish Republican, she did not take her seat), and was later the first woman TD (Irish MP) and the first woman Minister in an Irish government. She was also one of the six women in the second Dáil (Irish Lower House of Parliament) who rejected the 1921 Anglo-Irish Treaty, took the anti-Treaty side in the civil war and was imprisoned by the Irish Free State for that stance. While Markievicz could not be said to have been written out of Irish history books – indeed, she is often the only revolutionary woman included in accounts of this era – the sanitization (and occasional demonization) of this rebel Countess has long been a trope in Irish history. For a centrist government to name the award after a revolutionary woman who had studied Marxist political theory, and was particularly influenced by the work of Maxim Litvinov, whom she read while in Holloway Prison in 1918, perhaps shows the 'forgetting' of her radical views on and support for the redistribution of vacant land, and her vision of a Bolshevik Irish state.[47] Indeed, a portrait of Markievicz, gifted to the UK Parliament by the Irish Oireachtas (Parliament) in 2018, to commemorate the centenary of her 1918 election win, shows her in a more respectable full-length ballgown (the 'docile' aristocrat) rather than in the usual image of the revolutionary Countess in her Irish Citizen Army uniform, holding a revolver, or the socialist Countess working in the soup kitchen set up by the Irish Women Workers' Union (IWWU) to feed the starving Dublin workers during the 1913 lock-out strike.

In Britain, the First World War has a huge cultural significance and its centenary was seen as a major event in British life.[48] In 2014, the British government saw it as a bonding exercise around a celebration of British values,[49] and the year began with a clumsy attempt to prevent historical debate, using the nationalist *Daily Mail* to construct a false consensus around a commemoration centred on celebrating the heroism and sacrifice of British soldiers.[50] MP Michael Gove, then Education Secretary, asked, 'Why does the left insist on belittling true British heroes?', which prompted a response from historians who pointed out that history is not a matter of supplying 'the right answer' but of interpretation

Figure 6.1. Boleslaw von Szankowski's portrait of Countess Constance Markievicz, 1901, reproduced with permission of the Hugh Lane Gallery, Dublin.

Figure 6.2. 'The Ripening Tide' poster, 1976, reproduced with permission of the Jackie Clarke Collection, Ballina, Co. Mayo.

based on evidence.[51] The whole affair highlighted the ideological nature of commemorative activities and how these could be manipulated to support a particular agenda. The centenary has been seen by many UK academics as an opportunity to broaden and shift the narrative, to move some stories from the margins to the centre and to set the terms of the debate for the next decades. Three major themes which had previously been excluded from popular history emerged: first, the global reach of the war and the contribution of colonial and Commonwealth troops, secondly gender, which had previously tended to look at women's experience in an undifferentiated way, and thirdly resistance to the war. The commemorations did indeed include new stories and pushed against the boundaries of British reluctance to engage with the world beyond its own borders, but in the end did little to question gendered assumptions about the experience of the war or its meaning, tending instead to highlight stories that reinforced existing gender norms, such as women in nursing, or stories that fitted with contemporary feminist interest in women taking over male roles during wartime or showing bravery comparable to that of men.[52]

In the British context, it is important to understand the 'impact agenda', under which academic research is expected to demonstrate a direct influence on the economy, policy or society. Measurable impact is rewarded by funding for universities and career success for individual researchers, and it has been a major factor in encouraging and supporting the intervention of academics in public debate rather than confined to closed workshops or learned publications.[53] This is reflected in the nature of funded projects during the centenary, which centre on five Engagement Centres co-funded by the Arts and Humanities Research Council (AHRC) and the Heritage Lottery Fund (HLF).[54] The emphasis is on co-production, on academics working closely with community partners to produce joint findings – purely academic projects are not funded. Of the five centres which act as hubs coordinating the activities of several universities, Voices of War and Peace lists a specific interest in 'Gender and the Home Front', often gendered female, while Gateways to War includes expertise on 'Conscientious Objectors and Military Tribunals', which essentializes war resistance as a predominantly male experience. These hubs have coordinated and funded a vast number and variety of commemorative activities that have brought together community and academic partners on an unprecedented scale. As well as the Engagement Hubs and separate HLF-funded projects, more than 400 of which feature women's war experience,[55] the main brokers in forming and reflecting public opinion are the British Broadcasting Corporation (BBC) and the Imperial War Museum (IWM), who have also cooperated and shared material during the centenary. However, the work of campaigning groups has also been significant in raising the profile of gendered resistance to war and offering an ongoing critique of aspects of commemorative practice that glorify war.

The BBC dedicated 2,500 hours of radio and TV broadcast between 2014 and 2018, including drama and supporting material on its website, to First World War commemoration.[56] Although a few academics like Professors Mary Beard and Alice Roberts have become well-known media figures, the BBC has a preference for celebrities as presenters, and academics have mainly acted as advisors or interviewees. Popular history books on war by television journalists Kate Adie and Jeremy Paxman became best sellers.[57] An exception is the academic David Olusoga, presenter of *The World's War* in 2014, whose book and programme interrupted the overwhelming focus on the British war experience.[58] In 2014, the BBC collaborated with academics to create four massive open online courses (MOOCs), including one on heroism hosted by researchers at the University of Leeds.[59] *Changing Faces of Heroism* critically interrogated the concept in France and Germany as well as Britain and included war resisters and women as heroic figures. The programme *Voices of the First World War* used BBC and IWM sound archives to 'tell the story of World War I through the voices of those who were there'.[60] The voices and topics chosen were predominantly male and focused on major battles, although the conscientious objector (CO) experience is covered in one of the episodes. *World War One at Home* was a project developed in collaboration with both the IWM and the AHRC and included local as well as national and international stories.[61] Conscientious objection was included as one of the themes, but the focus was on 'the individuals who made a stand against conscription' and neither included the organizations supporting these individual men nor situated the COs within the context of a broader war resistance, where women played a leading role. Women were well represented in the project, with a wide variety of experiences showcased, but their prominence in opposing the war was overlooked and the majority of the stories chosen fit into the celebratory narrative showing bold girls and women creating spaces for themselves in male territory.[62]

A civil war museum has never been established in Finland; the memories have been too painful. However, during the commemorative years of the civil war in 2008 and again in 2018, dozens of short-term exhibitions were opened in museums all over the country, dealing with either the local perspective or the civil war more broadly. A central theme of the exhibitions was the aim to understand both sides of the war while avoiding conscious confrontations. In these exhibitions, the role of women was also highlighted, and they were seen as active subjects, not just passive objects. In addition to cultural history museums, the theme of the civil war was discussed in public galleries, such as the City of Turku Art Museum (WAM), whose aim in the civil war exhibition was to remind visitors of ongoing civil conflicts around the world. According to folklorist Ulla-Maija Peltonen, dealing with historical trauma requires remembering and critically confronting the issue that caused the trauma. Then repetition and dismantling of the trauma become the most important means of overcoming it.[63] In dismantling traumas, cultural experiences can also be valuable. During the memorial year 2018, many theatres included in their repertoires history-based plays about the civil war. The stories of women featured in many performances. For example, the musical *Girls 1918* at the Tampere Workers' Theatre, and *The Blood Roses* at Kom Theatre in

Figure 6.3. Grim memories and harsh experiences of a civil war will always overshadow a nation for a long time. The means of both research and art are needed to dismantle the national burden of the war. In Finland, in the Tampere Workers' Theatre the brutal destinies of young female soldiers were the focus of the musical *Girls 1918*. The distinctive feature of this musical was the combination of dark historical stories and modern rap music. Photograph: Kari Sunnari/ The Tampere Workers' Theatre.

Helsinki were both box office hits. Both were based on a novel of the same name by Anneli Kanto, which narrated the story of young female soldiers and their brutal fate. In addition to professional theatres, the theme of the civil war and women was also taken up by other interested parties. For example, the Helsinki City Museum produced the play *The Spring of Hate – Helsinki 1918*, written by Sirpa Kähkönen. Smaller provincial theatres also wanted to take on a new, local perspective. For example, in Turku, the premiere of Jo-Jo Teatteri talked about the girls who had worked at the local cotton factory and who became female soldiers, and Tehdas Theatre depicted how the mistress of the house and her maid had ended up in different prison sides in the play *The Colours are Freedom – Red and White*.[64]

In Finland, the civil war has also been dealt with through various immersive events. For example, artist Kaisa Salmi produced *Fellman's Field – A Living Monument of 22,000 People* as a work of performance in Lahti on 28 April 2013. Here it was staged in the same field where 22,000 Red women, men and children had waited for their interrogation and sentencing for six days in April–May 1918. The performance was attended by thousands of people, united by a desire to remember the victims of the civil war and reconcile the injustices that took place. The reception of the event was controversial. Some thought it was tearing open old wounds for no good purpose.[65]

Figure 6.4. This picture is a still frame from the documentary film *Fellman's Field* (in Finnish *Fellmanin pelto*) by Kaisa Salmi. In 2013, artist Kaisa Salmi directed a performance called Fellman's field – monument of 22,000 people. The event was attended by more than 10,000 people from all over Finland. The immersive performance was based on the events in the civil war's largest prison camp, where 22,000 Red prisoners spent several days in poor conditions on this same field waiting for their hearings. Reproduced with permission of the artist Kaisa Salmi.

In Manchester, England, in 2014, a group of local volunteer researchers decided to explore alternative narratives of the years 1914–18 using the city and the surrounding textile towns of the North-West as examples of local and individual sites of resistance to the war. Many of the anti-war women in the North-West were under surveillance by the Special Branch and MI5, and a number of women were imprisoned as a result of their anti-war activities. Of course, there was sizeable opposition to the war across the country and a local, regional and national network of anti-war activists existed, but this research enabled an exploration of the networks of local resistance in more depth and the creation of spaces to commemorate this resistance. The research shone a light on the largely forgotten Women's Peace Crusade (WPC) which, although a national campaign, spread like wildfire through the industrial north: one of its main protagonists was Selina Cooper from Nelson. Firstly, a film was made about the Crusade with more than 100 volunteers from Manchester, Blackburn, Bolton, Rochdale, Oldham and Nelson who acted in the film, and twenty researchers who pored over local archives and newspapers to discover some of the socialist women active in each town: Lydia Leach from Blackburn, Elsie Winterbottom from Oldham, and Gertrude Ingham and Selina Cooper. As part of a process of commemoration, a group of

Figure 6.5. Peace Crusade Choir, 2018, photography by and permission from Ali Ronan.

volunteers from Nelson bid successfully for a grant from the HLF. This funded the appointment of project facilitator, Charlotte Bill, and the creation of a series of exhibitions and displays. There was an exhibition celebrating Cooper's life, there were display boards illustrating the story of the socialist and anti-militarist conscientious objectors in north-east Lancashire during the First World War, and a set of banners telling the history of the socialist Clarion Movement. The only existing Clarion clubhouse is located just outside Nelson, near the village of Newchurch on Pendle Hill in Lancashire.

The commemoration in Nelson focused on the above-mentioned socialist and pacifist Selina Cooper (1864–1946). Cooper moved from Cornwall with her family to Nelson in 1875 and she worked full-time from the age of thirteen, joining the Nelson branch of the Cotton Workers Union and in 1891 leading a dispute over the lack of decent toilet facilities for women weavers. Like many working-class women in Nelson, she attended education classes at the local Women's Co-operative Guild and was involved in the local Independent Labour Party (ILP). She worked closely with other socialists locally like Gertrude Ingham, whose son Alex was imprisoned. In 1900, she joined the North of England Society for Women's Suffrage, helping to organize a petition that was signed by women working in the Lancashire cotton mills and was chosen as one of the delegates to present it to the House of Commons. In 1911, she became a national organizer for the National Union of Women's Suffrage Societies and was involved in the Election Fighting Fund, which was an informal project between the Labour Party and the NUWSS to encourage the election of pro-suffrage candidates. During the First World War, Cooper was a pacifist, totally opposed to military conscription. In 1917, she organized a huge WPC procession in Nelson. After the war, Cooper continued to be actively involved in local, national, and international politics, joining the committee of the Nelson branch of the League of Nations Union and the local No More War Movement. She organized the Nelson contingent of the Peacemakers' Pilgrimage in 1926 and was part of a Women Against War and Fascism delegation to Germany in 1934. This commemoration of Cooper has been another important breakthrough in the slow but determined process of remembering women who have been largely forgotten in the patriotic narrative of the First World War. It follows on from the campaigns in Manchester and other cities to remember suffrage and socialist women whose activism has often been overshadowed by the pro-war Pankhursts and the militant suffragette campaign. Sylvia Pankhurst's pacifism and socialism, although recognized, are often side-lined. Pankhurst was a regular visitor to Manchester and the Lancashire cotton towns, speaking at numerous meetings of anti-war organizations.

In the case of the First World War, gender history scholarship is well-established in Germany (and Austria), with several influential and respected researchers publishing on various gender aspects of the war experience.[66] This has meant that there was at the very least a token inclusion of women's war work in the commemoration of the war itself in 2014–18. However, this is not the case when it comes to the history of the revolution of 1918. There is very little gendered history of the revolution and what there is has not yet established itself in the public imagination,[67] with several scholars remaining unconvinced that women played key roles in the revolutionary events or that their contribution has anything to tell us about its nature and scope.[68] Without feminist pressure – as happened in Ireland – and underpinning research, it is perhaps not surprising that German museums could largely ignore the gender dimensions of the revolution and overlook women's roles. As a result, museums generally presented the male experience of the revolution as the whole experience without reflecting on gender at all. The presentation of the revolution often took its narrative from contemporaneous accounts, which are steeped in normative gender discourse, meaning that the museums have often reproduced these prejudices uncritically and presented the women as bystanders, motivated by supposedly feminine qualities of curiosity and political naivety. This encourages the idea that women are a-historical, as if outside of history, since they are only described according to stereotypical and supposedly unchangeable criteria. This danger has been noted by Brigitte Studer in her 2021 book.[69] The image of the revolutionary presented in exhibitions in Germany during 2018–19 was very narrow and gendered male: offering us either men with guns on barricades or fiery revolutionaries spreading the word as in the interactive project 'The rolling revolution' (*Die Revolution rollt*) that traced the progress of the revolution through the railways stations of Germany in November 2018, or in the case of Munich, of the soldier poet, the visionary, the dreamer.[70] Neither of these tropes are inclusive, and their dominance means that revolutionary women can only become briefly visible as a kind of drag king, if they adopt male roles and poses. As Moritz Föllmer's study has shown, this trope also hides a number of masculine roles and identities essential to an understanding of the revolution, so if our aim is to understand fully the nature and scope of these important events, challenging the narrow representation of a single revolutionary identity must be a priority.[71]

The history of the revolution is still present in Germany as a bone of contention, especially between different factions on the left, and there is also a strong regional flavour to commemorations. Three areas that were central to the revolution are: Kiel as the birthplace of the revolution; Munich, where the People's State of Bavaria (November 1918–April 1919) and then the two Bavarian Council

Republics (April–May 1919) were established and defended until their final defeat by government forces; and Berlin, where the Republic was proclaimed on 9 November 1918. In the naval city of Kiel, commemorations centred on the sailors' uprising, which is claimed as the catalyst and cornerstone of German democracy, positioning Kiel as the de facto birthplace of modern Germany.[72] Kiel's year of commemoration included a major new exhibition at the Maritime Museum as well as a touring version that travelled round the towns and cities of Schleswig-Holstein, several public talks and exhibitions and a newly commissioned opera, *False Betrayal* (*Falscher Verrat*), which premiered in Kiel in November 2018. The opera's plot centred on a love triangle involving a revolutionary sailor and a ship's officer vying for the affection of a female prostitute. Attempts at feminist interventions were largely unsuccessful in challenging the preferred focus on the sailors' experience. Although women were present in the Maritime Museum exhibition, they were cast as bystanders and as beneficiaries of the male-led uprising rather than political actors in their own right, while the touring exhibition featured eye-witness accounts from an exclusively male perspective. This was a missed opportunity to present a more nuanced and complete understanding of the revolutionary context that required a large amount of civilian support and years of anti-war activism, much of it by socialist women and girls, to enable the sailors' uprising to spread so swiftly to the

Figure 6.6. Rehearsal image from *Women of Aktion* by Bent Architect, 2018, photography by and permission from Karol Wyszynski.

local population and then to the rest of Germany. One of the few exceptions was a new play, funded by the AHRC and based on research by Ingrid Sharp and Corinne Painter, that was performed in Kiel as part of the commemorative events. The play, *Women of Aktion*, by the Bradford theatre collective Bent Architect, offered a rare female-centred perspective, telling the story of five women, three from Kiel and two based in Munich, who had played a significant role in the revolution, including strategic planning, communication, logistics and supplies.[73]

In Berlin, the revolution was more or less erased, with commemorative activities and exhibitions choosing dates that meant it did not need to engage with the revolution. At the German Historical Museum, which although situated in Berlin can be seen as representative of the nation, the exhibition *1917: Revolution, Russia and Europe* stopped short at 1917 after the Russian revolution,[74] while the exhibition *Democracy 2019 Weimar: On the Nature and Influence of Democracy*[75] centred the debate on the question of German democracy during the successful transition from Empire to Republic during the first, relatively bloodless, month of the revolution rather than engaging with the contentious history of the subsequent violent suppression of revolutionary forces by the governing Social Democratic Party (SPD). Likewise, the public history project *100 Years of Revolution Berlin* side-stepped controversy by focusing mainly on November and December 1918, thus avoiding having to deal with the SPD's suppression of the revolution using violent right-wing troops.[76] Dividing the project into seven themes like seven injunctions that the public has to follow ('Versammelt euch', 'Macht Frieden!', 'Mischt euch ein!', 'Informiert euch!', 'Keine Gewalt!', 'Beteiligt alle!', 'Solidarisiert euch!' - 'Gather together', 'Make Peace!', 'Get involved!', 'No Violence!', 'Take part!', 'Declare Solidarity!'), the project reduced major episodes of violence like the 'January Uprising' and the 'March Days' in Berlin to a discussion about solidarity as the cement of democracy. This approach to the revolution also fails to show revolutionary women participating somewhere else than in the fight for the right to vote. In Munich, the stress was on the figure of Kurt Eisner and on the poets, theorists and dreamers of the revolution – all of whom were men.[77] For example, the exhibition *Poetry is Revolution* considers the work of Eisner, Erich Mühsam, Gustav Landauer and Ernst Toller.[78]

The Irish Decade of Centenaries

In Ireland, the Decade of Commemorations or Decade of Centenaries began in 2012. Through the years 2012–23,[79] various pivotal events that marked the decade 1912–23 were chosen for national commemoration. Commemoration, as argued by the Irish President, Michael D. Higgins, offered 'the opportunity to reflect, to look deeply at change over time, to provide an understanding of where they have been, where they are today, and why'.[80] During 2020 and 2021, towards the end of the Decade of Commemoration, the President hosted a number of *Machnamh 100* seminars which were addressed by scholars, researchers, cultural commentators, archivists and historians on various aspects of commemorations. So far, these seminars have looked at the challenges of Public Commemorations, including remembering those who were excluded, as 'ethical remembering requires us to include those who may hitherto have been excluded from official, formal accounts of history' in order to produce a 'more comprehensive and balanced perspective on the independence struggle'.[81] As well as looking at the mainstream political campaigns during this period, the context of Empire, the First World War, and the Partition of the island of Ireland in 1921, the President also invited scholars to give papers on issues of 'Land, Social Class, Gender and the Sources of Violence'.[82] These seminars reflected, as the President noted, the 'inclusion of marginalised voices, the disenfranchised, voices from below in our recollections of the past. It must include the essential part played by women in the period … the role of class, and an openness to stories of "the Other", the stranger, the enemy of yesterday'.[83]

While the *Machnamh 100* seminars strove, and to a large degree achieved, this broad and inclusive concept of commemoration and remembrance, the Decade of Centenaries, as it began in 2012, reflected a much narrower, much more mainstream narrative of commemoration. In this section, we will discuss how the centrality of women to the commemorative events of the Irish Decade of Centenaries came about, and the impact that inclusion of women's voices does have and will continue to have, on the broader writing of history. In 2011, an Expert Advisory Group on Centenary Commemorations was set up by the then Taoiseach (Prime Minister) to advise government on historical matters relating to the Decade of Centenaries, and to consult widely with academic, community and voluntary groups and members of the public to ensure that significant events were commemorated accurately, proportionately and appropriately in tone.[84] Its first statement of intent in 2012 signalled that all commemorations would 'be measured and reflective' and 'informed by a full acknowledgement of the complexity of historical events … of multiple readings of history, and of multiple identities and traditions which are part of the Irish historical experiences'.[85] The first mention of a woman in the list of planned commemorations was for six years later, in 2018, and was to be the commemoration of the 1918 'General Election with new franchise including women'.[86] The activities of suffrage, trade union and nationalist women prior to 1918 were overlooked, and the 'multiple identities' referred to here were not especially inclusive of women's histories and experiences. One of the first centenaries to deal with histories outside of the mainstream political and military centenaries was that of the 1913 lock-out strike in Dublin.

Dublin, Ireland's largest city, had, in 1913, high levels of unemployment, poverty, and terrible living conditions for the poor. The city was never fully industrialized, and many workers were unskilled labourers on day wages or factory workers on terrible pay and conditions. Over the previous five years, since the forming of the Irish Transport and General Workers' Union (ITGWU) in 1908, trade union leaders worked at mobilizing the city's large unskilled workforce; by 1913, the ITGWU was the largest and most militant union in the country. While it did not admit women, a sister organization, the Irish Women Workers' Union (IWWU), had been set up in 1913 to advocate for the rights of women workers. On the platform at the meeting to launch the IWWU on 5 September 1911 were women activists from socialist, nationalist and feminist backgrounds. One speaker was the well-known feminist, and leader of the militant suffrage Irish Women's Franchise League (IWFL) Hanna Sheehy Skeffington, who called on all to work together 'for the welfare of both sexes'.[87] Another speaker, Countess Markievicz, a member of the militant separatist, feminist organization Inghinidhe na hÉireann (Daughters of Ireland), told the audience that 'as you are aware women have at present no vote, but a union such as now being formed will not alone help you obtain better wages, but will also be a means of helping you get votes'.[88] Delia Larkin, leader of the IWWU, and sister of Jim Larkin, leader of the ITGWU, said that women workers were weary of 'toiling to fill the pockets of unscrupulous employers receiving for their labours not sufficient to enable them to exist'.[89] The presence of militant feminist, socialist and nationalist women demonstrated that despite their differences, female political activists were determined to work together in Ireland. By 1913 they had a chance to show their unity of purpose.

One of the largest employers of women workers in Dublin was Jacob's Biscuit factory; the *Irish Worker* (edited by Jim Larkin) regularly complained about the treatment of women workers by Jacob's and other employers. These complaints led to a series of strikes at Jacob's throughout 1912 and the employers began a campaign of intimidation of their women workers. They wanted to prevent them from joining the IWWU and even demanded that they stay away from Liberty Hall, the headquarters it shared with the ITGWU. The cause of labour and the cause of women were becoming more united; as the suffrage paper, the *Irish Citizen*, noted, by September 1913, 'the men of Mr Larkin's union ... frequently [acted] ... to protect Suffragettes from ... hooliganism'.[90] As both the IWWU and the ITGWU became more militant, employers reacted by becoming more virulently anti-union, many demanding that their workers leave their unions. By August 1913, a standoff developed between the employers and the unions, leading to a lock-out of unionized workers on 15 August. By that date, the links between militant and radical suffrage women and labour women were well advanced, and throughout the lock-out the work of women was central to the campaign to win union recognition.

The lock-out would last five bitter months, ending in January 1914 when it was evident the workers had lost the dispute. During the strike, the participation of IWWU women, suffrage campaigners and socialist women was central. Women took their place on the picket lines, worked at the soup kitchen in Liberty Hall to feed the starving families of striking workers, and joined the newly formed workers' militia, the Irish Citizen Army (ICA), which was set up to defend workers against attacks from the Dublin Metropolitan Police and strike-breakers. This was a space where the working women of the IWWU came into contact with the middle-class radical feminist and nationalist women, creating female activist networks which were to prove very vital in the coming revolution. This was also a space where links with radical British women were made and political Irishwomen collaborated with socialist women in the UK on plans to aid the children of strikers. British socialist and suffragist Dora Montefiore, accompanied by activist Lucille Neal and trade union organizer Grace Neal, arrived in Dublin on 18 October 1913, determined to provide respite for workers' children 'from the hardship of the industrial dispute' which was ongoing.[91] The plan, called the 'Save the Kiddies Scheme', was to offer holidays for the workers' children in the homes of British workers, as a respite from the poverty, hunger and violence around them. In collaboration with Delia Larkin and the women activists in Liberty Hall, homes were located, and a list of needy children drawn up. As Montefiore said, 'Dublin mothers were prepared to trust the English mothers', which demonstrates, as Karen Hunt notes, the visceral power of solidarity.[92]

However, this power of solidarity could not stand before the disapproval of the Irish Catholic hierarchy. The Archbishop of Dublin declared the Save the Kiddies Scheme a 'most mischievous development' as there was no guarantee that the Dublin children would be sent to Catholic families.[93] Despite continued efforts by Montefiore and her supporters, the scheme was defeated, by 'book, bell and candle'.[94] Montefiore's intervention in Dublin in 1913 did 'illustrate the interconnections between the struggle of labour and women', and as she explained herself, her inspiration was the efforts of 'New York Socialists' to evacuate children from the 'violent industrial dispute in Lawrence, Massachusetts in 1912'.[95] As Hunt explains, while the scheme was an example of working-class solidarity, it was also 'solidarity with a gender dimension'.[96] Meetings to raise funds for the scheme were addressed by socialist, feminist and Irish trade union leader James Connolly, as well as suffrage speakers Charlotte Despard and Sylvia Pankhurst, and IWWU leader Delia Larkin.[97] Although ultimately a failure, the scheme was, as Hunt argued, 'an act of working-class solidarity organised by women which sought to show why a transnational red flag solidary organisation was a necessity ... as the world wandered to war'.[98]

In 2013, the centenary of this 1913 lock-out dominated the commemoration landscape. The Irish government, trade unions, museums, libraries and history societies all held commemorative events, from August 2013 through to January 2014. The Irish President, a labour politician in his former life, led the state commemoration on Saturday 31 August 2013 – the centenary of 'Bloody Sunday' 1913, when the Dublin police attacked a meeting of striking workers on O'Connell Street, killing three. He laid a wreath at the statute of Jim Larkin, which stands among many statues of male political, civic and cultural leaders on O'Connell Street – there are no statues of women. Trade union and socialist women were, however, part of the 2013 commemorations. In March 2013, a plaque to the IWWU was unveiled at Liberty Hall – the headquarters of Ireland's largest trade union, SPITU, into which the IWWU was subsumed in the 1980s. At the launch, feminist historian Margaret MacCurtain insisted: 'Women like Delia Larkin, Hanna Sheehy Skeffington, Louie Bennet, Helena Molony, Mary Galway, Rosie Hackett and a host of others have become part of the school curriculum because other women will not let them be forgotten.'[99] By that date, Rosie Hackett, in 1913 a young working-class IWWU member and Jacob's factory worker, had become well known to the Irish public, because of a bridge. In 2012, Dublin City Council set up a Commemorative Naming Committee for a new bridge being constructed over the River Liffey, adjacent to Liberty Hall.

To that date, no bridge over the river had been named after a woman: most were named after famous male writers, politicians or revolutionaries. As would be expected, a number of male politicians, literary figures and trade unions activists were put forward in the media as potential candidates but when the Naming Committee made public its call for nominations, an extraordinary campaign took off to name the bridge after an unknown, ordinary, female trade union activist and 1916 rebel, Rosie Hackett. Several young feminist and labour activists began a hugely effective social media, mainstream media and lobbying campaign in support of Rosie Hackett. They set up a Facebook page 'Rosie Hackett Bridge Campaign', wrote articles in newspapers, and had historians, including co-author of this chapter, Mary McAuliffe, address packed meetings on the subject of Hackett and on the non-representation of women generally in commemorative and memorial spaces. They lobbied national and local politicians and gathered thousands of signatures in support of their campaign. Hackett, they said, captivated them with 'her humble working-class roots, her defiant and unrelenting sense of justice and her undaunted struggle for her vision of a more equal and just society'.[100] Despite some 'indignant backlash' that a major bridge should be named after an unknown woman, the campaign succeeded, and on 2 September 2013 Dublin City Council announced that the bridge would be named after Rosie Hackett.[101] This very public campaign in 2013 marked a sea change in the inclusion of women in Ireland's commemorative landscape, even when the state and its institutions lagged behind. In 2014, with no state commemoration of the centenary of the formation of the largest militant nationalist women's organization, Cumann na mBan (Council of Women), the Women's History Association of Ireland (WHAI) organized three days of commemorative events in April of that year. As well as holding a major two-day conference, the WHAI worked with Glasnevin cemetery, where many of the revolutionary leaders, men and women, are buried, to organize a national commemoration of Cumann na mBan at which the President of Ireland laid a wreath in their memory.[102]

The success of these events encouraged more focus on the role of women during this period of Irish history. One of the major commemorative projects for 2016, and the centenary of the Easter Rising, was the Richmond Barracks renovation project. The Barracks was where all the 1916 rebels were taken after their surrender at the end of Easter week, 1916, among them seventy-seven women. When the Barracks project was announced in 2014, the role of women was not mentioned, but as noted by Laura McAtackney, by 2016 and the opening of the Barracks, 'The women of 1916 and the Irish Revolution' was one of the core themes.[103] 'Clearly,' she writes, 'there were changes in both personnel and the public discourse between 2014 and 2016 to refocus ... Richmond Barracks from a normative history to a site that explicitly engages with the previously marginalised roles of women.'[104] The '77 women' book and exhibition, as well as the '77 women' quilt project are all now central to the Barracks heritage site. However, this had not been part of the state plan for the barracks, rather it was a

Figure 6.7. Revolutionary women of Easter 1916, Dublin, autumn 1916, reproduced with permission of Kilmainham Gaol Museum.

Figure 6.8. The '77 women' of 1916 quilt, Richmond Barracks Exhibition, 2016, reproduced with permission of Richmond Barracks, photograph by Dan Butler.

collaborative effort between a group of feminists, academics, activists and artists who came together as a planning subgroup during the development phase of the Barracks.[105] This subgroup engaged academics to research and write the book on the seventy-seven Easter Rising women, and a local artist to work with seventy-seven local activists to create a commemorative quilt.

Many of the contemporary activists and the seventy-seven women of 1916 came from feminist, trade union and socialist backgrounds, and issues of work, equality and inclusion were similar for the 2016 and 1916 women. This more direct activism and engagement by feminist academics and campaigners has impacted, in a central way, on the inclusion of women's histories in the Decade of Centenaries. It continued in 2015 when the Irish National Theatre, the Abbey Theatre, announced their season for 2016, which would focus on the centenary of the Easter Rising, called *Waking the Nation*. While the programme included many plays and events of interest, it had '18 men on the programme in terms of writers and directors and just two women – and all the plays were written by men, apart from one play referred to as a "monologue for children"'.[106] In response to the privileging of the male voice and the exclusion of women's voices, a meeting of women producers, artists, writers, activists and academics was held at the Abbey Theatre on 12 November 2015 where *Waking the Feminists* was launched. #*WakingTheFeminists* was set up as a 'one-year grassroots campaign ... November 2015 to November 2016 and had huge success in advancing equality for women in Irish theatre'.[107] Its impact was global, with major Hollywood actors such as Meryl Streep tweeting support. In response to the exclusion of women's voices the Arts Council of Ireland funded *Waking the Feminists* to commission a piece of research into gender balance in Irish theatre.[108]

Not only did the controversy centre on the exclusion of women's voices in Irish theatre and culture but was also part of the broader discussion about the exclusion/inclusion of women in the Decade of Centenaries. A public consultation process was launched by the government in November 2017 'to stimulate a public conversation around how the significant historical events between 1918 and 1923 might be appropriately remembered'.[109] Some the telling themes referenced in the submissions received were 'the role of women and the role of the labour movement', which demonstrated that, by 2017, much had changed, and gender and class had become central to the centenary of the Irish revolutionary movement. The Decade of Centenaries 2021 Programme reflected this insistence on the inclusion of women – one of its eight main themes being the 'experiences of women'.[110] As part of this, the state invested in several woman-centred centenary projects, including funding for *Mná100* (Mná is the Irish for women), a dedicated online resource 'to document women in our history, particularly their contribution during the Irish Revolutionary period, 1912–1923'.[111] Funding, €25,000 to each recipient, was also made available for the Markievicz Award, for artists to reflect on 'the role of women in the period covered by the decade of centenaries 2012–2023 and beyond'.[112] Other funded projects, including new and expanded permanent exhibitions at both national and local museums, as well as the continuing digitization of records in the Military Archives, have also been impacted by the continuing focus on women. For instance, in January 2020, the National Museum of Ireland (NMI) launched its revamped permanent exhibition *Irish Wars, 1919 to 1923*, which was 'substantially reimagined' as part of the museum's 'decade of centenaries commemorations'.[113] An expanded subsection dealt with a 'new kind of war' entitled 'Women and Violence in the Irish Wars'.[114] The experiences and contributions of women in Ireland's revolutionary decade are currently, in 2022, in many ways central to the narratives. This was achieved not by a state-driven desire to include women, but by the numerous campaigns by feminists, activists and gender historians who demanded that women's contributions, activities and legacies were deserving of commemoration.

By any reckoning, it seems that demands to include women in Ireland's Decade of Centenaries have been a success. Indeed, in more recent additions to revolutionary historiography, by male and female scholars, the roles and contributions of political and militant women, women's suffrage, trade union and republican activism, and the experiences of women, including the violence they suffered, are no longer marginalized. This is something which feminist historians have been working towards for more than five decades, since 1983 with the publication of the first major history on revolutionary women, including Cumann na mBan, Margaret's Ward's *Unmanageable Revolutionaries: Women and Irish Nationalism*, or indeed since 2000 and the publication of Louise Ryan's ground-breaking article on gendered violence against women during the War of Independence, '"Drunken Tans": Representations of Sex and Violence in the Anglo-Irish War (1919–21)', published in the *Feminist Review*.[115] Since then, several books and articles, many by feminist scholars, have looked at the role of Ireland's pro-suffrage, socialist and revolutionary women. Archives which allow further knowledge of women's revolutionary activities have also been opened, catalogued and/or digitized, including the vast Military Pensions Applications Files, which serve to broaden our understanding of the role of women in this period.[116] In 2021, there were more than 13,300 pension files, of which 3,758 relate to women, with more to be released. These files are from women, the majority (2,362) members of Cumann na mBan, from all classes and all areas of the country. While most of the successful female applications were granted the lowest grade of pension (grade E), the files are important in revealing who these women were, what they said they did, what motivated them, the violence and traumas many suffered, and the legacies of their involvement in their later lives. These and other archives have transformed the historiography of mainstream revolutionary narratives, as well as knowledge of political and militant women's motivations, involvement, activities, suffering and legacies, and continue to do so. However, while funding for these archival projects is to be welcomed, the histories of other women and their archives continue to be resisted by the state. Even as more records of revolutionary women become available, the archives of those women who were institutionalized in Ireland's infamous Magdalen Laundries and Mother and Baby Institutions remain closed. In the state reports on the treatment of women and children in these institutions, which have bookended the Decade of Centenaries, the McAleese Inquiry into the Magdalen Laundries (2013) and the Mother and Baby Home Commission (2021),[117] official archival materials, state records, records of the religious congregations, local archives, and the testimonies of state officials and members of the religious orders who ran these institutions were privileged over the testimonies of survivors. However, in 2022, despite all that has been achieved with the inclusion of some women in Irish histories, the trauma memories, testimonies, and histories of some 'inconvenient' Irish women are still being sanitized, managed and marginalized. Furthermore, despite the successful inclusion of women in many aspects of Ireland's Decade of Centenaries, vigilance is still necessary. In February 2022, the centenary of the split in Cumann na mBan, the largest militant female republican organization, which rejected the Anglo-Irish Treaty by a large majority, passed unobserved by any state remembrance. The split between political and militant women would be central to the coming civil war in 1922–3, a war often recalled as being 'brother against brother', when 'sister against sister' was as relevant and central to the histories. The battle for female inclusion in historical narratives and commemorations continues.

Conclusion

What conclusions can be drawn from these case studies? Women were nowhere represented as central to – or even influential in – the revolutionary events of the First World War era. Even where women were present, they were peripheral and could be removed or overlooked without affecting the narrative. Even where published sources were readily available, the choice was made to exclude women. In Schleswig-Holstein, the travelling exhibition on the November 1918 revolution (as opposed to the fixed Maritime Museum exhibition) did not contain even a single eyewitness account by a woman. As the aim was to create a link between the revolution and civic-mindedness in the present day, the un-reflected absence of role models for women and girls is disturbing. This imbalance was also reflected in the '100 years of Revolution Berlin' project: of more than 250 exhibitions, guided tours and open discussions, just twelve were dedicated to women's experiences, and of these, eight were about the right to vote. The only representation in Germany that centred revolutionary women was in the feminist-informed exhibition *Damenwahl!* in Frankfurt, but this was a specific exhibition about female suffrage rather than an attempt to show women's revolutionary roles.[118] Another aspect of the commemorations has been the dominance of male expertise, whether in journalistic debates or in academic conferences, where women were often outnumbered ten to one, and often relegated to a single panel discussing women's experiences of revolution. This was then reflected in the publications arising from the conferences which offered a similarly undifferentiated view in a lone chapter on women, often with a generic title such as 'women in the revolution'. The example from Berlin fits this pattern, with just one panel on 'Women in the Revolution', which is where female scholars Dania Alasti and Gisela Notz were to be found.[119] On the other hand, several panels featured male historians such as Robert Gerwarth, Wolfgang Niess or Mark Jones. In Ireland, anger at the absence of female historians from panels on the revolutionary period led to the creation, in 2016, of a twitter account @ManelWatchIre, set up to name and shame manels (all male panels). This has had some impact, as it would be a very foolhardy organizer who would put together a revolutionary manel now!

However, unless feminist scholars and activists insist on inclusion, women often remain marginalized. So, how do we explain the choices that at every level excluded women on into the twenty-first century? In Germany, for instance, the research context on the revolution is problematic, and the interpretation of events contested on party lines. For Wolfgang Niess, writing in 2018, the revolution has been interpreted in a variety of ways, most of them negative, and heavily influenced by party affiliation.[120] Indeed, German scholarship has only recently begun to look beyond questions of responsibility and blame to consider the revolution in a broader context, with the publication of Alexander Gallus' edited volume *The Forgotten Revolution* (*Die vergessene Revolution*) in 2010 kick-starting the trend.[121] The work of Kathleen Canning has been especially important in providing a gender perspective and a more capacious understanding of revolution in terms of time and spaces that allows women to become visible.[122] In the context of the centenary, a new interpretation of the revolution has emerged as in fact representing the catalyst for and cornerstone of German democracy. Unsurprisingly perhaps, this take is more popular in Kiel than elsewhere, and much of the commemoration in other parts of Germany skilfully avoided engaging with the revolution as outlined above. In his speech to mark the founding of the Weimar Republic, German President Frank-Walter Steinmeier, too, chose to bypass the revolution entirely and erase the new Republic's revolutionary roots. Instead, he characterized the Weimar Republic as 'an experiment in democracy' that had begun on 9 November 1918, apparently for no particular good reason. Steinmeier instead situated the revolution in the Republic's progressive constitution: 'Anyone looking at the constitution today will be amazed at how progressive its aims were and how topical they still are. Yes, what was written there was truly revolutionary.'[123] Without any sort of context to explain why the constitution may have reflected its revolutionary roots and taken a distinctly progressive position on workers' rights and universal adult suffrage, the document is indeed surprising.

There is still a long way to go before the full range of women's experiences during and after the war is included in the commemorative practices within nation-states and internationally. Our case studies have shown significant variation between the national contexts discussed in this chapter, with some signs that gendered perspectives and narratives explored in feminist research can carry over into public histories and reach a receptive audience. The importance of feminist challenge to dominant and largely male-centric narratives and commemorative practice is illustrated in particular by the Irish case which offers a possible model for coordinated and varied interventions by gender, women's and feminist historians in public debate through cultural and artistic as well as historical methods. This is further underlined when we consider how central women's scholarship has been to expanding public history narratives around the First World War and associated revolutions to include gender perspectives. However, in several national contexts, applying a gender lens specifically to the history of the revolutionary period post-1917 is less well-established and it has been harder to gain recognition of women's political agency and activism as revolutionaries. This could be in part due to the relative lack of scholarship on revolutionary women compared to several decades of academic interest in women's roles and experiences during the war period itself. The opportunity, as Sylvia Schraut and Sylvia Paletschek noted, 'to inscribe the female experience into memory culture' is inextricably linked to contemporary feminist and gender politics and, more especially, to the work of gender historians in these periods of history.[124] While contemporary feminism and gender politics play a part in demanding that women be included in commemorations, if gender historians are not at the forefront of research on revolutionary movements and experiences, the activism, contributions, impacts and legacies of revolutionary women will continue to be marginalized and excluded.

Notes

1 Socialist Women and the Great War, 1914–21: Protest, Revolution and Commemoration

1 Dora B. Montefiore, 'Women and the Crimmitschau strike', *New Age*, 28 January 1904, 58–9. Available at https://www.marxists.org/archive/montefiore/1904/01/crimmitschau-strike.htm (accessed 1 April 2022).
2 On Montefiore, see June Hannam and Karen Hunt, *Socialist Women: Britain, 1880s to 1920s* (London and New York: Routledge, 2002), esp. 126, 179–80.
3 On the Crimmitschau strike, see Sean Dobson, *Authority and Upheaval in Leipzig, 1910–1920: The Story of a Relationship* (New York: Columbia University Press, 2001), 119.
4 Kathleen Canning, *Languages of Labor and Gender: Female Factory Work in Germany, 1850–1914* (Ithaca, NY and London: Cornell University Press, 1996), 261.
5 Ibid., 262.
6 Dobson, *Authority and Upheaval*, 119.
7 See, for instance, the critical comments of Ardis Cameron, 'Bread and Roses Revisited: Women's Culture and Working-Class Activism in the Lawrence Strike of 1912', in Ruth Milkman (ed.), *Women, Work, and Protest: A Century of US Women's Labor History*, new ed. (London and New York: Routledge, 2013 [1985]), 42–61 (here 44).
8 Eric Hobsbawm, 'Man and Woman in Socialist Iconography', *History Workshop Journal*, 6 (1978), 121–38.
9 Sheila Rowbotham, *Daring to Hope: My Life in the 1970s* (London: Verso, 2021), 2.
10 Nan Sloane, *Uncontrollable Women: Radicals, Reformers and Revolutionaries* (London: I.B. Tauris, 2022).
11 Ibid., 22. See also Olwen H. Hufton, *Women and the Limits of Citizenship in the French Revolution* (Toronto: University of Toronto Press, 1992).
12 Marianne Pollak, 'Barrikadenbräute', *Arbeiter-Zeitung*, 11 March 1928, 18.
13 Maryann Gialanella Valiulis, *The Making of Inequality: Women, Power and Gender Ideology in the Irish Free State, 1922–1937* (Dublin: Four Courts Press, 2019), 44.
14 Hans von Hentig, 'Die revolutionäre Frau', *Schweizerische Zeitschrift für Strafrecht*, 36 (1923), 29–45 (here 29, 43–4). Cited in Brigitte Studer, 'Rosa Grimm (1875–1955): Als Frau in der Politik und Arbeiterbewegung – Die Grenzen des weiblichen

Geschlechts', in Sibylle Benz et al. (eds.), *Auf den Spuren weiblicher Vergangenheit* (Zurich: Chronos, 1988), 163–82 (here 169).

15 For the concept of 'memory-work' (*Erinnerungsarbeit*), we are influenced by the ideas of the German sociologist Frigga Haug. See her essay collection *Beyond Female Masochism: Memory-Work and Politics*, transl. by Rodney Livingstone (London: Verso, 1992).

16 Dania Alasti, *Frauen der Novemberrevolution: Kontinuitäten des Vergessens* (Münster: Unrast Verlag, 2018), 72.

17 See here Veronika Helfert, *Frauen, wacht auf! Eine Frauen- und Geschlechtergeschichte von Revolution und Rätebewegung in Österreich, 1916–1924* (Göttingen: Vandenhoeck & Ruprecht, 2021), 67.

18 Sloane, *Uncontrollable Women*, 26; Hufton, *Women and the Limits of Citizenship*, 152.

19 Haug, *Beyond Female Masochism*, x.

20 Rosa Leviné-Meyer, *Inside German Communism: Memoirs of a Party Life in the Weimar Republic*, edited and introduced by David Zane Mairowitz (London: Pluto Press, 1977), 142. Also cited in Brigitte Studer, *Reisende der Weltrevolution: Eine Globalgeschichte der Kommunistischen Internationale* (Berlin: Suhrkamp, 2020), 39.

21 Moritz Föllmer, 'The Unscripted Revolution: Male Subjectivities in Germany, 1918–1919', *Past & Present*, 240.1 (2018), 161–92.

22 See Helfert, *Frauen, wacht auf!*, 132–3; and Matthew Stibbe, Corinne Painter and Ingrid Sharp, 'History beyond the Script: Rethinking Female Subjectivities and Socialist Women's Activism during and after the German Revolution of 1918–1919', in Christopher Dillon and Kim Wünschmann (eds.), *Living the German Revolution of 1918–19: Expectations, Experiences, Responses* (Oxford: Oxford University Press, forthcoming).

23 Phrase taken from Olga Shparaga, *Die Revolution hat ein weibliches Gesicht: Der Fall Belarus*, transl. from Russian to German by Volker Weichsel (Berlin: Suhrkamp, 2021), 42–3.

24 Temma Kaplan, 'Women and Communal Strikes in the Crisis of 1917–1922', in Renate Bridenthal, Claudia Koonz and Susan Stuard (eds.), *Becoming Visible: Women in European History*, Vol. 2 (Boston, MA: Houghton Mifflin, 1987), 429–49 (here 430).

25 Arlette Farge and Natalie Zemon Davis (eds.), *History of Women in the West, Volume III: Renaissance and the Enlightenment Paradoxes* (Paris: Plon 1995), 491–3.

26 Joan W. Scott, 'Gender: A Useful Category of Historical Analysis', *American Historical Journal*, 91.5 (1986), 1030–75 (here 1075).

27 Caroline Arni, 'Zeitlichkeit, Anachronismus und Anachronien: Gegenwart und Transformation der Geschlechtergeschichte aus geschichtstheoretischer Perspektive', *L'Homme: Europäische Zeitschrift für feministische Geschichtswissenschaft*, 18.2 (2007), 53–76.

28 Gabriella Hauch, 'Feministische Melancholie – ein Geleit', foreword to Helfert, *Frauen, wacht auf!*, 14.
29 Omer Bartov and Eric D. Weitz (eds.), *Shatterzone of Empires: Coexistence and Violence in the German, Habsburg, Russian, and Ottoman Borderlands* (Bloomington and Indianapolis: Indiana University Press, 2013). See also the various contributions to *Military Occupations in First World Europe*, special issue of *First World War Studies*, 4.1 (2013), guest-edited by Sophie de Schaepdrijver.
30 Leonard V. Smith, *Sovereignty at the Paris Peace Conference of 1919* (Oxford: Oxford University Press, 2018).
31 Nick Baron and Peter Gatrell (eds.), *Homelands: War, Population and Statehood in Eastern Europe and Russia, 1918–1924* (London: Anthem Press, 2004). For an examination of both the former territories of Tsarist Russia and other parts of Europe and the Middle East, see also Marcus Payk and Roberta Pergher (eds.), *Beyond Versailles: Sovereignty, Legitimacy, and the Formation of New Polities after the Great War* (Bloomington and Indianapolis: Indiana University Press, 2019).
32 Smith, *Sovereignty*, 10.
33 For an incisive feminist critique of the gendered assumptions behind these ways of interpreting sovereignty, see Glenda Sluga, 'Female and National Self-Determination: A Gendered Re-Reading of "the Apogee of Nationalism"', *Nations and Nationalism*, 6.4 (2000), 495–521.
34 Daniel Gaido and Cintia Frencia, '"A Clean Break": Clara Zetkin, the Socialist Women's Movement, and Feminism', *International Critical Thought*, 8.2 (2018), 277–303.
35 This is also the position taken by Nan Sloane in her recent study of radical women in late eighteenth- and early nineteenth-century Britain – see Sloane, *Uncontrollable Women*, esp. 256–7.
36 Lotte Pirker (1877–1963), '"So wurde ich eine der vielen Novembersozialistinnen"', in Peter Eigner and Günter Müller (eds.), *Hungern – Hamstern – Heimkehren: Erinnerungen an die Jahre 1918 bis 1921* (Vienna: Böhlau 2017), 93–106 (here 96).
37 For a trenchant critique of this approach, see Marilyn J. Boxer, 'Rethinking the Socialist Construction and International Career of the Concept "Bourgeois Feminism"', *American Historical Journal*, 112 (2007), 131–58.
38 Werner Thönnessen, *The Emancipation of Women: The Rise and Decline of the Women's Movement in German Social Democracy, 1863–1933*, transl. by Joris de Bres (London: Pluto Press, 1973 [1969]), 62.
39 Gaido and Frencia, '"A Clean Break"', 288–94. See also Chapter 2 of this volume.
40 Ann Taylor Allen, *Women in Twentieth-Century Europe* (Basingstoke: Palgrave Macmillan, 2007), 35.
41 Boxer, 'Rethinking the Socialist Construction', 157. See also Geoff Eley, *Forging Democracy: The History of the Left in Europe, 1850–2000* (Oxford: Oxford University Press, 2002), here esp. 112–13.

42 Gisela Bock, 'Das politische Denken des Suffragismus: Deutschland um 1900 im internationalen Vergleich' (1999), reproduced in Gisela Bock, *Geschlechtergeschichten der Neuzeit: Ideen, Politik, Praxis* (Göttingen: Vandenhoeck & Ruprecht, 2014), 168–203 (here 195).
43 Ibid., 197–8.
44 Leila J. Rupp, *Worlds of Women: The Making of an International Women's Movement* (Princeton, NJ: Princeton University Press 1997), 22.
45 Gisela Bock, *Frauen in der europäischen Geschichte: Vom Mittelalter bis zur Gegenwart* (Munich: C.H. Beck, 2000), 209–10.
46 Selina Todd, *The People: The Rise and Fall of the Working Class, 1910–2010* (London: John Murray, 2014), 17.
47 Hannam and Hunt, *Socialist Women*, 90.
48 See Geoffrey Mitchell (ed.), *The Hard Way Up: The Autobiography of Hannah Mitchell – Suffragette and Rebel* (London: Faber and Faber, 1968), 126.
49 Jill Liddington and Jill Norris, *'One Hand Tied Behind Us': The Rise of the Women's Suffrage Movement* (London: Virago, 1978), 260.
50 Mary Cullen, 'Women, Emancipation and Politics, 1860–1984', in J. R. Hill (ed.), *A New History of Ireland. Vol. VII: Ireland 1921–1984* (Oxford: Oxford University Press, 2003), 852.
51 The concept of *Doigkeit* is discussed directly by Cornelia Naumann in her recent novel based on the true story of Lerch's life – see Cornelia Naumann, *Der Abend kommt so schnell: Sonja Lerch – Münchens vergessene Revolutionärin* (Meßkirch: Gmeiner, 2018), esp. 166–9. It also has some similarities with the Belorussian concept of тутесьчы or *tutesjschy* (being from here and now), as discussed by Shparaga, *Die Revolution hat ein weibliches Gesicht*, 174; and with the 'libertarian left' notion of politics focused on the '"now" of daily living', as referenced by Rowbotham, *Daring to Hope*, 118.
52 Kathleen Canning, 'Gender and the Imaginary of Revolution in Germany', in Klaus Weinhauer, Anthony McElligott and Kirsten Heinsohn (eds.), *Germany, 1916–23: A Revolution in Context* (Bielefeld: transcript Verlag, 2015), 103–26 (here 112). On Zetkin as an 'inveterate Marxist', see Jean H. Quataert, 'Unequal Partners in an Uneasy Alliance: Women and the Working Class in Imperial Germany', in Marilyn J. Boxer and Jean H. Quataert (eds.), *Socialist Women: European Socialist Feminism in the Nineteenth and Early Twentieth Centuries* (New York: Elsevier, 1978), 112–45 (here 116).
53 Boxer, 'Rethinking the Socialist Construction', 133–4.
54 Canning, 'Gender and the Imaginary of Revolution in Germany', esp. 106–8, 112–25.
55 On the Galileo circle, see Judith Szapor, *Hungarian Women's Activism in the Wake of the First World War: From Rights to Revanche* (London: Bloomsbury, 2018), 33–4, 58–9; Veronika Helfert, 'Eine demokratische Bolschewikin: Ilona Duczynska Polanyi (1897–1967)', *Österreichische Zeitschrift für Geschichtswissenschaft* (ÖZG), 26.2

(2015), 166–89 (here 173–4); and Gareth Dale, 'Karl Polanyi in Budapest: On his Political and Intellectual Formation', *European Journal of Sociology/Archives européennes de sociologie/Europäisches Archiv für Soziologie*, 50.1 (2009), 97–130.

56 Madeleine Hurd, *Public Spheres, Public Mores, and Democracy: Hamburg and Stockholm, 1870–1914* (Ann Arbor, MI: University of Michigan Press, 2000), 129–30.

57 Constance Markievicz, 'Women, Ideals and the Nation', lecture delivered in 1909 to the Students' National Literary Society, Dublin, available at https://digital.library.villanova.edu/Item/vudl:526517#?c=&m=&s=&cv=1&xywh=-2300%2C0%2C6472%2C2870 (accessed 1 April 2022).

58 Thomas Lindenberger, *Straßenpolitik: Zur Sozialgeschichte der öffentlichen Ordnung in Berlin 1900 bis 1914* (Bonn: J.H.W. Dietz Nachfolger, 1995), 324.

59 Among other examples, see 'Das Frauenstimmrecht in Finnland und Australien', *Arbeiterinnen-Zeitung*, 18 January 1910, 8–9.

60 Amerigo Caruso, *'Blut und Eisen auch im Innern': Soziale Konflikte, Massenpolitik und Gewalt in Deutschland vor 1914* (Frankfurt/Main and New York, 2021), 94–5.

61 Dora B. Montefiore, *From a Victorian to a Modern* (London: E. Archer, 1927), 119.

62 Gaido and Frencia, '"A Clean Break"', 287.

63 Eley, *Forging Democracy*, 113.

64 Bock, *Frauen in der europäischen Geschichte*, 214. See also Hufton, *Women and the Limits of Citizenship*, esp. 137–54.

65 Marilyn J. Boxer, 'Socialism Faces Feminism: The Failure of Synthesis in France, 1879–1914', in Boxer and Quataert (eds.), *Socialist Women*, 75–111 (here 86).

66 Jad Adams, *Women and the Vote: A World History* (Oxford: Oxford University Press, 2014), 115, 177–83.

67 Ibid., 181.

68 Bock, *Frauen in der europäischen Geschichte*, 213.

69 See also Chapter 2 in this volume.

70 Jan Claas Behrends, 'A Laboratory of Modern Politics: The Russian Revolution and its International Legacy', in Stefan Rinke and Michael Wildt (eds.), *Revolutions and Counter-Revolutions: 1917 and Its Aftermath from a Global Perspective* (Frankfurt/Main and New York: Campus Verlag, 2017), 79–101 (here 79). See also Susan Buck-Morss, *Dreamworld and Catastrophe: The Passing of Mass Utopia in East and West* (Cambridge, MA and London: MIT Press, 2000).

71 See Matthew Stibbe, Veronika Helfert and Olga Shnyrova, 'Women and Socialist Revolution, 1917–1923', in Ingrid Sharp and Matthew Stibbe (eds.), *Women Activists Between War and Peace: Europe, 1918–1923* (London: Bloomsbury Academic, 2017), 123–72 (here 128 and ff.).

72 See Erez Manela, *The Wilsonian Moment: Self-Determination and the International Origins of Anticolonial Nationalism* (Oxford, 2007), esp. 37–8, 139.

73 Caruso, *'Blut und Eisen'*, 39.

74 Henriette Roland-Holst, *Generalstreik und Sozialdemokratie*, with a foreword by Karl Kautsky, revised and expanded edition (Dresden: Kaden, 1906 [1905]), XIV.
75 See, however, the important corrective offered by Maria Todorova, *The Lost World of Socialists at Europe's Margins: Imagining Utopia, 1870s–1920s* (London: Bloomsbury, 2020).
76 The next congress of the IWSA, or rather of its successor organization, the IAWSEC (International Alliance of Women for Suffrage and Equal Citizenship), to take place in a non-Western capital was the twelfth congress in Istanbul in 1935. See Rupp, *Worlds of Women*, 302.
77 See, for instance, Hedwig Richter, *Demokratie: Eine deutsche Affäre* (Munich: C.H. Beck, 2020). See also Richter's essay 'Lange vorbereitet und kein Grund zur Aufregung – das Frauenwahlrecht', in Thomas Stamm-Kuhlmann (ed.), *November 1918: Revolution an der Ostsee und im Reich* (Cologne and Weimar: Böhlau, 2020), 87–101.
78 See, for example, Dave Sherry, *Empire and Revolution: A Socialist History of the First World War* (London: Bookmark Publications, 2014).
79 Leviné-Meyer, *Inside German Communism*, 143.
80 Caruso, 'Blut und Eisen', 102.
81 Stefan Berger, 'Die deutsche Revolution 1918/19 in ihren europäischen Kontexten', in Frank Bischoff, Guido Hitze and Wilfried Reininghaus (eds.), *Aufbruch in die Demokratie. Die Revolution 1918/19 im Rheinland und in Westfalen: Beiträge der Tagung am 8. und 9. November 2018 in Düsseldorf* (Münster, 2019), 17–29.
82 See also Stefan Berger and Klaus Weinhauer (eds.), *A Period of Global Revolutions (1905–1920): Foreshadowing the Twentieth Century or Ending a Longer Revolutionary Tradition*, forthcoming.
83 Caruso, 'Blut und Eisen', 58–60.
84 Anja Huber, *Fremdsein im Krieg: Die Schweiz als Ausgangs- und Zielort von Migration, 1914–1918* (Zurich: Chronos, 2018), 48–9.
85 Boxer, 'Socialism Faces Feminism', 82.
86 Caruso, 'Blut und Eisen', 65, 90–9.
87 Cameron, 'Bread and Roses Revisited', 56–7.
88 Ibid., 44.
89 Mary McAuliffe and Liz Gillis, *Richmond Barracks – We were there: 77 women of the Easter Rising* (Dublin: Four Courts Press, 2016), 16.
90 Senia Pašeta, *Irish Nationalist Women, 1900–1918* (Cambridge: Cambridge University Press, 2013), 123.
91 Caruso, 'Blut und Eisen', 45, 265.
92 See, for instance, Gregor Schöllgen (ed.), *Escape into War? The Foreign Policy of Imperial Germany* (Oxford: Berg, 1990).
93 Benjamin Ziemann, *Gewalt im Ersten Weltkrieg: Töten – Überleben – Verweigern* (Essen: Klartext, 2013); Robert Gerwarth and John Horne (eds.), *War in Peace:*

Paramilitary Violence in Europe After the Great War (Oxford: Oxford University Press, 2013); Jochen Böhler, Włodzimierz Borodziej and Joachim von Puttkamer (eds.), *Dimensionen der Gewalt: Ostmitteleuropa zwischen Weltkrieg und Bürgerkrieg 1918–1921* (Berlin: Metropol Verlag, 2020); Sven Oliver Müller and Christin Pschichholz (eds.), *Gewaltgemeinschaften? Studien zur Gewaltgeschichte im und nach dem Ersten Weltkrieg* (Frankfurt/Main and New York: Campus Verlag, 2021).

94 Donald Bloxham and Robert Gerwarth, 'Introduction', in Donald Bloxham and Robert Gerwarth (eds.), *Political Violence in Twentieth-Century Europe* (Cambridge: Cambridge University Press, 2011), 1–39 (here 35). See also, more recently, Robert Gerwarth, 'The Role of Violence in the European Counter-Revolution, 1917–1939', in Rinke and Wildt (eds.), *Revolutions and Counter-Revolutions*, 141–59, here esp. 156–8.

95 Among the many different studies, see in particular Joanna Bourke, *Dismembering the Male: Men's Bodies, Britain, and the Great War* (Chicago, IL: Chicago University Press, 1996); Sabine Kienitz, *Beschädigte Helden: Kriegsinvalidität und Körperbilder 1914–1923* (Paderborn: Schöningh, 2008); Heather Perry, *Recycling the Disabled: Army, Medicine, and Modernity in WWI Germany* (Manchester: Manchester University Press, 2015); Tracey Loughran, *Shell-Shock and Medical Culture in First World War Britain* (Cambridge: Cambridge University Press, 2017).

96 Benjamin Ziemann, *Contested Commemorations: Republican War Veterans and Weimar Political Culture* (Cambridge: Cambridge University Press, 2013), esp. 154–8; Chris Millington, *From Victory to Vichy: Veterans in Inter-war France* (Manchester: Manchester University Press, 2013), 33; Julia Eichenberg and Natali Stegmann, 'Divided by War, United by Welfare: The International Labour Organization Promoting War Invalids' Internationalism', *European Review of History: Revue européenne d'histoire*, advanced publication online, 13 January 2022, https://www.tandfonline.com/doi/full/10.1080/13507486.2021.1979936 (accessed 1 April 2022).

97 See, as a good example, Robert L. Nelson, *German Soldier Newspapers of the First World War* (Cambridge: Cambridge University Press, 2011).

98 Annette Becker, *Oubliés de la grande guerre: Humanitare et culture de guerre – populations occupeés, déportés civils, prisonniers de guerre* (Paris: Noêsis, 1998). Alan Kramer, *Dynamic of Destruction: Culture and Mass Killing in the First World War* (Oxford: Oxford University Press, 2007), 244–51; and Matthew Stibbe, 'Gendered Experiences of Civilian Internment during the First World War: A Forgotten Dimension of Wartime Violence', in Ana Carden-Coyne (ed.), *Gender and Conflict since 1914: Historical and Interdisciplinary Perspectives* (Basingstoke: Palgrave Macmillan, 2012), 14–28, also touch briefly on gender-based violence, but few other studies do. A research project into sexual violence in First World War Austria-Hungary and territories occupied by its armies has nonetheless been in progress since 2020. See https://hist-kult.univie.ac.at/forschung/forscherinnengruppen/sexuelle-gewalt-im-ersten-weltkrieg (accessed 1 April 2022).

99 See, for instance, Mary McAuliffe, 'The Homefront as Battlefront: Women, Violence and the Domestic Space during War in Ireland 1919-1921', in Linda Connolly (ed.), *Women and the Irish Revolution: Feminism, Activism, Violence* (Newbridge, Co. Kildare: Irish Academic Press, 2019), 164-82; and Mary McAuliffe, 'The Forcible Hair Cutting of the Cullen Sisters of Keenaghan, Co Tyrone: Gendered Violence against Women', in Darragh Gannon and Fearghal McGarry (eds.), *Ireland 1922: Independence, Partition, and Civil War* (Dublin: Royal Irish Academy, 2022), 136-40. Also Justin Dolan Stover, 'Families, Vulnerability and Sexual Violence During the Irish Revolution', in Jennifer Evans and Ciara Meehan (eds.), *Perceptions of Pregnancy from the Seventeenth to the Twentieth Century* (London: Palgrave Macmillan, 2017), 57-76; Louise Ryan, '"Drunken Tans": Representations of Sex and Violence in the Anglo-Irish War (1919-21)', *Feminist Review*, 66 (2000), 73-92; and Julia Eichenberg, 'The Dark Side of Independence: Religiously and Ethnically Motivated Violence in Poland and Ireland, 1918-1923', *Contemporary European History*, 19.3 (2010), 231-48.

100 See Mary E. Cox, *Hunger in War and Peace: Women and Children in Germany, 1914-1924* (Oxford: Oxford University Press, 2019).

101 'Die Mutter stellt sich an', *Arbeiter-Zeitung*, 30 September 1916, 4.

102 Ziemann, *Gewalt im Ersten Weltkrieg*, 10, 12, citing respectively Michael Geyer. 'Eine Kriegsgeschichte, die vom Tod spricht', in Thomas Lindenberger and Alf Lüdtke (eds.), *Physische Gewalt: Studien zur Geschichte der Neuzeit* (Frankfurt/Main: Suhrkamp, 1995), 136-61 (*Tötungsgewalt*); and Heinrich Popitz, *Phänome der Macht*, 2nd ed. (Tübingen: J.C.B. Mohr, 1992), 48 (*absichtliche körperliche Verletzung anderer*).

103 Cox, *Hunger in War and Peace*, 53.

104 Ibid., 115, 122.

105 Ibid., 122, n. 84.

106 Implacabilis (i.e. Karl Liebknecht), 'Antimilitarismus!', first published in *Die Jugendinternationale*, 1-2 (September-December 1915), reproduced in *Gegen den Pazifismus! Für die Bewaffnung des Proletariats! Drei Aufsätze von N. Lenin, Leo Trotski, Karl Liebknecht* (Berlin: Verlag der Jugendinternationale, 1920), 5-19 (here 12).

107 Ibid., 7.

108 Rowbotham, *Daring to Hope*, 5, 59, 287.

109 Ibid., 99.

110 See, for example, Stephen Reicher, 'Mass Action and Mundane Reality: An Argument for Putting Crowd Analysis at the Centre of the Social Sciences', *Contemporary Social Science*, 6.3 (2011), 433-49. Also the collaborative research project 'Reading the Riots: Investigating England's Summer of Disorder' conducted by the London School of Economics and The Guardian Newspaper, Reading the

riots, https://eprints.lse.ac.uk/46297/1/Reading%20the%20riots(published).pdf (accessed 7 January 2022).
111 See the works listed in note 93 above.
112 Lara Vapnek, 'The 1919 International Congress of Working Women: Transnational Debates on the "New Woman Worker"', *Journal of Women's History*, 26.1 (2014), 160–84, here 167–8.
113 Susan Zimmermann, *Frauenpolitik und Männergewerkschaft: Internationale Geschlechterpolitik, IGB-Gewerkschafterinnen und die Arbeiter- und Frauenbewegungen der Zwischenkriegszeit* (Vienna: Löcker Verlag, 2021), 93–142.
114 Alexandra Kollontai and Polina Vinogradskaia (eds.), *Otchet o pervoi mezhdunarodnoi konferentsii kommunistok* (Report on the First International Conference of Communist Women) (Moscow: Gosizdatelstvo, 1921). With many thanks for this information to Ivelina Masheva.
115 Kevin McDermott and Jeremy Agnew, *The Comintern: A History of International Communism from Lenin to Stalin* (London: Macmillan, 1996), 34.
116 In this sense, the conclusions reached by George L. Mosse, *Fallen Soldiers: Reshaping the Memory of the World Wars* (Oxford: Oxford University Press, 1990), still stand.
117 Michelle Perrot, quoted in Fátima Mariano and Helena da Silva, 'From Memory to Reality: Remembering the Great War in Portugal and Gender Perspectives', *L'Homme: European Journal of Feminist History*, 19.2 (2018), 51–63 (here 51–2).
118 Oona Frawley (ed.), *Women and the Decade of Commemorations* (Bloomington, IN: Indiana University Press, 2021), 7.
119 See, for instance, Sheila Rowbotham, *Hidden from History: 300 years of Women's Oppression and the Fight Against It* (London: Pluto Press, 1973). Also Carol R. Berkin and Clara M. Lovett (eds.), *Women, War, and Revolution* (New York and London: Holmes & Meier, 1980).
120 The pioneering work here was Ute Daniel's *The War from Within: German Working-Class Women in the First World War*, transl. by Margaret Ries (Oxford: Berg, 1997 [1989]).
121 See Cynthia Enloe, *The Curious Feminist: Searching for Women in a New Age of Empire* (Berkeley, CA: University of California Press, 2004); idem, *Bananas, Beaches and Bases: Making Feminist Sense of International Politics*, 2nd ed. (Berkeley, CA: University of California Press, 2014 [1989]); idem, *Globalization and Militarism: Feminists Make the Link*, 2nd ed. (Lanham, MD: Rowman & Littlefield, 2016 [2007]).
122 Enloe, *Globalization*, 6.
123 Ibid., 54.
124 This approach is demonstrated in J. Ann Tickner and Laura Sjoberg (eds.), *Feminism and International Relations: Conversations about the Past, Present and Future* (London and New York: Routledge, 2013).

125 Enloe, *Bananas*, 17.
126 As an example of a more global approach, see Mona L. Siegel, *Peace on Our Terms: The Global Battle for Women's Rights After the First World War* (New York: Columbia University Press, 2020).

2 Socialist Women and 'Urban Space': Protest, Strikes and Anti-Militarism, 1914–18

1 Olga Shparaga, *Die Revolution hat ein weibliches Gesicht: Der Fall Belarus*, transl. from Russian to German by Volker Weichsel (Berlin: Suhrkamp, 2021), 15.
2 For an example of the default characterization of the revolutions of 1917–19 as male, see Richard Bessel, 'Revolution', in Jay Winter (ed.), *The Cambridge History of the First World War. Volume II: The State* (Cambridge: Cambridge University Press, 2014), 126–44 (here esp. 131); and for an explicit identification of the November 1918 German Revolution as male, see Benjamin Ziemann, 'Germany, 1914–1918: Total War as a Catalyst of Change', in Helmut Walser Smith (ed.), *The Oxford Handbook of Modern German History* (Oxford: Oxford University Press, 2011), 378–99 (here 387).
3 Julian Aulke, *Räume der Revolution: Kulturelle Verräumlichung in Politisierungsprozessen während der Revolution 1918–1920* (Stuttgart: Franz Steiner, 2015).
4 Ibid., 22. More generally, see Simon Gunn, 'The Spatial Turn', in Simon Gunn and Robert J. Morris (eds.), *Identities in Space: Contested Terrains in the Western City since 1850* (Aldershot: Ashgate, 2001), 1–14. A compelling comparative case study is provided by Klaus Weinhauer, 'World War I and Urban Societies: Social Movements, Fears, and Spatial Order in Hamburg and Chicago (c.1916–1923)', in Stefan Rinke and Michael Wildt (eds.), *Revolutions and Counter-Revolutions: 1917 and Its Aftermath from a Global Perspective* (Frankfurt/Main and New York: Campus Verlag, 2017), 287–306.
5 Karl Liebknecht, *Militarism and Anti-Militarism: With Special Regard to the International Young Socialist Movement* (Glasgow: Socialist Labour Press, 1917), 176. First published in German in 1907.
6 See Implacabilis (i.e. Karl Liebknecht), 'Antimilitarismus!', first published in *Die Jugendinternationale*, 1–2 (September–December 1915), reproduced in *Gegen den Pazifismus! Für die Bewaffnung des Proletariats! Drei Aufsätze von N. Lenin, Leo Trotski, Karl Liebknecht* (Berlin: Verlag der Jugendinternationale, 1920), 5–19.
7 For the best example of the latter approach, see Leila J. Rupp, *Worlds of Women: The Making of an International Women's Movement* (Princeton, NJ: Princeton University Press, 1997).

8   Edward W. Soja, *Postmodern Geographies: The Reassertion of Space in Critical Social Theory* (London: Verso, 1989), 92.
9   See Mary E. Cox, *Hunger in War and Peace: Women and Children in Germany, 1914–1924* (Oxford: Oxford University Press, 2019), esp. 129.
10 Sean Dobson, *Authority and Upheaval in Leipzig, 1910–1920: The Story of a Relationship* (New York: Columbia University Press, 2001), 159.
11 Ute Daniel, *The War from Within: German Women in the First World War*, transl. by Margaret Ries (Oxford: Berg, 1997 [1989]), 246.
12 For an introduction to this genre, see the pioneering volumes edited by Jay Winter and Jean-Louis Robert, *Capital Cities at War, Vol. 1: Paris, London, Berlin, 1914–1919* and *Vol. 2: A Cultural History* (Cambridge: Cambridge University, 1997–2007). Important studies that focus specifically on women's war experiences in the urban realm include Belinda J. Davis, *Home Fires Burning: Food, Politics, and Everyday Life in World War I Berlin* (Chapel Hill, NC: University of North Carolina Press, 2000); Maureen Healy, *Vienna and the Fall of the Habsburg Empire: Total War and Everyday Life in World War I* (Cambridge: Cambridge University Press, 2004); Christiane Sternsdorf-Hauck, *Brotmarken und rote Fahnen: Frauen in der bayerischen Revolution und Räterepublik 1918/19*, revised ed. (Cologne: Neuer ISP Verlag, 2008 [1989]); and the relevant contributions to Sybille Kraft (ed.), *Zwischen den Fronten: Münchner Frauen in Krieg und Frieden 1900–1950* (Munich: Buchendorfer, 1995). For a perspective from a neutral country, see Håkan Blomqvist, *Potatisrevolutionen och Kvinnouppploppet på Södermalm 1917* (The Potato Revolution and the Women's Uprising on Södermalm Island in Central Stockholm in 1917) (Stockholm: Hjalmarson & Högberg Bokförlag, 2017).
13 Pierre Purseigle, 'An Urban Geography of the World at War, 1911–1923', in Nico Wouters and Laurence van Ypersele (eds.), *Nations, Identities and the First World War: Shifting Loyalties to the Fatherland* (London: Bloomsbury Academic, 2018), 235–53 (here 243).
14 Eckhard Müller, 'Clara Zetkin und die Internationale Frauenkonferenz im März 1915 in Bern', in Ulla Plener (ed.), *Clara Zetkin in ihrer Zeit: Neue Fakten, Erkenntnisse, Wertungen* (Berlin: Dietz, 2008), 54–71 (here 62). The exact number of delegates was possibly a bit higher, with twenty-seven voting on the main conference resolutions.
15 Martin Grass, '"Werte Genossin . . .": Brev från Clara Zetkin till den svenska arbetarrörelsen', *Arbetarhistoria*, 136 (2010), 49–60 (here 57).
16 Müller, 'Clara Zetkin', 56, 60.
17 June Hannam and Karen Hunt, *Socialist Women: Britain, 1880s to 1920s* (London and New York: Routledge, 2002), 177, 198, n. 42; Christine Collette, *For Labour and For Women: The Women's Labour League, 1906–1918* (Manchester: Manchester University Press, 1989), 173.
18 On the presence of revolutionaries in Switzerland, and the broader demographic impact of the war on Swiss society, see Anja Huber, *Fremdsein im Krieg: Die Schweiz als Ausgangs- und Zielort von Migration, 1914–1918* (Zurich: Chronos, 2018).

19 *Die Vorkämpferin*, 1 December 1914. On conflicts between *Die Gleichheit* and the German military censors after August 1914, see Werner Thönnessen, *The Emancipation of Women: The Rise and Decline of the Women's Movement in German Social Democracy, 1863–1933*, transl. by Joris de Bres (London: Pluto Press, 1973 [1969]), 79.

20 Eckhard Müller, 'Clara Zetkins Vernehmungen zur Verbreitung des Flugblattes "Frauen des arbeitenden Volkes!"', *Jahrbuch für Forschungen zur Geschichte der Arbeiterbewegung*, 1 (2010), 93–114 (here 95).

21 See 'Die Frauen-Friedensversammlung in Zürich', *Die Vorkämpferin*, 1 January 1915, 1.

22 See the letters reproduced in Marga Voigt (ed.), *Clara Zetkin: Die Kriegsbriefe (1914–1918)*, Vol. 1 (Berlin: Dietz, 2016), 104, 106–7.

23 See, for instance, R. C. Elwood, *Inessa Armand: Revolutionary and Feminist* (Cambridge: Cambridge University Press, 1992), 157.

24 Clara Zetkin, 'Internationale sozialistische Frauenkonferenz in Bern: Offizieller Verhandlungs-bericht', *Berner Tagewacht*, 3 April 1915, Beilage, 1.

25 R. Craig Nation, *War on War: Lenin, the Zimmerwald Left, and the Origins of Communist Internationalism* (Chicago, IL: Haymarket Books, 2009), 70.

26 Elwood, *Inessa Armand*, 158.

27 See Institut für Marxismus-Leninismus beim Zentralkomitee der SED (ed.), *Dokumente und Materialien zur Geschichte der deutschen Arbeiterbewegung, Vol. 1: Juli 1914-Oktober 1917* (East Berlin: Dietz, 1958), 125, n. 1.

28 Zetkin, 'Internationale sozialistische Frauenkonferenz' (as note 24 above).

29 Toni Sender, *The Autobiography of a German Rebel* (London: The Labour Book Service, 1940), 65.

30 Dobson, *Authority and Upheaval*, 161.

31 Ute Daniel, 'Frauen', in Gerhard Hirschfeld, Gerd Krumeich and Irina Renz (eds.), *Enzyklopädie Erster Weltkrieg* (Paderborn: Schöningh, 2003), 116–34 (here 125–7). See also Jill Liddington and Jill Norris, *'One Hand Tied Behind Us': The Rise of the Women's Suffrage Movement* (London: Virago, 1978), 253–4.

32 Henriette Fürth, *Die deutschen Frauen im Kriege* (Tübingen: Mohr, 1917), 59. Cited in Ute Frevert, *Women in German History: From Bourgeois Emancipation to Sexual Liberation*, transl. by Stuart McKinnon-Evans (Oxford: Berg, 1997 [1989]), 165.

33 Dobson, *Authority and Upheaval*, esp. 172–3, 293–5.

34 Dania Alasti, *Frauen der Novemberrevolution: Kontinuitäten des Vergessens* (Münster: Unrast, 2018), 63.

35 Liddington and Norris, *'One Hand Tied Behind Us'*, 255.

36 Dobson, *Authority and Upheaval*, esp. 173.

37 On the NCF, see Cyril Pearce, *Comrades in Conscience: The Story of an English Community's Opposition to the Great War* (London: Francis Boutle, 2001), esp. 151–4.

38 See the Peace Pledge Union website at https://menwhosaidno.org/context/women (accessed 1 April 2022).
39 René Dubach, *'Strizzis, Krakeeler und Panduren': Aktivitäten des Staatsschutzes vom Landesstreik bis zum roten Zürich* (Zurich: Offsetdruckerei, 1996), 67–8. See also Schweizerisches Bundesarchiv Bern, E21#1000/131#10684*, Az 06.2.3.2-2, Untersuchung gegen die Sozialistische Jugendorganisation und ihre Presse, sowie Ausweisung ausländischer Agitatoren, 1918–1921, Mappe Ausweisung Bertha Volk.
40 Sheila Rowbotham, *Daring to Hope: My Life in the 1970s* (London: Verso, 2021), 133.
41 Ibid., 115.
42 Cox, *Hunger in War and Peace*, 233.
43 Weinhauer, 'World War I and Urban Societies', esp. 292–3.
44 Davis, *Home Fires Burning*, 83.
45 See the unsigned police report dated 17 May 1916 in Landesarchiv Berlin (henceforth LAB), A Pr. Br. Rep. 030, Nr. 15818, Bl. 7.
46 Ibid. On the 1916 disturbances in Leipzig, see also Dobson, *Authority and Upheaval*, 145–6.
47 Daniel, *The War from Within*, 164; Weinhauer, 'World War I and Urban Societies', 293.
48 Dobson, *Authority and Upheaval*, 146.
49 Daniel, *The War from Within*, 241.
50 See, for instance, the case of Johanna Stöckel, arrested and held in protective custody in Mannheim, Germany, after returning from a trip to Switzerland on suspicion of having arranged 'the publication of a highly anti-German and inflammatory brochure written by herself' ('die Veröffentlichung einer im hohen Grade deutschfeindlichen und aufhetzerischen, von ihr verfassten Broschüre'), as outlined in a letter from the Bavarian envoy in Baden to the Bavarian State Ministry, 28 February 1918. Copy in Bayerisches Hauptstaatsarchiv Munich – Abt. II: Neuere Bestände, MInn 66272.
51 Sender, *Autobiography*, 65.
52 Yvonne Svanström, *Offentliga kvinnor: Prostitution i Sverige, 1812–1918* (Public Women: Prostitution in Sweden, 1812–1918) (Stockholm: Ordfront, 2006), 100.
53 Ibid., 161.
54 As claimed by the USPD deputy Wilhelm Dittmann in the Reichstag in 1916 – see his own illegally distributed pamphlet, *Drei Reden über Belagerungszustand, Zensur und Schutzhaft: Gehalten am 18. Januar, 24. Mai und 28. Oktober 1916 vor dem Reichstage* (Bern: Freier Verlag, 1918), esp. 66–8.
55 Weinhauer, 'World War I and Urban Societies', 292.
56 Amerigo Caruso, *'Blut und Eisen auch im Innern': Soziale Konflikte, Massenpolitik und Gewalt in Deutschland vor 1914* (Frankfurt/Main and New York: Campus Verlag, 2021), 33.

57 Sophie Ennenbach, 'Lebenserinnungen', n.d., in Stiftung Archiv der Parteien und Massenorganisationen der ehemaligen DDR im Bundesarchiv, Berlin-Lichterfelde (henceforth SAPMO-BArch), SgY 30/0197, Bl. 13.
58 Sender, *Autobiography*, 74.
59 Ennenbach, 'Lebenserinnerungen', Bl. 13.
60 See the Berlin police report dated 4 March 1916 in LAB, A Pr. Br. Rep. 030, Nr. 15817, Bl. 26–8.
61 Martha Arendsee, 'Vom Kampf gegen den ersten imperialistischen Krieg: Erinnerungen', n.d., in SAPMO-BArch, SgY 30/0017, Bl. 25–6.
62 Ennenbach, 'Lebenserinnerungen', Bl. 15.
63 See, for instance, Maria Meier, *Von Notstand und Wohlstand: Die Basler Lebensmittelversorgung im Krieg, 1914–1918* (Zurich: Chronos, 2020).
64 See H. R. Fuhrer, 'Weltkrieg, Erster. Militärische Lage', in *Historisches Lexikon der Schweiz*, Vol. 13 (Basel and Berlin: Schwabe Verlag, 2014), 368.
65 See Regula Stämpfli, 'Von der Grenzbesetzung zum Aktivdienst: Geschlechterpolitische Lösungsmuster in der schweizerischen Sozialpolitik (1914–1945)', in Hans Jörg Gilomen, Sébastien Guex and Brigitte Studer (eds.), *Von der Barmherzigkeit zur Sozialversicherung: Umbrüche und Kontinuitäten vom Spätmittelalter bis zum 20. Jahrhundert* (Zurich: Chronos, 2002), 373–86 (here 375).
66 See Erich Gruner, *Arbeiterschaft und Wirtschaft in der Schweiz. Vol. 1: Demographische, wirtschaftliche und soziale Basis und Arbeitsbedingungen* (Zurich: Chronos, 1987), 226–7; and Brigitte Studer, 'Arbeiterinnen zwischen Familie, Erwerbsarbeit und Gewerkschaft, 1880–1945', in *Verflixt und zugenäht! Frauenberufsbildung – Frauenerwerbsarbeit 1888–1988: Berufs, Fach- und Fortbildungsschule Bern* (Zurich: Chronos, 1988), 55–64 (here 59–60).
67 See 'Unser schweizerischer Frauentag', *Die Vorkämpferin*, 1 April 1915, 2. For German women, see Dobson, *Authority and Upheaval*, 173, 295.
68 For further examples of such cooperation, see Chapter 4 of this volume.
69 A copy of the petition can be found in LAB, A Rep. 060-53 MF 4219–20.
70 Helen Boak, *Women in the Weimar Republic* (Manchester: Manchester University Press, 2013), 31.
71 On Crawfurd and the Glasgow rent strike, see Hannam and Hunt, *Socialist Women*, 147–52, here esp. 149. Also Kenny MacAskill, *Glasgow 1919: The Rise of Red Clydeside* (London: Biteback Publishing, 2019), 68, 85–97.
72 Elizabeth Crawford, *The Women's Suffrage Movement in Britain and Ireland: A Regional Survey* (London and New York: Routledge, 2008), 242.
73 Sandra Stanley Holton, *Feminism and Democracy: Women's Suffrage and Reform Politics in Britain, 1900–1918* (Cambridge: Cambridge University Press, 2003), 124.
74 MacAskill, *Glasgow 1919*, 299.
75 Hannam and Hunt, *Socialist Women*, 151.

76 Ibid., 152.
77 Further details in Irene Andersson, 'Kvinnor mot krig: Aktioner och nätverk för fred 1914–1940' ('Women against War: Actions and networks for peace, 1914–1940'), PhD Dissertation, Lund University, 2001, esp. 57–114.
78 Ibid., 107.
79 Irene Andersson, 'Patterns from the Guardians of Neutrality: Women Social Democrats in Sweden and their Resistance against Civil Defense, 1939–1940', in Maartje Abbenhuis and Sara Buttsworth (eds.), *Restaging War in the Western World: Noncombatant Experiences, 1890–Today* (Basingstoke: Palgrave Macmillan, 2009), 41–60 (here 43).
80 Daniel, *The War from Within*, 167.
81 See the reports written by Constable (*Polizei-Wachtmeister*) Lang of the political police department in Düsseldorf, 20 June 1916, containing a copy of a confiscated pro-Spartacist flyer, 'Ein Sieg der Jugend in Braunschweig' and by Police Officer (*Kriminalschutzmann*) Wilhelm Dittmann of the Berlin political police, 20 September 1916, in LAB, A Pr. Br. Rep. 030, Nr. 15818, Bl. 268–70, 291–2.
82 Ibid., report by Constable Lang, Bl. 270.
83 See Regula Pfeifer, 'Frauen und Protest: Marktdemonstrationen in der deutschen Schweiz im Kriegsjahr 1916', in Albert Tanner and Lise Head-König (eds.), *Frauen in der Stadt – Les femmes dans la ville* (Zurich: Chronos, 1992), 93–109. Also Béatrice Ziegler, *Arbeit – Körper – Öffentlichkeit: Berner und Bieler Frauen zwischen Diskurs und Alltag (1919–1945)* (Zurich: Chronos Verlag, 2007), 331.
84 Caruso, 'Blut und Eisen', 39.
85 Ibid., 59.
86 Staatsarchiv Zurich, P 239.13 a, Kommunisten etc., Jugendorganisation, sozialdemokratische Partei, sozialdemokratische Eintracht, 1916, Mappe Sozialdemokratische Jugend-Organisation und andere soz. Vereinigungen betr. Demonstrat.-Versammlungen und Umzüge.
87 Claes Brundenius, 'Social Democracy and the Fate of the Swedish Model', in Claes Brundenius (ed.), *Reflections on Socialism in the Twenty-First Century: Facing Market Liberalism, Rising Inequalities and the Environmental Imperative* (Cham: Springer, 2020), 47–102 (here 50).
88 See also Daniel, *The War from Within*, esp. 241–50.
89 Brundenius, 'Social Democracy', 50, n. 7.
90 Dan Diner, *Das Jahrhundert verstehen, 1917–1989: Eine universalhistorische Deutung* (Munich: Luchterhand, 1999), 84.
91 Veronika Helfert, *Frauen, wacht auf! Eine Frauen- und Geschlechtergeschichte von Revolution und Rätebewegung in Österreich, 1916–1924* (Göttingen: Vandenhoeck & Ruprecht, 2021), 86–7, 119.
92 Cläre Casper-Derfert, unpublished memoirs, 14 April 1958, in SAPMO-BArch, SgY 30/0148, Bl. 19.

93 Alasti, *Frauen der Novemberrevolution*, 69.
94 Helfert, *Frauen, wacht auf!*, 132. On Hornik-Strömer, see also Chapter 5 in this volume.
95 Weipert, 'Widerstand im Zentrum der Macht', 221.
96 Casper-Derfert, unpublished memoirs, Bl. 20.
97 Alasti, *Frauen der Novemberrevolution*, 67–8.
98 Helfert, *Frauen, wacht auf!*, 136–7.
99 On the methodological difficulties of using apparently gender-neutral sources to gauge the number of female participants in any given demonstration, strike or food riot, see Helfert, *Frauen, wacht auf!*, 52, 138–9 and 168–70. Helfert points out that the inherent tendency of contemporary reports to use the generic masculine when speaking of 'workers', 'strikers' or 'youths', and the deployment of words like 'crowds' or 'masses' as opposed to more gender-specific terminology, tends linguistically to reinforce the often false impression of 'woman-lessness' or 'absence of women' (*Frauenlosigkeit*) in such events.
100 Ursula Herrmann, 'Sozialdemokratische Frauen in Deutschland im Kampf um den Frieden vor und während des Ersten Weltkrieges', *Zeitschrift für Geschichtswissenschaft*, 33.3 (1985), 213–30 (here 228).
101 Alasti, *Frauen der Novemberrevolution*, 67. See also 'Forderugen der streikenden Berliner Arbeiter vom 29. Januar 1918', in *Dokumente und Materialien zur Geschichte der deutschen Arbeiterbewegung*, Vol. 2, 75. For universal, including female, suffrage as one the demands of the workers' strike in Vienna in January 1918, see Helfert, *Frauen, wacht auf!*, 134, 171.
102 Daniel, *The War from Within*.
103 See the figures in Herrmann, 'Sozialdemokratische Frauen', 228, n. 73.
104 On the USPD, see also Thönnessen, *The Emancipation of Women*, 81; and Peter Kohlbrodt, 'Die proletarische Frauenbewegung in Deutschland am Vorabend und während der Novemberrevolution (Herbst 1917 bis Anfang Mai 1919)', PhD dissertation, Pädagogische Hochschule Clara Zetkin, Leipzig, 1981.
105 See the figures in Herrmann, 'Sozialdemokratische Frauen', 225, n. 56, citing Kohlbrodt's work above.
106 Helfert, *Frauen, wacht auf!*, 120 and 168.
107 Cox, *Hunger in War and Peace*, 32–3.
108 Ulf Wickbom, 'Hungerkravallerna 1917: Söderhamns bortglömda kvinnor' ('The Hunger Riots 1917: Söderhamn's Forgotten Women'), unpublished manuscript prepared for the Sandarne Cultural and Historical Association (KULT) and ABF Hälsingekusten (the Workers' Education Union of the Hälsinge Coast), 2, 13.
109 See, for example, Ingvar Flink, *Hungerdemonstrationerna i Västervik 1917* (Västervik: Norra Kalmar läns folkrörelsearkiv, 1982).
110 Olwen Hufton, 'Women in Revolution, 1789–1796', *Past and Present*, 53 (1971), 90–108 (here 91).

111 Idem., *Women and the Limits of Citizenship in the French Revolution* (Toronto: University of Toronto Press, 1992), 39.
112 Ibid., 46.
113 Interview conducted by Anna Hammerin with Ulf Wickbom, Swedish journalist and author, Stockholm, 13 December 2019 (for an upcoming documentary film).
114 *Söderhamns Tidning* (Söderhamn Gazette), 18 April 1917.
115 Interview with Ulf Wickbom, 13 December 2019 (as note 113 above).
116 Ibid.
117 Blomqvist, *Potatisrevolutionen och Kvinnouppploppet*, 13, 17.
118 Ibid., 30.
119 Bernard Degen and Christian Koller, 'Protest und Streiks in der Schweiz in der zweiten Hälfte des Ersten Weltkriegs', *Journal of Modern European History*, 17.1 (2019), 64–82 (here 75).
120 Stadtarchiv Zurich, V.E.a.8.27, 464, Frauendemonstration.
121 For an example of such literature, see Cesare Lombroso and Rodolfo Laschi, *Delitto Politico e le Rivoluzioni in rapporto al diritto, all'antropologia criminale ed alla scienza di governo* (Turin: Fratelli Bocca, 1890). Translated into German as *Der politische Verbrecher und die Revolutionen* (Hamburg: Verl.-Anst. und Druckerei, 1891–2); and into French as *Le crime politique et les révolutions* (Paris: Germer Ballière, 1891–2).
122 See 'Die Frauendemonstration vor dem Zürcher Kantonsrat', *Die Vorkämpferin*, 1 July 1918, 3.
123 Michael Brenner, *Der lange Schatten der Revolution: Juden und Antisemiten in München 1918–1923* (Berlin: Jüdischer Verlag im Suhrkamp Verlag, 2019), 25–6, 35, 60.
124 For a recent novel based on Lerch's life story, see Cornelia Naumann, *Der Abend kommt so schnell: Sonja Lerch – Münchens vergessene Revolutionärin* (Meßkirch: Gmeiner, 2018).
125 Brenner, *Der lange Schatten*, 177. See also Albert Earle Gurganus, 'Sarah Sonja Lerch, née Rabinowitz: The Sonja Irene L. of Toller's *Masse-Mensch*', *German Studies Review*, 28.3 (2005), 607–20 (here 612).
126 Alasti, *Frauen der Novemberrevolution*, 69–70.
127 Gurganus, 'Sarah Sonja Lerch', 614.
128 Brenner, *Der lange Schatten*, 178.
129 On the *Landesstreik*, see Willi Gautschi, *Der Landesstreik 1918*, mit einem Nachwort von Hans Ulrich Jost, 4th edition (Zurich: Chronos, 2018 [1988]). Also Degen and Koller, 'Protest und Streiks', 77–80; Roman Rossfeld, Christian Koller and Brigitte Studer (eds.), *Der Landesstreik: Die Schweiz in 1918* (Baden: Hier und Jetzt, 2018).
130 Universitätsbibliothek Basel, Landesstreik 1918, Flugblätter 'An das arbeitende Volk der Schweiz', Aufruf zum unbefristeten Landesstreik vom 11. November 1918.

131 Frauenkommission der sozialdemokratischen Partei der Schweiz, 'An die Arbeiterinnen und Arbeiterfrauen', *Volksrecht*, No. 263, 11 November 1918, 4.
132 The Social Democratic Teachers' Association of Zurich already foresaw this possibility in 1917, noting that if a general strike were to take place, they would need to stand by to take care of the children and teach them about the strike. See Schweizerisches Sozialarchiv Zurich, Ar 201.525.1, Sozialdemokratische Lehrervereinigung, Protokollbuch 1906–1920, Versammlung vom 13. Juni 1917.
133 See 'Aufgaben der Frauen', *Die Vorkämpferin*, 1 December 1918, 6.
134 See Katharina Hermann, 'Weiber auf den Geleisen: Frauen im Landesstreik', in Rossfeld, Koller and Studer (eds.), *Der Landesstreik*, 217–40 (here 232).
135 Liddington and Norris, *'One Hand Tied Behind Us'*, 257–8.
136 In this sense, Gautschi's distinction between 'purely pacifist' anti-militarism and 'bolshevik' anti-militarism may lack nuance. See Gautschi, *Der Landesstreik*, 79–80.
137 'Der Massenaufstand', *Arbeiterinnen-Zeitung*, 29 January 1918. Cited in Helfert, *Frauen, wacht auf!*, 135.
138 Daniel, *The War from Within*, 250.
139 Christopher Dillon, '"The Revolutionary Flame Burns also in the Provinces": The Bavarian Revolutions of 1918-19', in Christopher Dillon and Kim Wünschmann (eds.), *Living the German Revolution 1918-19: Expectations, Experiences, Responses* (Oxford: Oxford University Press, forthcoming). We would like to thank Christopher Dillon for allowing us to see an advance draft of this chapter.
140 Ibid.
141 Helfert, *Frauen, wacht auf!*, 122.
142 Ibid., 314.
143 *Labour Leader*, 2 August 1917. Melksham was a textile town in Wiltshire specializing in woollen cloth making.
144 *Labour Leader*, 30 May 1918.
145 *Labour Leader*, 12 September 1918.
146 *Labour Leader*, 10 September 1917.
147 *Labour Leader*, 30 August 1917.
148 Liddington and Norris, *'One Hand Tied Behind Us'*, 256.
149 Ibid., 256–7.
150 On Anna Hornik-Strömer, see also Chapter 5 of this volume.
151 Matt Perry, *'Red Ellen' Wilkinson: Her Ideas, Movements and World* (Manchester: Manchester University Press, 2014), 161–5.
152 Ibid., 73–4. See also Chapter 4 of this volume.
153 See WILPF Resolutions drawn up in Zurich and presented in May 1919 to the Peace Conference in Paris, at https://wilpf.org/wp-content/uploads/2012/08/WILPF_triennial_congress_1919.pdf (accessed 1 April 2022), here 3, 5.
154 Ibid., 7.

155 See Reichsausschuß deutscher Frauen zur Befreiung unserer Gefangenen, Berlin-Wilmersdorf, 28 April 1919, in LAB, A Rep. 060-53, MF 4224, Bl. 12. Also Brian K. Feltman, '"Heraus mit unseren Gefangenen!" The German Home Front and the International Campaign for Prisoner of War Repatriation, 1918–1919', in Marcel Berni and Tamara Cubito (eds.), *Captivity in War during the Twentieth Century: The Forgotten Diplomatic Role of Transnational Actors* (London: Palgrave Macmillan, 2021), 47–72.

156 Sender, *Autobiography*, 145.
157 Dobson, *Authority and Upheaval*, 283.
158 Cox, *Hunger in War and Peace*, 48, 248, 264–5.
159 Andersson, 'Kvinnor mot krig', 121.
160 Idem., 'Patterns from the Guardian of Neutrality', 44.
161 Cox, *Hunger*.
162 Dobson, *Authority and Upheaval*, 228.
163 Ibid., 295.
164 See, for instance, Stefan Berger, 'Die deutsche Revolution 1918/19 in ihren europäischen Kontexten', in Frank Bischoff, Guido Hitze and Wilfried Reininghaus (eds.), *Aufbruch in die Demokratie: Die Revolution 1918/19 im Rheinland und in Westfalen – Beiträge der Tagung am 8. und 9. November 2018 in Düsseldorf* (Münster: Aschendorff, 2019), 17–29.
165 Carl Schmitt, *Political Theology: Four Chapters on the Concept of Sovereignty* (1922), transl. by George Schwab with a foreword by Tracy B. Strong (Chicago, IL and London: University of Chicago Press, 2005), 5.

3 Socialist Women and Revolutionary Violence, 1918–21

1 The spelling 'Steinbrink' also exists, but is less prevalent (see Georg Ledebour, *Der Ledebour-Prozess: Gesamtdarstellung des Prozesses gegen Ledebour wegen Aufruhr etc. vor dem Geschworenengericht Berlin-Mitte vom 19. Mai bis 23. Juni 1919* (Berlin: Verlagsgenossenschaft Freiheit, 1919), 215–16). In the judgment of the Berlin Court of Justice, the first name *Charlotte* is never mentioned. While Helga Grebing uses the first name *Hilde* in her booklet *Frauen in der deutschen Revolution* (Heidelberg: Stiftung Reichspräsident-Friedrich-Ebert-Gedenkstätte, 1994), it does not appear in the archival and published primary material used for this chapter, while *Charlotte* appears in the memoirs of Lotte Pulewka, who recalls a 'comrade Lotte Steinbring' in 1958. See Stiftung Archiv der Parteien und Massenorganisation der ehemaligen DDR im Bundesarchiv Berlin (henceforth SAPMO), SgY 30/503.
2 Grebing, *Frauen in der deutschen Revolution*, 6.
3 SAPMO, SgY 30/503, 31.

4 Ledebour, *Der Ledebour-Prozess*, 392–9.
5 This can be seen in many other cases of women arrested for participating in resistance movements or armed conflicts. See, for example, the conflicting accounts of her own use of arms by the Social Democrat Maria Emhart, the only woman to be tried for treason and being a leader (*Rädelsführer*) at the 1936 socialist trials in Vienna. Lena Köhler, *Die Konstruktion von Erinnerung: Geschlecht, Sozialismus und Widerstand gegen den Austrofaschismus anhand der Selbstzeugnisse Maria Emharts* (Vienna: LIT Verlag, 2020), 60–84.
6 SAPMO, SgY 30/57, Helene Behr, 1.
7 Helen Boak, *Women in the Weimar Republic* (Manchester: Manchester University Press, 2013), 64.
8 See, for instance, Donald Bloxham and Robert Gerwarth, 'Introduction', in Donald Bloxham and Robert Gerwarth (eds.), *Political Violence in Twentieth-Century Europe* (Cambridge: Cambridge University Press, 2011), 1–10; Robert Gerwarth and John Horne, 'Paramilitarism in Europe after the Great War: An Introduction', in Robert Gerwarth and John Horne (eds.), *War in Peace: Paramilitary Violence in Europe after the Great War* (Oxford and New York: Oxford University Press, 2012), 1–20; and Mark Jones, *Founding Weimar: Violence and the German Revolution of 1918–1919* (Cambridge: Cambridge University Press, 2016).
9 Apart from the above-mentioned works, see also Robert Gerwarth, *November 1918: The German Revolution* (Oxford and New York: Oxford University Press, 2020); Julian Aulke, *Räume der Revolution: Kulturelle Verräumlichung in Politisierungsprozessen während der Revolution 1918–1920* (Stuttgart: Franz Steiner Verlag, 2015); Benjamin Ziemann, 'Germany 1914–1918: Total War as a Catalyst of Change', in Helmut Walser Smith (ed.), *The Oxford Handbook of Modern German History* (Oxford and New York: Oxford University Press, 2011), 378–99.
10 Christine Sylvester, *War as Experience: Contributions from International Relations and Feminist Analysis* (London: Routledge, 2013), 5.
11 Gerhard Botz, *Gewalt in der Politik: Attentat, Zusammenstöße, Putschversuche, Unruhen in Österreich 1918–1939* (Munich: Fink, 1983), 25–8.
12 SAPMO, SgY 30, No. 1188, 504, 167.
13 Judith Szapor, *Hungarian Women's Activism in the Wake of the First World War: From Rights to Revanche* (London: Bloomsbury, 2018), 80.
14 Tiina Lintunen, 'Women at War', in Tuomas Tepora and Aapo Roselius (eds.), *The Finnish Civil War: History, Memory, Legacy* (Leiden: Brill, 2014), 201–29; Tuomas Hoppu, *Sisällissodan naiskaartit: Suomaeflaisnaiset aseissa 1918* (Helsinki: Gummerus, 2017); Anu Hakala, *Housukaartilaiset: Maarian punakaartin naiskomppania Suomen sisällissodassa* (Helsinki: Like, 2006); Tiina Lintunen, *Punaisten naisten tiet: Valtiorikosoikeuteen vuonna 1918 joutuneiden Porin seudun naisten toiminta sota-aikana, tuomiot ja myöhemmät elämänvaiheet* (Turku: University of Turku, 2015).

15 Over the past four decades, there has been a determined push by gender and feminist historians to both recover and rewrite women's roles during the revolutionary decade (and beyond), 1912–22, in Ireland. One of the first major works published on Irish revolutionary women was Margaret Ward, *Unmanageable Revolutionaries: Women and Irish Nationalism* (London: Pluto Press, 1983). Other publications include Rosemary Cullen Owens, *Smashing Times: A History of the Irish Women's Suffrage Movement 1889–1922* (Dublin: Attic Press, 1984); Sinead McCoole, *No Ordinary Women: Irish Female Activists in the Revolutionary Years* (Dublin: The O'Brien Press, 2003); Louise Ryan and Margaret Ward (eds.), *Irish Women and Nationalism: Soldiers, New Women and Wicked Hags* (Dublin: Irish Academic Press, 2004); Cal MacCarthy, *Cumann na mBan and the Irish Revolution* (Cork: Collins, 2007); Ann Matthews, *Renegades: Irish Republican Women 1900–1922* (Cork: Mercier, 2010); Senia Pašeta, *Irish Nationalist Women 1900–1918* (Cambridge: Cambridge University Press, 2013); Mary McAuliffe and Liz Gillis, *Richmond Barracks 1916: We were there: 77 Women of the Easter Rising* (Dublin: Four Courts Press, 2016); Margaret Ward, *Fearless Woman: Hanna Sheehy Skeffington, Feminism and the Irish Revolution* (Chicago, IL: The University of Chicago Press, 2020). Other publications such as Roy Foster, *Vivid Face: The Revolutionary Generation in Ireland, 1890–1923* (London: Allen Lane, 2014) include much material on the lives of men and women of this revolutionary generation who were 'linked together by youth, radicalism, subversive activities, enthusiasm and love' (inside page flap).

16 Chapter 5 of this volume looks more closely at the connection between memory, historiography and revolution.

17 Veronika Helfert, *Frauen, wacht auf! Eine Frauen- und Geschlechtergeschichte von Revolution und Rätebewegung in Österreich, 1916–1924* (Göttingen: Vandenhoeck & Ruprecht, 2021), 74–7.

18 Brigitte Studer, *Reisende der Weltrevolution: Eine Globalgeschichte der Kommunistischen Interanationale* (Berlin: Suhrkamp, 2020), 39.

19 Coline Cardi and Geneviève Pruvost, 'Introduction générale: Penser la violence des femmes: enjeux politiques et épistémologiques', in Coline Cardi and Geneviève Pruvost (eds.), *Penser la violence des femmes* (Paris: La Découverte, 2012), 13–64.

20 Neithard Bulst, Ingrid Gilcher-Holtey and Heinz-Gerhard Haupt, 'Einleitung', in Neithard Bulst, Ingrid Gilcher-Holtey and Heinz-Gerhard Haupt (eds.), *Gewalt im politischen Raum: Fallanalysen vom Spätmittelalter bis ins 20. Jahrhundert* (Frankfurt/Main and New York: Campus, 2010), 7–23 (here 11).

21 Adelheid Popp, *Frauen der Arbeit, schließt euch an! Ein Mahnruf* (Vienna: Brand, 1919), 5.

22 Pia Schölnberger, *Das Anhaltelager Wöllersdorf 1933–1938: Strukturen, Brüche, Erinnerungen* (Vienna: LIT Verlag, 2015), 105–6.

23 Emily Gioielli, The woman with no first name, online since 15 August 2017, https://fernetzt.univie.ac.at/the-woman-with-no-first-name (accessed 9 August 2022). On sexualized violence in the First World War, see, for example, Antoine Rivière, '"Special decisions": Children Born as the Result of German Rape and Handed Over to Public Assistance during the Great War (1914–18)', in Raphaëlle Branche and Fabrice Virgili (eds.), *Rape in wartime* (Basingstoke: Palgrave Macmillan, 2012), 184–200; Ruth Harris, 'The "Child of the Barbarian": Rape, Race and Nationalism in France during the First World War', *Past & Present*, 141 (1993), 170–206. Recently, a research group on 'Sexual Violence in the First World War' has been established at the University of Vienna, whose spokesperson is Christa Hämmerle. Sexualized violence within the Habsburg Army and its use as a weapon of war has been little researched so far (https://hist-kult.univie.ac.at/forschung/forscherinnengruppen/sexuelle-gewalt-im-ersten-weltkrieg, accessed 3 June 2022).

24 Birgit Sauer, 'Migration, Geschlecht, Gewalt: Überlegungen zu einem intersektionellen Gewaltbegriff', *Gender: Zeitschrift für Geschlecht, Kultur und Gesellschaft*, 3.2 (2011), 44–60; Pierre Bourdieu, 'Symbolische Gewalt und politische Kämpfe', in Pierre Bourdieu, *Mediationen: Zur Kritik der scholastischen Vernunft* (Frankfurt/Main: Suhrkamp, 2001), 210–46; Cardi and Pruvost, 'Introduction générale: Penser la violence des femmes', 13–64.

25 Alf Lüdtke, *The History of Everyday Life: Reconstructing Historical Experiences and Ways of Life* (Princeton, NJ: Princeton University Press, 1995), 313–14.

26 We are focusing mainly on the representations of revolutionary women in the enemy press. On the question of how women revolutionaries were treated in their own ranks, see for the Finnish case, for example, Hoppu, *Sisällissodan naiskaartit*, and for the Austrian case, Helfert, *Frauen, wacht auf!*.

27 Pertti Haapala and Marko Tikka, 'Revolution, Civil War, and Terror in Finland in 1918', in Gerwarth and Horne (eds.), *War in Peace*, 74–9.

28 Haapala and Tikka, 'Revolution, Civil War, and Terror in Finland in 1918', 74–9; Risto Alapuro, *State and Revolution in Finland* (Berkeley, CA: University of California Press, 1988), 145, 160; Pertti Haapala, 'The Expected and Non-expected Roots of Chaos: Preconditions', in Tepora and Roselius (eds.), *The Finnish Civil War*, 21–50 (here 40–50); Tuomas Hoppu, 'Sisällissodan puhkeaminen', in Pertti Haapala and Tuomas Hoppu (eds.), *Sisällissodan pikkujättiläinen* (Helsinki: WSOY, 2009), 92–111 (here 92–3); Pertti Haapala, 'Vuoden 1917 kriisi', in Haapala and Hoppu (eds.), *Sisällissodan pikkujättiläinen*, 58–89 (here 80); Marko Tikka, 'Warfare and Terror in 1918', in Tepora and Roselius (eds.), *The Finnish Civil War*, 90–118 (here 118).

29 McAuliffe and Gillis, *Richmond Barracks 1916*, 16.

30 Mary Cullen, 'Women, Emancipation and Politics, 1860–1984', in J.R. Hill (ed.), *A New History of Ireland, Vol VII, Ireland 1921–1984* (Oxford: Oxford University Press, 2003), 826–91 (here 846–7).

31 Ibid.
32 These strikes are discussed in more detail in Chapter 2 of this volume.
33 Peter Borowsky, *Schlaglichter historischer Forschung: Studien zur deutschen Geschichte im 19. und 20. Jahrhundert* (Hamburg: Hamburg University Press, 2005), 21–3.
34 Helfert, *Frauen, wacht auf!*, 173–98.
35 Gabriella Hauch, *Frauen.Leben.Linz: Eine Frauen- und Geschlechtergeschichte im 19. und 20. Jahrhundert* (Linz: Archiv der Stadt Linz, 2013), 185–242.
36 Hannah Arendt, *On Violence* (New York: Harcourt, Brace & World, 1970), 8.
37 Belinda Davis, Thomas Lindenberger and Michael Wildt, 'Einleitung', in Belinda Davis, Thomas Lindenberger and Michael Wildt (eds.), *Alltag, Erfahrung, Eigensinn: Historisch-anthropologische Erkundungen* (Frankfurt/Main and New York: Campus, 2008), 11–28 (here 20).
38 E. W., 'Der offene Brief einer Frau an einen Kriegshetzer', *Arbeiterinnen-Zeitung*, 1 January 1918.
39 'Die Proklamierung der deutsch-österreichischen Republik', *Arbeiterinnen-Zeitung*, 19 November 1918.
40 Maria Lähteenmäki, *Vuosisadan naisliike: Naiset ja sosialidemokratia 1900-luvun Suomessa* (Helsinki: Sosialidemokraattiset Naiset, 2000), 75.
41 Marjaliisa Hentilä, Matti Kalliokoski, and Armi Viita, *Uuden ajan nainen: Hilja Pärssisen elämä* (Helsinki: Siltala, 2018), 207–8.
42 Lähteenmäki, *Vuosisadan naisliike*, 77–8.
43 Hilde Wertheim-Hofmann, *Probleme der Klassengesellschaft* (Vienna: Münster, 1925), 99–100.
44 'Die Revolution in Deutschland', *Die Revolutionäre Proletarierin*, 15 March 1919.
45 Veronika Helfert, 'Between Pacifism and Militancy: Socialist Women in the First Austrian Republic, 1918–1934', *Diplomacy & Statecraft*, 31.4 (2020), 648–72.
46 Bini Adamczak, *Beziehungsweise Revolution: 1917, 1968 und kommende*, 3rd ed. (Stuttgart: Suhrkamp, 2018), 138.
47 Käthe Pick, 'Der österreichische Rätekongreß' (1920), in Günter Hillmann (ed.), *Die Rätebewegung II* (Reinbek bei Hamburg: Rowohlt, 1972), 93–9 (here 98).
48 Hilde Wertheim, 'Vorwort', in O.W. Kuusinen, *Die Revolution in Finnland: Eine Selbstkritik* (Vienna: Verlag der Arbeiter-Buchhandlung, 1920), 3–9.
49 Barbara Evans Clements, *Bolshevik Women* (Cambridge: Cambridge University Press, 1997), 19.
50 Matthew Stibbe, Olga Shnyrova and Veronika Helfert, 'Women and the Socialist Revolution, 1917–1923', in Ingrid Sharp and Matthew Stibbe (eds.), *Women Activists Between War and Peace: Europe, 1918–1923* (London and New York: Bloomsbury, 2017), 123–72.
51 The Proclamation of Independence, Ireland, 1916. This document was signed by seven (male) signatories and leaders of the militant nationalist and socialist groups

who participated in the Easter Rising, 1916. Among the seven signatories was socialist and feminist James Connolly, who was most likely influential in including the sections that promised universal suffrage, as well as 'religious and civil liberty, equal rights, and equal opportunities to all its citizens' (1916).

52 *Suomen Kansanvaltuuskunnan Tiedonantaja*, 15 April 1918.
53 Rochelle Goldberg Ruthchild, 'Women's Suffrage and Revolution in the Russian Empire, 1905-1917', in Karen Offen (ed.), *Globalizing Feminisms 1789-1945* (London and New York: Routledge, 2010), 257-74 (here 270).
54 Florian Wenninger, '"Die Zilli schießt": Frauen in den Februarkämpfen 1934', *Österreichische Zeitschrift für Geschichtswissenschaft* (ÖZG), 27.3 (2016), 117-44.
55 SAPMO, SgY 30/1188, 167 and 504.
56 *Tägliche Rundschau*, 12 January 1919; *Germania*, 10 March 1918.
57 Landesarchiv Berlin (henceforth LAB), A Rep. 358-01 n. 321.
58 *Työmies*, 12 April 1918.
59 Lintunen, *Punaisten naisten tiet*, 36; Hoppu, *Sisällissodan naiskaartit*, 35-45.
60 Hoppu, *Sisällissodan naiskaartit*, 70-1.
61 Lintunen, *Punaisten naisten tiet*, 36.
62 Vera Bianchi, 'Geschlechterverhältnisse im Spanischen Bürger*innenkrieg: *Milicianas* (Milizionärinnen) zwischen Heroisierung und Schützengraben', 27.3 (2016), 145-59.
63 SAPMO, SgY 30/129 Cläre Casper-Derfert; SgY 30 Nr504 Cläre Quast, 9.
64 *Germania*, 10 January 1919.
65 Arbeitskreis verdienter Gewerkschaftsveteranen beim Bundesvorstand des FDGB (ed.), *1918: Erinnerungen von Veteranen der deutschen Gewerkschaftsbewegung an die Novemberrevolution (1914-1920)* (East Berlin: Tribüne, 1960), 311-21.
66 *Vossische Zeitung*, 11-13 March 1919; *BZ am Mittag*, 12 January 1919.
67 Heinrich Hillmayr, *Roter und Weisser Terror in Bayern nach 1918: Ursachen, Erscheinungsformen u. Folgen d. Gewalttätigkeiten im Verlauf d. revolutionären Ereignisse nach d. Ende d. Ersten Weltkrieg* (Munich: Nusser, 1974), 153.
68 Hoppu, *Sisällissodan naiskaartit*, 270.
69 Ibid.; Lintunen, 'Women at War', 226.
70 André Keil and Matthew Stibbe, 'Ein Laboratorium des Ausnahmezustands: Schutzhaft während des Ersten Weltkriegs und in den Anfangsjahren der Weimarer Republik – Preußen und Bayern 1914 bis 1923', *Vierteljahrshefte für Zeitgeschichte*, 68.4 (2020), 535-73 (here 553).
71 LAB, A Rep. 358-01, no. 433, Sklarz wegen Gefangenenbefreiung aus dem Polizeigefängnis, November 1918, 92.
72 Staatsarchiv Munich (henceforth StAM), Staatsanwaltschaft I, no. 1947 – Strafverfahren gegen Ernst Bauer und Ida Bauer wegen Beihilfe zum Hochverrat.

73 Gemma Clarke, *Everyday Violence in the Irish Civil War* (Cambridge: Cambridge University Press, 2014), 192.
74 'Galway Women & "Bobbing"', https://www.galwaycitymuseum.ie/blog/galway-women-bobbing/?locale=en (accessed 7 April 2021).
75 Hilary Dully (ed.), *On Dangerous Ground: A Memoir of the Irish Revolution by Máire Comerford* (Dublin, Lilliput Press, 2021), 166–7.
76 T. K. Wilson, *Frontiers of Violence, Conflict and Identity in Ulster and Upper Silesia, 1918–1922* (Oxford: Oxford University Press, 2010), 120.
77 Lil Conlon, *Cumann Na MBan and the Women of Ireland: 1913–25* (Kilkenny: Kilkenny People Limited, 1969), 224.
78 *Irish Examiner*, 1 March 1920.
79 Louise Ryan, '"Drunken Tans": Representations of Sex and Violence in the Anglo-Irish War (1919–21)', *Feminist Review*, 66 (2000), 73–95 (here 83).
80 Helen Litton (ed.), *Kathleen Clarke: Revolutionary Woman* (Dublin: The O'Brien Press, 2008), 244–5.
81 *Irish Bulletin*, 9 July 1921.
82 Erskine Childers, *Military Rule in Ireland* (Dublin: Talbot Press, 1920), 11–12.
83 Ibid., 12.
84 Ryan, '"Drunken Tans"', 83.
85 Justin Dolan Stover, 'Families, Vulnerability and Sexual Violence during the Irish Revolution', in Jennifer Evans and Ciara Meehan (eds.), *Perceptions of Pregnancy from the Seventeenth to the Twentieth Century* (London: Palgrave Macmillan, 2017), 57–75 (here 62).
86 Louise Ryan, '"Furies" and "Die Hards": Women and Irish Republicanism in the Early Twentieth Century', *Gender and History*, 11.2 (1999), 256–75 (here 263).
87 Dolan Stover, 'Families, Vulnerability and Sexual Violence', 59.
88 Ibid., 63.
89 Ville Kivimäki, 'Ryvetetty enkeli: Suomalaissotilaiden neuvostoliittolaisiin naissotilaisiin kohdistama seksuaalinen väkivalta ja sodan sukupuolittunut mielenmaisema', *Naistutkimus – Kvinnoforskning*, 20.3 (2007), 19–32 (here 26, 28).
90 Lintunen, 'Women at War', 225–6; Kivimäki, 'Ryvetetty enkeli', 26–8; Susan R. Grayzel, *Women's Identities at War: Gender, Motherhood, and Politics in Britain and France during the First World War* (Chapel Hill, NC: University of North Carolina Press, 1999), 50–2.
91 Lintunen, 'Women at War', 225; Virva Liski, *Vankileirin selviytyjät: Tuhat naista Santahaminassa 1918* (Helsinki: Into Kustannus, 2020), 145.
92 Liski, *Vankileirin selviytyjät*, 145–7.
93 LAB, A Rep. 358-01 Nr. 433, Sklarz wegen Gefangenenbefreiung aus dem Polizeigefängnis.
94 Jones, *Founding Weimar*, 251–85.

95 Arbeitskreis verdienter Gewerkschaftsveteranen, *1918*, 319–20.
96 Martin Conway and Robert Gerwarth, 'Revolution and Counter-Revolution', in Bloxham and Gerwarth (eds.), *Political Violence*, 140–75 (here 140).
97 'Statement of atrocities on women in Ireland made and signed by Mrs. Hanna Sheehy-Skeffington' (1920), reproduced in Margaret Ward (ed.), *Hanna Sheehy Skeffington: Suffragette and Sinn Féiner: Her Memoirs and Political Writings* (Dublin: UCD Press, 2017), 182–6.
98 *American Commission on Conditions in Ireland Interim Report*, May 1921, 54.
99 M. Connory, Report to the Executive Irish White Cross, (Military Archives), 1922, 1.
100 Conlon, *Cumann Na MBan*, 224.
101 Lindsey Earner-Byrne, 'The Rape of Mary M.: A Microhistory of Sexual Violence and Moral Redemption in 1920s Ireland', *Journal of the History of Sexuality*, 24.1 (2015), 75–98 (here 86).
102 Hans von Hentig, 'Die revolutionäre Frau', *Schweizerische Zeitschrift für Strafrecht/ Revue pénale suisse*, 36.1/2 (1923), 29–45 (here 34).
103 *Berliner Tagblatt*, 10 March 1919.
104 Otto Bauer, *Die österreichische Revolution* (Vienna: Verlag der Wiener Volksbuchhandlung, 1923), 121.
105 Kathleen Canning, *Gender History in Practice: Historical Perspectives on Bodies, Class and Citizenship* (Ithaca, NY: Cornell University Press, 2006), 62.
106 Aulke, *Räume der Revolution*, 141.
107 Jean-Clément Martin, 'De la violence des femmes pendant la période révolutionnaire: un paradoxe persistant', in Cardi and Pruvost (eds.), *Penser la violence des femmes*, 95–184.
108 Stuart Hall, 'The Spectacle of the "Other"', in Stuart Hall (ed.), *Representation: Cultural Representations and Signifying Practices* (Thousand Oaks, CA: The Open University, 2003), 258–9.
109 *Suomen Kuvalehti* 19/1918, 11 May 1918.
110 Lintunen, *Punaisten naisten tiet*, 44–55.
111 *Uusi Päivä*, 16 April 1918.
112 *Keskisuomalainen*, 12 April 1918.
113 The Finnish National Archive, vryo 24419 and vryo 18297.
114 *Germania*, 10 March 1918.
115 *Tägliche Rundschau*, 10 March 1919.
116 *Berliner Tageblatt*, 13 January 1919.
117 *Tägliche Rundschau*, 10 March 1919.
118 *Tägliche Rundschau*, 13 January 1919.
119 See also StAM, Polizeidirektion I, Nr. 3124 Denkschrift der Polizeidirektion München, 57–82.

120 *Tägliche Rundschau*, 8 March 1919.
121 LAB, A Rep. 358-01, Nr. 466.
122 StAM I, N. 2077.
123 Ibid.
124 'Jünglinge aus dem Osten – Hysterische Damen: Beiträge zur Naturgeschichte der österreichischen Bolschewiken', *Christlich-soziale Arbeiter-Zeitung*, 2 February 1918; 'Tirol und die Friedländer', *Neues Montagblatt*, 7 July 1919.
125 Elfriede Friedländer, *Sexualethik des Kommunismus: Eine prinzipielle Studie* (Vienna: Neue Erde, 1920).
126 'Aus dem Gerichtssaale', *Linzer Volksblatt*, 19 March 1922.
127 'Elfriede Friedländer', *Wiener Caricaturen*, 10 August 1919; 'Ruth Fischer, die Überkommunistin – abgetan?', *Kikeriki*, 25 July 1926.
128 Tiina Lintunen and Kimmo Elo, 'Valtiorikosoikeuteen joutuneiden punaisten naisten verkostot Porin alueella vuonna 1918', *Historiallinen Aikakauskirja*, 116.2 (2018), 139–52.
129 *Turun Sanomat*, 17 July 1918.
130 Lintunen, *Punaisten naisten tiet*, 171, 174, 180–1.
131 Maryann Gialanella Valiulis, 'Virtuous Mothers and Dutiful Wives; the Politics of Sexuality in the Irish Free State', in Maryann Gialanella Valiulis (ed.), *Gender and Power in Irish History* (Dublin: Irish Academic Press, 2009), 100–14 (here 102).
132 See Jason Knirck, *Women of the Dáil: Gender, Republicanism and the Anglo-Irish Treaty* (Dublin, Irish Academic Press, 2006), 160–2.
133 Marie Coleman, 'Compensating Irish Female Revolutionaries, 1916–1923', *Women's History Review*, 27.6 (2017), 915–34 (here 918).
134 Ibid., 930.
135 Ibid., 921.
136 Caitriona Beaumont, 'Women, Citizenship and Catholicism in the Irish Free State, 1922–1948', *Women's History Review*, 6.4 (1997), 563–85 (here 563).
137 Studer, *Reisende der Weltrevolution*, 39.

4 Suffrage, Democracy and Citizenship

1 Rosa Luxemburg, 'Women's Suffrage and Class Struggle', in Peter Hudis and Kevin B Anderson (eds.), *The Rosa Luxemburg Reader* (New York: The Monthly Review Press, 2004), 237–42 (here 238).
2 Kathleen Canning, 'Claiming Citizenship. Suffrage and Subjectivity after the First World War', in Kathleen Canning, Kerstin Brandt and Kristin McGuire (eds.), *Weimar Publics/Weimar Subjects: Rethinking the Political Culture of Germany in the 1920s* (New York: Berghahn Books, 2010), 116–37 (here 131).

3   Birgitta Bader-Zaar, 'Women's Citizenship and the First World War: General Remarks and a Case Study of Women's Enfranchisement in Austria and Germany', *Women's History Review*, 25:2 (2016), 274–95; Hedwig Richter and Kerstin Wolff (eds.), *Frauenwahlrecht: Demokratisierung der Demokratie in Deutschland und Europa* (Hamburg: Hamburger Edition, 2018). See also Pat Thane, 'What Difference Did the Vote Make?', in Amanda Vickery (ed.), *Women, Privilege, and Power: British Politics, 1750 to the Present* (Stanford, CA: Stanford University Press, 2001), 253–88.
4   Jane Slaughter and Robert Kern (eds.), *European Women on the Left: Socialism, Feminism, and the Problems Faced by Political Women, 1880 to the Present* (Westport, CT: Greenwood Press, 1981), 5.
5   The idea for an international women's day associated with the demand for female suffrage originated in American Social Democracy and its adoption by Zetkin illustrates the transnational influences within women's movements.
6   Rochelle Goldberg Ruthchild, 'From West to East: International Women's Day, the First Decade', *Aspasia*, 6 (2012), 1–24 (here 3).
7   William A. Pelz, *A People's History of the German Revolution* (London: Pluto Press, 2018), 115.
8   See for example Karen Hunt, *Equivocal Feminists: The Social Democratic Federation and the Woman Question, 1884–1911* (Cambridge: Cambridge University Press, 1996), especially Chapter 6.
9   Karen Hunt and June Hannam, *Socialist Women: Britain 1880s–1920s* (London and New York: Routledge, 2002).
10 Jill Liddington and Jill Norris, *One Hand Tied Behind Us: The Rise of the Women's Suffrage Movement* (London: Virago, 1978), 15.
11 Jo Vellacott, *Pacifists, Patriots and the Vote: The Erosion of Democratic Suffragism in Britain During the First World War* (Basingstoke: Palgrave Macmillan, 2007).
12 Sandra Holton, *Feminism and Democracy: Women's Suffrage and Reform Politics in Britain, 1900–1918* (Cambridge: Cambridge University Press, 1986).
13 Other relevant books that add to an understanding of the complexities of the British situation might include Claire Eustance, Joan Ryan and Laura Ugolini (eds.), *A Suffrage Reader: Charting Directions in British Suffrage History* (London: Leicester University Press, 2000); Sandra Holton, *Suffrage Days: Stories from the Women's Suffrage Movement* (London and New York: Routledge, 1996); Les Garner, *Stepping Stones to Women's Liberty: Feminist Ideas in the Women's Suffrage Movement, 1900–1918* (London: Heinemann, 1984) Jill Liddington, *The Life and Times of a Respectable Rebel: Selina Cooper, 1864–1946* (London: Virago, 1984).
14 For an overview, see Angelika Schaser, 'Zur Einführung des Frauenwahlrechts vor 90 Jahren am 12. November 1918', *Feministische Studien*, 27.1 (2009), 97–110; and Kerstin Wolff, 'Noch einmal von vorn erzählt: Die Geschichte des Kampfes um das Frauenwahlrecht in Deutschland' in Richter and Wolff (eds.), *Frauenwahlrecht*, 35–56.

15 These include Richter and Wolff (eds.), *Frauenwahlrecht*; Birte Förster, *1919: Ein Kontinent erfindet sich neu* (Stuttgart: Reclam, 2018).
16 Hedwig Richter, *Demokratie: Eine deutsche Affäre* (Munich: C.H. Beck, 2020).
17 Axel Weipert, 'Frauen für die Räte, die Frauen in die Räte? Konzept und Praxen von Frauen in der Rätebewegung 1918–1920', *Ariadne: Forum für Frauen- und Geschlechtergeschichte*, 73–4 (2018), 40–4.
18 Between 1874 and 1917 the percentage of eligible voters was around 6 per cent of the population. See, among others, Gábor Gyáni and György Kövér, *Magyarország társadalomtörténete* (The Social History of Hungary) (Budapest: Osiris, 1998), 107.
19 Benjamin Ziemann, 'Germany 1914–1918. Total War as a Catalyst of Change', in Helmut Walser Smith (ed.), *The Oxford Handbook of Modern German History* (Oxford: Oxford University Press, 2011), 378–99 (here 387).
20 Pelz, *A People's History of the German Revolution*, 110.
21 See Werner Thönnessen, *The Emancipation of Women: The Rise and Decline of the Women's Movement in German Social Democracy, 1863–1933*, transl. by Joris de Bres (London: Pluto Press, 1973 [1969]).
22 Christl Wickert, *Unsere Erwählten: Sozialdemokratische Frauen im Deutschen Reichstag und im Preussischen Landtag 1919–1933* (Göttingen: Sovec, 1986).
23 Karen Hagemann, *Frauenalltag und Männerpolitik* (Bonn: J.H.W. Dietz Nachf., 1990); Julia Sneeringer, *Winning Women's Votes: Propaganda and Politics in Weimar Germany* (Chapel Hill, NC and London: The University of North Carolina Press, 2002).
24 'Die erste Parlamentsrede einer Frau in Deutschland', *Die Gleichheit*, 14 March 1919, 89–93.
25 *Die Gleichheit*, No. 5, 6 December 1918, 33. Quoted in Hagemann, *Frauenalltag und Männerpolitik*, 516.
26 Clara Zetkin, 'Die Revolution und die Frauen', *Die Rote Fahne*, 22 November 1918, 10.
27 Sneeringer, *Winning Women's Votes*, 53.
28 Robert F. Wheeler, 'German Women and the Communist International: The Case of the Independent Social Democrats', *Central European History*, 8.2 (1975), 113–39.
29 Sneeringer, *Winning Women's Votes*, 7; Helen Boak, 'Women in Weimar Germany: The "Frauenfrage" and the Female Vote', in Richard Bessel and Edgar Feuchtwanger (eds.), *Social Change and Political Development in Weimar Germany* (London: Croom Helm, 1981), 155–73.
30 Gisela Bock, 'Frauenwahlrecht – Deutschland um 1900 in vergleichender Perspektive', in Michael Grüttner, Rüdiger Hachtmann and Heinz-Gerhard Haupt (eds.), *Geschichte und Emanzipaton: Festschrift für Reinhard Rürup* (Frankfurt/Main: Campus Verlag, 1999); Sabine Hering, *Die Kriegsgewinnlerinnen* (Pfaffenweiler: Centaurus, 1990), 138.
31 Ibid., 138.

32 See Ingrid Sharp, 'Overcoming Inner Division: Post-Suffrage Strategies in the Organised German Women's Movement', *Women's History Review*, 23.3 (2014), 347–54.
33 See Kerstin Wolff, 'Wir wollen die Wahl haben: Wie die Frauen im deutschen Kaiserreich für das politische Wahlrecht stritten', *Ariadne: Forum für Frauen- und Geschlechtergeschichte*, 73–4 (2018), 22–31 (here 30).
34 Rochelle Goldberg Ruthchild, 'Women's Suffrage and Revolution in the Russian Empire, 1905–1917', *Aspasia*, 1 (2007), 1–35.
35 See for example Judit Acsády, 'In a Different Voice: Responses of Hungarian Feminism to the First World War', in Alison Fell and Ingrid Sharp (eds.), *The Women's Movement in Wartime: International Perspectives* (Basingstoke: Palgrave Macmillan, 2007), 105–23; Judith Szapor, 'Sisters or Foes; The Shifting Frontlines of the Hungarian Women's Movement, 1896–1918', in Bianca Pietrow-Ennker and Sylvia Paletschek (eds.), *Women's Emancipation Movements in the Nineteenth Century: A European Perspective* (Stanford University Press, 2004), 189–205; Julie V. Gottlieb and Judith Szapor with Tiina Lintunen and Dagmar Wernitznig, 'Suffrage and Nationalism in Comparative Perspective' in Ingrid Sharp and Matthew Stibbe (eds.), *Women's Movements and Female Activists in the Aftermath of WWI* (London: Bloomsbury Academic, 2017), 29–75.
36 Dóra Czeferner, *Kultúrmisszió vagy propaganda? Feminista lapok és olvasóik Bécsben és Budapesten* (Budapest: Bölcsészettudományi Kutatóközpont, Történettudományi Intézet, 2021).
37 Ibid.
38 Irén Simándi, *Küzdelem a nők parlamenti választójogáért Magyarországon 1848–1938* (Budapest: Gondolat, 2009).
39 Judith Szapor, *Hungarian Women's Activism in the Wake of the First World War: From Rights to Revanche* (London: Bloomsbury Academic, 2018).
40 Ágoston Péterné, *A magyar szocialista nőmozgalom története* (Budapest: Népszava, 1947).
41 Magda Aranyossi, *Lázadó asszonyok: A Magyar nőmunkásmozgalom története 1867–1919* (Budapest: Kossuth, 1963).
42 Susan Zimmermann, 'Frauenbestrebungen und Frauenbewegungen in Ungarn: Zur Organisationsgeschichte der Jahre 1848 bis 1918', in Beáta Nagy and Margit S. Sárdi (eds.), *Szerep és alkotás: Női szerepek a társdalomban és az alkotóművészetben* (Debrecen: Csokonai, 1997), 175–205 ; idem, *Die bessere Hälfte: Frauenbewegungen und Frauenbestrebungen im Ungarn der Habsburgermonarchie 1848 bis 1918* (Vienna: Promedia, 1999).
43 Andrea Pető and Judith Szapor, 'The State of Women's and Gender History in Eastern Europe: The Case of Hungary', *Journal of Women's History*, 19.1 (2007), 160–6.
44 For an activist account of this development, equally threatening to the academic infrastructure of women's history, see Andrea Pető, 'Report from the Trenches: The

Debate around Teaching Gender Studies in Hungary', https://www.boell.de/en/2017/04/10/report-trenches-debate-around-teaching-gender-studies-hungary (accessed 4 March 2022).
45 Examples include Slovene political activists/intellectuals from the inter-war era: Zofka Kveder, Franja Tavčar, Minka Govekar, Cilka Krek, Pavla Hočevar, Ivanka Anžič Klemenčič, Josipina Vidmar, Marica Nadlišek Bartol, Ada Kristan and Alojzija Štebi.
46 Jovanka Kecman, *Žene Jugoslavije u radničkom pokretu i ženskim organizacijama 1918–1941* (Yugoslav Women in the Labour Movement and Women's Organizations 1918–41) (Belgrade: Narodna knjiga – Institut za savremenu istoriju, 1978).
47 Lydia Sklevicky, *Konji, žene, ratovi* (Horses, Women, Wars) (Zagreb: Ženska infoteka, 1996).
48 Marta Verginella (ed.), *Dolga pot pravic žensk: Pravna in politična zgodovina žensk na Slovenskem* (The Long Road to Women's Rights: Legal and Political History of Women in Slovenia) (Ljubljana: Znanstvena založba Filozofske fakultete – Studia humanitatis, 2013).
49 Milica Antić Gaber (ed.), *Ženske na robovih politike* (Women on the Fringes of Politics) (Ljubljana: Sophia, 2011); and *Naše žene volijo!* (Our Women Vote!) (Ljubljana: Urad za žensko politiko, 1999).
50 Ida Ograjšek Gorenjak, *Opasne iluzije: Rodni stereotipi u međuratnoj Jugoslaviji* (Dangerous Illusions: Gender Stereotypes in Inter-War Yugoslavia) (Zagreb: Srednja Europa, 2014).
51 For example, Irena Selišnik, *Prihod žensk na oder slovenske politike* (The Arrival of Women on the Stage of Slovenian Politics) (Ljubljana: Sophia, 2008), deals with the political beginnings of women in Slovenia and focuses primarily on the period before 1918. Sabrina P. Ramet (ed.), *Gender Politics in the Western Balkans: Women and Society in Yugoslavia and the Yugoslav Successor States* (Pennsylvania, PA: The Pennsylvania State University, 1999) is an important overview of women's consciousness in the lands of the South Slavs from the early years of the twentieth century to the end of the century. Some of the Croatian cases of gender history are also well represented in Andrea Feldman (ed.) *Žene u Hrvatskoj: Ženska i kulturna povijest* (Women in Croatia: Women's and Cultural History) (Zagreb: Institut Vlado Gotovac, 2004). An important contribution to Serbian women's history is the second volume of a three-volume historiographical project, entitled *Srbija u modernizacijskim procesima 19. i 20. veka*. Latinka Perović's volume, *Položaj žene kao merilo modernizacije* (Belgrade: Institut za noviju istoriju Srbije, 2008), is dedicated to economic, social and political conditions of Serbian women in the nineteenth and twentieth centuries.
52 Béla Bodó, *The White Terror: Political and Antisemitic Violence in Hungary, 1919–1923* (New York and London: Routledge, 2019), especially Chapter 6.
53 Thönnessen, *The Emancipation of Women*, 80.

54 Clara Zetkin, 'Women's Right to Vote' (1907), reproduced in Clara Zetkin, *Selected Writings* (Philip S. Foner: Aakar Books, 2012), 98–107.
55 Resolutions of the 1st Congress, The Hague 1915 WILPF International (online) at https://www.wilpf.org/wp-content/uploads/2012/08/WILPF_triennial_congress_1915.pdf (accessed 4 July 2022).
56 See Marilyn J. Boxer and John S. Partington, *Clara Zetkin: National and International Contexts* (London: Socialist History Society, 2013).
57 K. Honeycutt, 'German Social Democracy and Women's Suffrage 1891–1918', *Journal of Central European History*, 15.3 (1980), 533–57 (here 552).
58 Hagemann, *Frauenalltag und Männerpolitik*, 550.
59 Wolff, 'Wir wollen die Wahl haben', 30.
60 Karen Honeycutt argues that the SPD were using female suffrage as a bargaining chip to achieve an expanded male franchise. Honeycutt, 'German Social Democracy and Women's Suffrage', 552.
61 Gorenjak, *Opasne iluzije*, 245.
62 Katalin N. Szegvári, *Numerus clausus intézkedések az ellenforradalmi Magyarországon* (Budapest: Akadémiai, 1988), 160–1; Anna Borgos, '"Put a stop to the excessive influx": The Rhetoric of Restriction Regarding Female and Jewish Students at Budapest University, 1900–1930', *Hungarian Studies Review*, 48.1 (2021), 48–78.
63 Cheryl Law, 'The old faith living and the old power there: the movement to extend women's suffrage', in Joannou Maroula and June Purvis (eds.), *The Women's Suffrage Movement: New Feminist Perspectives* (Manchester University Press, Manchester, 1998).
64 MSWSS Annual report 1917, M50/1/5/3.
65 Karen Hunt, 'Class and Adult Suffrage in Britain During the Great War', in June Purvis and June Hannam (eds.), *The British Women's Suffrage Campaign: National and International Perspectives* (London and New York: Routledge, 2020), 136–54 (here 136).
66 Letter to Helena Swanwick, DMAR/4/23, 6 October 1916.
67 This was part of the wording of Margaret Ashton's resolution (the Manchester resolution) to the NUWSS Special Council in June 1915. The resolution was lost. Ashton had resigned from the NUWSS in 1915 along with many members of the Executive Council in defiance of Fawcett's sympathy with the war.
68 Closing argument of Dr. Béla Gonda, Papers of Gizella Berzeviczy, Archives of the Institute of Political History, Budapest, fond 822, unit 8.
69 Mór Bihari, 'Berzeviczy Gizella forradalmi pályafutása (1878–1954)', *Pedagógiai Szemle*, 14.1 (1964), 48–59, provides biographical details for Berzeviczy, while keeping to what was then the official party line.
70 See Thönnessen, *The Emancipation of Women*.

71 1918 General Election: Battersea North: Mrs Charlotte Despard (Labour) Belfast, Victoria: Miss Winifred Carney (Sinn Fein) Birmingham, Ladywood: Mrs Margery Corbett Ashley (Liberal) Brentford and Chiswick: Mrs Rachel Strachey (Independent) Chelsea: Miss Emily Phipps (Independent) *Dublin, St Patricks: Countess Constance Markievicz (Sinn Fein)* Enfield: Mrs Janet McEwan (Liberal) Glasgow, Bridgeton: Miss Eunice G Murray (Independent) Kennington: Mrs Alice Lucas (Conservative) – delayed election due to death of previous Tory candidate (who was Lucas's husband) Manchester, Rusholme: Mrs Emmeline Pethick-Lawrence (Labour) Hendon: Mrs Edith How-Martyn (Independent) Mansfield: Mrs Violet Carruthers (Liberal) Portsmouth South: Miss Alison Garland (Liberal) Richmond, Surrey: Mrs Nora Dacre Fox (Independent) Smethwick: Miss Christabel Pankhurst (Women's party) University of Wales: Mrs Millicent Mackenzie (Labour) Stourbridge: Mrs Mary Macarthur (Labour).

72 Sylvia Schraut, 'Angekommen im demokratisierten "Männerstaat"? Weibliche Geschichten in der Weimarer Republik', *Ariadne: Forum für Frauen- und Geschlechtergeschichte*, 73–4 (2018), 8–18 (here 9).

73 Anna Blos, 'Der Fraueneinfluss bei den Wahlen', *Die Gleichheit*, No. 27 (1920), cited in Thönnessen, *The Emancipation of Women*, 128.

74 Sneeringer, *Winning Women's Votes*, 281.

75 Ibid., 51–9.

76 For a fuller discussion of these complexities, see Isidora Grubački, 'The Emergence of the Yugoslav Interwar Liberal Feminist Movement and the Little Entente of Women: An Entangled History Approach (1919–1924)', *Feminist Encounters: A Journal of Critical Studies in Culture and Politics*, 4.2 (2020), article no. 27.

77 See, for example, Katarina Bogdanović, 'Ženska politička prava' ('Women's Political Rights'), *Ženski pokret*, III, 26 June 1920, 11–13.

78 Gorenjak, *Opasne iluzije*, 114.

79 Alojzija Štebi, *Demokratizem in ženstvo* (Democracy and Women) (Ljubljana: Slovenska socialna matica, 1918), 3.

80 Franc Rozman (ed.), *Korespondenca Albina Prepeluha-Abditusa* (Correspondence of Albin Prepeluh Abditus) (Ljubljana: Arhivsko društvo Slovenije, 1991), 70.

81 For detailed biographies of Alojzija Štebi, see Darinka Drnovšek, 'Alojzija Štebi: Borka za pravice žensk in mladine' ('Alojzija Štebi: Fighter for the Rights of Women and Youth'), in Serša Budna Kodrič (ed.), *Splošno žensko društvo, 1901–1945: od dobrih deklet do feministk* (Ljubljana: Arhiv Republike Slovenije, 2003), 188–209; and Irena Selišnik, 'Alojzija Štebi, socialna feministka in ena prvih političark v Sloveniji' ('Alojzija Štebi, a Social Feminist and one of the First Politicians in Slovenia'), in Antić Gaber (ed.), *Ženske na robovih politike* (Ljubljana: Sophia, 2011), 41–59.

82 Historical Archives of Ljubljana, ZAL LJU 285, Splošno žensko društvo, Box 7, Danica Hrstić writing in 19 September 1921. Quoted in Selišnik, 'Alojzija Štebi', 52.
83 Jovanka Kecman, *Žene Jugoslavije u radničkom pokretu i ženskim organizacijama 1918–1941* (Yugoslav Women in the Labour Movement and Women's Organizations 1918–41) (Belgrade: Narodna knjiga – Institut za savremenu istoriju, 1978), 182; and Selišnik, 'Alojzija Štebi', 52.
84 National and University Library of Ljubljana (NUK), Manuscript Collection, Fond of Erna Muser, MS 1432 VIII 1.22 Alojzija Štebi.
85 Angela Vode, *Spomin in pozaba* (Memory and Oblivion) (Ljubljana: Krtina, 2000), 95.
86 Angela Vode, 'Socializem in žena' ('Socialism and Woman'), *Naprej: Glasilo jugoslovanske socialno-demokratične stranke* (Forward: Newspaper of the Yugoslav Social Democratic Party), IV, 9 April 1920, 1.
87 Angela Vode, 'Sestram', *Naprej: Glasilo jugoslovanske socialno-demokratične stranke*, IV, 29 April 1920, 1.
88 Vode, *Spomin in pozaba*, 101.
89 Angela Vode, *Žena v sedanji družbi* (Woman in Today's Society) (Maribor: Žena in dom, 1934), 36.
90 Ibid., 53.
91 Ibid., 71.
92 NUK, Manuscript Collection, Fond of Erna Muser, MS 1432 VIII, 1. 9. Kos Leopoldina.
93 For an account of working women's lives during this period, see Ute Daniel, *The War from Within: German Working-Class Women in the First World War*, transl. by Margaret Ries (Oxford: Berg, 1997). See also Chapter 2 in this volume for a discussion of police repression of working class protests.
94 From 1923, there was another international association, the so-called Little Entente, which brought together women's organizations from Yugoslavia, Czechoslovakia, Romania, Bulgaria, Greece and Poland, whose first assembly was held in November 1923 in Bucharest, followed by a meeting in Belgrade the following year. See Grubački, 'The Emergence of the Yugoslav Interwar Liberal Feminist Movement'.
95 Gorenjak, *Opasne iluzije*, 121.
96 See Boxer and Partington, *Clara Zetkin: National and International Contexts*; Karen Honeycut, 'Clara Zetkin: A Socialist Approach to the Problem of Women's Oppression' in Slaughter and Kern *European Women on the Left*, 29–50; Daniel Gaido and Cintia Frencia, '"A Clean Break": Clara Zetkin, the Socialist Women's Movement, and Feminism', *International Critical Thought*, 8.2 (2018), 277–300.
97 See Goldberg Ruthchild, 'Women's Suffrage and Revolution'.
98 See Women's International League newssheet Vol. 1, 10 and Vol. 3.
99 Resolutions of the Zurich Congress 1919, https://www.wilpf.de/wp-content/uploads/2020/08/WILPF_1919-Congress.pdf (accessed 6 June 2022).

100 WIL newssheet Vol. 3 No 1. April 1918 R188351 Manchester City Library Archives.
101 Ibid.
102 'The French only permitted two delegates and Italy just one, Rosa Genoni, who got a passport by declaring she was going to study fashion. This may seem like camouflage but Signora Genoni is trying her best to keep her pledge as she is making a study between sessions of the attractive hats and blouses in the shop windows.' *Chicago Tribune*, 17 May 1919 Archives, University of Colorado at Boulder Libraries.
103 WILPF series 1. Folder 14. Christian World? Archives University of Colorado, Boulder Library.
104 Open Letter to German and Austrian Women, published in *Jus Suffragii*, December 1914.
105 *New York Times*, 22 June 1919, 11.
106 Letter from Florence Kelley to Mary Rozet Smith of the National Consumer League, 22 May 1919, in *Selected Letters of Florence Kelley 1969–1931*, ed. by Kathryn Kish Sklar and Beverley Palmer (Chicago, IL: University of Illinois Press, 2009), 240.
107 Report of the International Congress of Women, Zurich, 12 to 17 May 1919 (Geneva, Switzerland: Women's International League for Peace and Freedom, 1920). English edition.
108 Canning et al., *Weimar Publics/Weimar Subjects*, 9.
109 Canning, 'Claiming Citizenship', 131.
110 Glenda Sluga, *Internationalism in the Age of Nationalism* (Philadelphia: University of Pennsylvania Press, 2013), 11–44.
111 On women and the League of Nations see Carol Miller, 'Geneva – the Key to Equality: Inter-War Feminism and the League of Nations', *Women's History Review*, 3 (1994), 219–45; Susan Pedersen, 'Back to the League of Nations: Review Essay', *American History Review*, 112 (2007), 1091–117; Leila J. Rupp, *Worlds of Women: The Making of an International Women's Movement* (Princeton, NJ: Princeton University Press, 1997), 210–22.
112 Dorothee Linnemann (ed.), *Damenwahl! 100 Jahre Frauenwahlrecht. Begleitbuch zur Ausstellung* (Frankfurt/Main: Historisches Museum Frankfurt, 2018).
113 '*Frauen machten aber Revolution und standen eben nicht am Strassenrand und bleiben schon gar nicht friedfertig zu Hause*', in Linnemann, *Damenwahl*, 120.
114 Ibid., 187.
115 Blaustrumpf Ahoi! '*Sie meinen es politisch*' *100 Jahre Frauenwahlrecht in Österreich* (Vienna: Löcker, 2019).
116 Szapor, *Hungarian Women's Activism*, 62.
117 Daniel Hicks, 'War and the Political Zeitgeist: Evidence from the History of Female Suffrage', *European Journal of Political Economy*, 31 (2013), 60–81.

5 Life Trajectories: Making Revolution and Breaking Boundaries

1. Mary Saran, *Never Give Up* (London: Oswald Wolf, 1976), 113.
2. Vladimira Jelovšek's Letter to Karmela Kosovel, 16 February 1919, National and University Library, Ljubljana (henceforth NUK), Manuscript Collection, Ms 1981 II (grammatical errors in original; translated by Manca G. Renko). Vladimira apparently died from influenza in somewhat suspicious circumstances in 1920, when she was nineteen years old. She moved to Prague with two male friends, who were both renowned Yugoslav (Croatian) communist activists, her lover Đuro Cvijić and their friend August Cesarec.
3. For example, Benjamin Ziemann, 'Germany 1914–1918: Total War as a Catalyst of Change', in Helmut Walser Smith (ed.), *The Oxford Handbook of Modern German History* (Oxford: Oxford University Press, 2011), 378–400 asserts this argument in the German case and Judith Szapor challenges this view of Hungarian inter-war politics in her book *Hungarian Women's Activism in the Wake of the First World War: From Rights to Revanche* (London: Bloomsbury, 2019).
4. Tazreena Sajjad, 'Women Guerillas: Marching Toward True Freedom?', *Agenda*, 18.59 (2011), 4–16, here 6.
5. By restricting politics to certain spheres, many political actions and actors are rendered apolitical. See Claudia Bruns, 'Wissen – Macht – Subjekt(e): Dimensionen historischer Diskursanalyse am Beispiel des Männerbunddiskurses im Wilhelminischen Kaiserreich', *Österreichische Zeitschrift für Geschichtswissenschaften*, 16.4 (2005), 106–22.
6. Quoted in Maroula Joannou, '"She who would be politically free herself must strike the blow": Suffragette Autobiography and Suffragette Militancy', in Julia Swindells (ed.), *The Uses of Autobiography* (London: Taylor and Francis, 1995), 31–55, here 41.
7. Maria Todorova, *The Lost World of Socialists at Europe's Margins: Imagining Utopia 1870s–1920s* (London: Bloomsbury, 2020), 262.
8. Ibid., 164.
9. Gabriella Hauch, 'Isa Strasser: Land ohne Schlaf (1970): Ein autobiographischer Roman über das Leben in Moskau in den 1920er Jahren' in Lisia Bürgi and Eva Keller (eds.), *Ausgeschlossen einflussreich: Handlungsspielräume an den Rändern etablierter Machtstrukturen: Festschrift für Brigitte Studer zum 65. Geburtstag* (Basel: Schwabe, 2020), 105–20.
10. Ruth Fischer's son described the different places and caring arrangements he experienced in his autobiography. See Houghton Library, Harvard University (HOU) b97-m 21. Gerald Friedlander, Vienna, Berlin, Paris, London: Growing Up in Interesting Times. Manuscript [1997?].

11 Veronika Helfert, *Frauen, wacht auf!: Eine Frauen- und Geschlechtergeschichte von Revolution und Rätebewegung in Österreich, 1916–1924* (Göttingen: Vandenhoeck and Ruprecht, 2021), 255.
12 Brigitte Studer, *Reisende der Weltrevolution: Eine Globalgeschichte der Kommunistischen Internationale* (Berlin: Suhrkamp, 2020), 83–7.
13 Chapter 3 examines how women were affected by, and at times the target of, revolutionary violence.
14 For a gendered history of these developments, see Szapor, *Hungarian Women's Activism*.
15 Ibid.
16 See Corinne Painter, 'Revolutionary Perspectives: German Jewish Women and 1918–19', *Journal of European Studies*, 51.2 (2021), 93–110.
17 Sidonie Smith and Julia Watson, *Reading Autobiography: A Guide for Interpreting Life Narratives* (Minneapolis, MN: University of Minnesota Press, 2001), 13–14.
18 Penny Summerfield, 'Culture and Composure: Creating Narratives of the Gendered Self in Oral History Interviews', *Cultural and Social History*, 1.1 (2004), 65–93, here 70–1.
19 Johanna Gehmacher, Elisa Heinrich and Corinna Oesch, *Käthe Schirmacher: Agitation und autobiografische Praxis zwischen radikaler Frauenbewegung und völkischer Politik* (Vienna: Böhlau, 2018), 513–28.
20 Martyn Lyons, '"Ordinary Writing" or How the "Illiterate" Speak to Historians', in Martyn Lyons (eds.), *Ordinary Writings, Personal Narratives: Writing Practices in 19th and early 20th Century Europe* (Bern: Peter Lang, 2007), 13–31; Barbara Caine, *Biography and History* (Basingstoke: Palgrave Macmillan, 2010), 5–6; Bernd Jürgen Warneken, 'Social Differences in the Autobiographic Representation of the Self', in Christa Hämmerle (ed.), *Plurality and Individuality: Autobiographical Cultures in Europe* (Vienna: IFK-Materialien, 1995), 7–14.
21 Joannou, '"She who would be politically free"', 32.
22 The reasons why gender has been neglected are different in each national context, and Chapter 4 discusses this in relation to suffrage. For an in-depth examination of the Hungarian case, see Andrea Pető and Judith Szapor, 'The State of Women's and Gender History in Eastern Europe: The Case of Hungary', *Journal of Women's History*, 19.1 (2007), 160–6.
23 Ernőné Müller, *Eszmélés* (Budapest: Kossuth, 1964), 190–3.
24 Ibid., 203.
25 Ibid., 197–9.
26 György Dalos, *A cselekvés szerelmese* (Budapest: Kossuth, 1984), 22–51.
27 Müller, *Eszmélés*, 383–4.
28 'Die Frauen und die Nationalversammlung: Das Frauenwahlrecht', *Die Revolutionäre Proletarierin: Beilage zur Sozialen Revolution*, 26.1/2 (8 February 1919), 5–6 (translated by Veronika Helfert).

29 See Helfert, *Frauen, wacht auf!*, 253–6.
30 Käthe Pick (Käthe Leichter), 'Der österreichische Rätekongreß: Die Rätebewegung II', ed. by Günter Hillmann (Reinbek bei Hamburg: Rowohlt, 1972), 93.
31 Ilona Ducynska, *Der demokratische Bolschewik: Zur Theorie und Praxis der Gewalt* (Munich: List, 1975), 110.
32 Käthe Leichter, *100.000 Kinder auf einen Hieb. Die Frau als Zuchtstute im Dritten Reich* (Sozialistische Kampfschriften 1) (Vienna: Verlag der Wiener Volksbuchhandlung, 1931).
33 Alexandra Kollontai and Polina Vinogradskaia (eds.), *Otchet o pervoi mezhdunarodnoi konferentsii kommunistok* (*Report on the First International Conference of Communist Women*) (Moscow: Gosizdatelstvo, 1921), pp. 25–7. With many thanks to Ivelina Masheva for the information.
34 Anna Hornik, *This is Austria: The Story of a Beautiful Country* (London: Austria Centre, 1942).
35 Anthony Grenville, 'The Politics of the Austrian Centre', in Marietta Bearman, Charmian Brinson, Richard Dove, Anthony Grenville and Jennifer Taylor (eds.), *Out of Austria: The Austrian Centre in London in World War II* (London and New York: Tauris Academic Studies, 2008), 22–52.
36 See, for instance, her articles in the pro-Communist trade union publication *die arbeit*, issues March and April 1949 as well as March 1950.
37 Irma Schwager, 'Anna Hornik-Ströhmer (1890–1966): Eine Frau, die nicht vergessen werden darf', *Mitteilungen der Alfred-Klahr-Gesellschaft*, 4 (2006), 21.
38 Helen Boak, 'Women in Weimar Politics', *European History Quarterly*, 20.3 (1990), 369–99.
39 Saran mentions the socialist and author Dora Russell, wife of Bertrand, and the anti-colonialist campaigner Rita Hinden, among many other names. Saran, *Never Give Up*, 75–7.
40 Saran, *Never Give Up*, 96.
41 Hilde Kramer, *Rebellin in München, Moskau und Berlin: Autobiographisches Fragment 1900–1924* (Berlin: BasisDruck, 2011).
42 Willi Eichler, Wilhelm Heidorn, Mary Saran and Minna Specht, *Re-making Germany* (London: International Publishing Company, 1945).
43 Anica Lokar, *Od Anice do Ane Antonovne* (Ljubljana: Mladinska knjiga, 2002), 12.
44 Ibid., 51.
45 Angela Vode, *Spomin in pozaba* (Ljubljana: Krtina, 2000), 97 and Gusti Jirku Stridsberg, *Mojih Pet življenj* (Maribor: Obzorja, 1983), 223.
46 Stridsberg, *Mojih Pet življenj*, 223.
47 Lokar, *Od Anice do Ane Antonovne*, 147.
48 Ibid., 70.

49 Letter from Anica Lokar to Danilo Lokar, 16 February 1953, NUK, Manuscript Collection, Ms 1389.
50 Letter from Anica Lokar to Danilo Lokar, 16 July 1963, NUK, Manuscript Collection, Ms 1389.
51 Letters from Anica Lokar to Danilo Lokar, 1 April 1952 and 23 December 1956, NUK, Manuscript Collection, Ms 1389.
52 Biblioteka ZRC SAZU, R 105/1, 2 (Archive of the Research Centre of the Slovenian Academy of Sciences and Arts).
53 Lokar, *Od Anice do Ane Antonovne*, 169.
54 Peter Haumer, 'Wer kennt schon Berta Pölz? Eine Reportage', in Theresa Adamski et al. (eds.), *Geschlechtergeschichten vom Genuss: Zum 60. Geburtstag von Gabriella Hauch* (Vienna: Mandelbaum, 2019), 222–36.
55 Sabine Lichtenberger, '"... durchaus nicht nur ernste Wissenschaftlerin und Politikerin". Eine Erinnerung an Käthe Leichter (1895–1942) und ihre Praxis eines genussvollen Lebens', in Theresa Adamski, Doreen Blake, Veronika Duma, Veronika Helfert and Michaela Neuwirth (eds.), *Geschlechtergeschichten vom Genuss: Zum 60. Geburtstag von Gabriella Hauch* (Vienna: Mandelbaum, 2019), 32–51, here 51.
56 Letter from Ilona Polanyi-Duczynska to Ernst K. Herlitzka, 8 June 1970, Verein für Geschichte der Arbeiterbewegung, Vienna, llona Duczysnka Papers, Box 3.
57 Kenneth McRobbie, 'Under the Sign of the Pendulum: Childhood Experience as Determining Revolutionary Consciousness: Ilona Duczynska Polanyi (1897–1978)', *Canadian Journal of History*, 42.2 (2006), 263–98.
58 Ilona Duczynska, 'Zum Zerfall der K.P.U.', Unser Weg, 4/5 (1922), 97–105.
59 György Dalos, *A cselekvés szerelmese* (Budapest: Kossuth, 1984).
60 Ducynska, *Der demokratische Bolschewik*, 290.
61 Saran, *Never Give Up*, 115.
62 Ibid., 117.
63 See for example Ellen Wilkinson (1891–1947) or Phillis Skinner (1874–1950).
64 See Zsófia Lóránd et al. (eds.), *Texts and Contexts from the History of Feminism and Women's Rights in East Central Europe* (Vienna: CEU Press, forthcoming).
65 Cläre Jung, *Paradiesvogel* (Hamburg: Nautilus, 1987).
66 Isa Strasser, Theresa Adamski et al., Brief an den Leser, in *Land ohne Schlaf: Roman* (Vienna: Europa, 1970), 9 (translated by Veronika Helfert).
67 Pavla Hočevar, *Pot se vije* (Trieste: ZTT, 1969), 98, 110.
68 Lokar, *Od Anice do Ane Antonovne*, 62.
69 Ibid., 69.
70 Ibid., 73.
71 Ibid., 88–96.
72 Stridsberg, *Mojih Pet življenj*, 178.

73 Lokar, *Od Anice do Ane Antonovne*, 115.
74 Ibid., 117.
75 Ibid., 126.
76 See Mario Kessler, *Ruth Fischer: Ein Leben mit und gegen Kommunisten (1895–1961)* (Vienna: Böhlau Verlag, 2013).
77 Magda Aranyossi (with the commentaries of Péter Nádas), *Én régi, elsüllyedt világom* (Budapest: Jelenkor, 2018). For a recent study on the post-war, Soviet-sponsored women's organizations across Europe, see Celia Donert and Christine Moll-Murata (eds.), 'Women's Rights and Global Socialism', *International Review of Social History*, 67.30 (2022).
78 Jolán Kelen, *Eliramlik az élet* (Budapest: Kossuth, 1976).
79 Ibid., 212–14.
80 Ibid., 226–8.
81 See for example Angela Vode, 'Socializem in žena' ('Socialism and Woman'), *Naprej: Glasilo jugoslovanske socialno-demokratične stranke* (*Forward: Newspaper of Yugoslav Social Democratic Party*), IV, 9 April 1920, 1 and *Žena v sedanji družbi* (*Woman in Today's Society*) (Maribor: Žena in dom, 1934).
82 Jung, *Paradiesvogel*, 61.
83 Rosa Luxemburg's 1897 marriage to Gustav Lübeck to gain German citizenship is a well-known example.
84 Enzo Traverso, *Left-Wing Melancholia: Marxism, History, and Memory* (New York: Columbia University Press, 2016), 3.

6 Commemorating Revolution, Commemorating Women

1 Lucy Noakes, 'Gender, War and Memory: Discourse and Experience in History', *Journal of Contemporary History*, 36.4 (2001), 663–72 (here 664).
2 Roisín Higgins, *Transforming 1916: Meaning, Memory and the Fiftieth Anniversary of the Easter Rising* (Cork: Cork University Press, 2012), 22.
3 Alan Kramer, 'Recent Historiography of the First World War (Part I)', *Journal of Modern European History / Zeitschrift für moderne europäische Geschichte / Revue d'histoire européenne contemporaine*, 12.1 (2014), 5–27 (here 15). See also Ian Ousby, *The Road to Verdun: France, Nationalism and the First World War* (London: Jonathan Cape, 2002).
4 Kramer, 'Recent Historiography', 15. The collection of essays is Gerhard Hirschfeld, Gerd Krumeich and Irina Renz (eds.), *Scorched Earth: The Germans on the Somme 1914–1918* (Barnsley: Pen & Sword, 2009).
5 Matt McDonald, 'Remembering Gallipoli: Anzac, the Great War and Australian Memory Politics', *Australian Journal of Politics and History*, 63.3 (2017), 406–18.

6 Kramer, 'Recent Historiography', 19.
7 Maggie Andrews, 'Poppies, Tommies and Remembrance: Commemoration is Always Contested', *Soundings: A Journal of Politics and Culture*, 58 (2014–15), 104–15 (here 105).
8 For a gendered comparison of European commemorative practice, see Christa Hämmerle, Ingrid Sharp and Heidrun Zettelbauer (eds.), *L'Homme, Zeitschrift für feministische Geschichtswissenschaft, 1914/18 – revisited*.
9 McDonald, 'Remembering Gallipoli', 417.
10 Tiina Lintunen and Anne Heimo, 'Monisärmäinen punainen historia', *Ennen ja nyt*, 21.4 (2021), 31; Pilvi Torsti, 'Historiapolitiikkaa tutkimaan – Historian poliittisen käytön typologian kehittelyä', *Kasvatus & Aika*, 2.2 (2008), 61–71; Jukka Rantala, 'Historiapolitiikkaa koulun opetussuunnitelman avulla', *Politiikka*, 60.2 (2018), 112–23; Pertti Grönholm ja Heino Nyyssönen, 'Historian käyttö ennen ja nyt – faktana ja fiktiona', *Kosmopolis*, 49.3 (2019), 7–27.
11 The Expert Advisory Group on Centenary Commemorations, https://www.decadeofcentenaries.com/expert-advisory-group (accessed 11 November 2021).
12 This was reflected in a conference convened by the Foreign Office in Berlin in December 2014, which sought to establish a common European narrative. An English version of 'Speech by Foreign Minister Frank-Walter Steinmeier at the "Europäische Erinnerungskulturen" (European Commemoration) conference in the Weltsaal at the Federal Foreign Office – Federal Foreign Office)' can be found at https://www.auswaertiges-amt.de/en/newsroom/news/141217-bm-erinnerungskulturen/267828 (accessed 4 June 2022).
13 James Wertsch, *Voices of Collective Remembering* (Cambridge: Cambridge University Press, 2002), 11.
14 Jenny Edkins, *Trauma and the Memory of Politics* (Cambridge: Cambridge University Press, 2003), 54.
15 Kalle Pihlainen, 'Historia, historiatietoisuus ja menneisyyden käyttö', *Kasvatus & Aika*, 5.3 (2011), 5–17.
16 Jorma Kalela, *Making History: The Historian and Uses of the Past* (London: Palgrave Macmillan, 2011). See also Lintunen and Heimo, 'Monisärmäinen punainen historia', 32.
17 Aleida Assmann and Sebastian Conrad (eds.), *Memory in a Global Age: Discourses, Practices and Trajectories* (Basingstoke: Palgrave Macmillan, 2010), 2.
18 Cynthia Enloe, *Bananas, Beaches and Bases: Making Feminist Sense of International Politics* (Berkeley, CA: University of California Press, 1990), 45.
19 Lintunen and Heimo, 'Monisärmäinen punainen historia', 32, 34.
20 Tiina Kinnunen, 'The Post-Cold War Memory Culture of the Civil War: Old-New Patterns and New Approaches', in Tuomas Tepora and Aapo Roselius (eds.), *The Finnish Civil War 1918* (Leiden: Brill, 2014), 401–39.

21 John R. Gillis (ed.), *Commemorations: The Politics of National Identity* (Princeton, NJ: Princeton University Press, 1994), 5.
22 Ibid.
23 Ibid., 10.
24 Aleida Assmann, 'Transnational Memories', *European Review*, 22.4 (2014), 546–56 (here 550).
25 Ibid.
26 Ibid., 555.
27 Niko Kannisto, *Vaaleanpunainen tasavalta: SDP, itsenäisyys ja kansallisen yhtenäisyyden kysymys vuosina 1918–1924* (Helsinki: Työväen historian ja perinteen tutkimuksen seura, 2016).
28 Edgar Wolfrum, Odila Triebel, Cord Arendes, Angela Siebold and Joana Duyster Borredà (eds.), *European Commemoration: Locating World War I* (Stuttgart: Institut für Auslandsbeziehungen, 2016), 7.
29 Ibid., 7.
30 Ibid., 6.
31 Ibid., 6.
32 Keith Jeffrey, 'Irish Varieties of Great War Commemoration', in John Horne and Edward Madigan (eds.), *Towards Commemoration: Ireland in War and Revolution, 1912–1923* (Dublin: Royal Irish Academy, 2013), 117–25 (here 120).
33 Wolfrum et al. (eds.), *European Commemoration*, 6.
34 Oona Frawley, *Women and the Decade of Commemorations* (Bloomington, IN: Indiana University Press, 2019), 16.
35 Ibid.
36 Christa Hämmerle, Ingrid Sharp and Heidrun Zettelbauer (eds.), *L'Homme, Zeitschrift für feministische Geschichtswissenschaft*, 29.2 (2018), 1914/18 – revisited.
37 Frawley, *Women and the Decade of Commemorations*, 18; Edkins, *Trauma and the Memory of Politics*.
38 Rebecca Graff McRae, *Remembering and Forgetting 1916: Commemoration and Conflict on a Post-Peace Process Ireland* (Dublin: Irish Academic Press, 2010), 2.
39 Ibid., 5.
40 Ibid., 123.
41 Jonathan Evershed, *Ghosts of the Somme: Commemoration and Culture War in Northern Ireland* (South Bend: University of Notre Dame Press, 2018).
42 Wolfrum et al. (eds.), *European Commemoration*, 6.
43 The Third Home Rule Bill, had it worked, would have secured a Parliament in Dublin with limited self-government. It was opposed by the Protestant Unionist minority and eventually shelved when war broke out in 1914. The 1913 lock-out strike was a violent conformation between employers and trade unions, which led to the employers 'locking out' the workers in Dublin from late August 1913 to January

1914, in a bitter dispute over trade union membership. The 1916 Rising was a weeklong rebellion to break the link with Britain, taking place from 24 to 29 April 1916. The Rising was defeated but directly led to the outbreak of an Independence War in 1919. This ended in 1921 with the Anglo-Irish Treaty, which cemented the existence of two States on the island of Ireland: the Irish Free State (now the Irish Republic) and Northern Ireland. A brief, bloody and bitter civil war consumed the Irish Free State at its foundation – in which the Free State emerged victorious.

44 Clare County Council Guidelines for Assistance: Decade of Centenaries Arts Project Awards 2021, https://www.clarecoco.ie/services/arts-recreation/arts-office/funding-and-opportunities/guidelines-for-decade-of-centenaries-arts-project-awards-2021-41496.pdf (accessed 4 June 2022).

45 Ibid.

46 The Markievicz Award, https://www.artscouncil.ie/Funds/Markievicz-Award (accessed 4 June 2022).

47 Lauren Arrington, 'Constance Markievicz and the Idea of Ireland', 37th Annual Constance Markievicz Lecture Irish Association of Industrial Relations, 29 November 2013, at https://www.ul.ie/iair/sites/default/files/2013%20lecture%20by%20Dr.%20Lauren%20Arrington.pdf (accessed 4 June 2022).

48 See Ingrid Sharp, 'How Do Germany and Britain Remember the First World War, and Can the Differences Explain Brexit?', *Beyond the Trenches*, 28 October 2016, at http://beyondthetrenches.co.uk/how-do-germany-and-britain-remember-the-first-world-war-and-can-the-differences-explain-brexit (accessed 12 March 2018).

49 https://www.gov.uk/government/news/government-announces-scheme-to-commemorate-ww1 (accessed 10 March 2018).

50 'Why Does the Left Insist on Belittling True British Heroes?', by Michael Gove, Education Secretary, http://www.dailymail.co.uk/news/article-2532923/Michael-Gove-blasts-Blackadder-myths-First-World-War-spread-television-sit-coms-left-wing-academics.html (accessed 12 March 2018).

51 Heather Jones, 'Goodbye To All That? Memory and Commemoration of the First World War', *Juncture*, 20.4 (2014), 287–91 (here 287).

52 For example, interest in Nurse Edith Cavell, arrested and executed in 1915 for her role in helping British soldiers escape from occupied Belgium.

53 See http://www.rcuk.ac.uk/innovation/impacts (accessed 12 March 2018).

54 These are: Voices of War and Peace, Birmingham; Gateways to War, Kent; Everyday Lives in War, Hertfordshire; The Centre for Hidden Histories, Nottingham; Living Legacies 1914–1918, Queen's University Belfast. See http://www.ahrc.ac.uk/research/fundedthemesandprogrammes/worldwaroneanditslegacy/worldwaroneengagementcentres (accessed 4 June 2022).

55 The HLF have funded a number of projects on the anti-war movement, including an award to a Peace Pledge Union project about conscientious objection and an

exhibition and performance at the Working Class Movement Library, which focused on conscientious objectors. See HLF projects https://www.hlf.org.uk/our-projects (accessed 8 May 2017).
56 BBC announces WW1 centenary programming, https://www.bbc.co.uk/mediacentre/latestnews/2013/world-war-one-centenary (accessed 4 June 2022). See also BBC World War One programmes, http://www.bbc.co.uk/programmes/p01nb93y (accessed 12 March 2018).
57 Kate Adie, *Fighting on the Home Front: The Legacy of Women in World War One* (London: Hodder, 2014); Jeremy Paxman, *Great Britain's Great War* (London: Viking, 2014).
58 David Olusoga, *The World's War. Forgotten Soldiers of Empire*, BBC 2 and book (London: Head of Zeus, 2015).
59 'BBC Teams Up with British Universities for Online Learning Pilot', http://www.bbc.co.uk/mediacentre/mediapacks/mooc/university-of-leeds (accessed 12 March 2018).
60 BBC Radio 4, *Voices of the First World War*, http://www.bbc.co.uk/programmes/b03t7p9l (accessed 7 April 2018).
61 BBC, *World War One at Home: Conscientious Objectors*, http://www.bbc.co.uk/programmes/p01nhwgx (accessed 7 April 2018).
62 *World War One at Home: Women*, http://www.bbc.co.uk/programmes/p01p329t (accessed 7 April 2018).
63 Ulla-Maija Peltonen, *Muistin paikat: Vuoden 1918 sisällissodan muistamisesta ja unohtamisesta* (Helsinki: Suomalaisen Kirjallisuuden Seura, 2003), 255–6.
64 Lintunen and Heimo, 'Monisärmäinen punainen historia', 39.
65 Ibid., 44.
66 Influential German scholarship on the First World War includes Ute Daniel, *The War from Within: German Working-Class Women in the First World War*, transl. by Margaret Ries (Oxford: Berg, 1997 [1989]); Karen Hagemann and Stefanie Schüler-Springorum (eds.), *Home/Front: The Military, War and Gender in Twentieth Century Germany* (Oxford: Berg, 2002); and Christa Hämmerle (ed.), *Heimat/Front: Geschlechtergeschichte/n des Ersten Weltkriegs in Österreich-Ungarn* (Vienna: Böhlau, 2014).
67 Exceptions to this include Kathleen Canning's publications: 'Das Geschlecht der Revolution – Stimmrecht und Staatsbürgertum 1918/19', in Alexander Gallus (ed.), *Die vergessene Revolution von 1918/19* (Göttingen: Vandenhoeck & Ruprecht, 2010), 84–116; 'Claiming Citizenship: Suffrage and Subjectivity in Germany after the First World War', in Kathleen Canning, Kerstin Barndt and Kristin McGuire (eds.), *Weimar Publics/Weimar Subjects: Rethinking the Political Culture of Germany in the 1920s* (New York and Oxford: Berghahn Books, 2010), 116–37; 'Gender and the Imaginary of Revolution in Germany', in Klaus Weinhauer, Anthony McElligott and Kirsten Heinsohn (eds.), *Germany, 1916–23: A Revolution in Context* (Bielefeld:

transcript, 2015), 103–26. On Austria, see Gabriella Hauch, *Frauen bewegen Politik: Österreich 1848–1938* (Innsbruck: StudienVerlag, 2009); and Veronika Helfert, *Frauen, wacht auf! Eine Frauen- und Geschlechtergeschichte von Revolution und Rätebewegung in Österreich, 1916–1924* (Göttingen: Vandenhoeck & Ruprecht, 2021).

68 Notably Benjamin Ziemann, 'Germany 1914–1918. Total War as a Catalyst of Change', in Helmut Walser Smith (ed.), *The Oxford Handbook of Modern German History* (Oxford: Oxford University Press, 2011), 378–99 (here 387).

69 Brigitte Studer, *Reisende der Weltrevolution: Eine Globalgeschichte der Kommunistischen Internationale* (Berlin: Suhrkamp, 2020).

70 https://www.historisches-lexikon-bayerns.de/images/2/2b/Rotgardist_Kaiser.jpg (accessed 4 June 2022). See also Volker Weidermann, *Dreamers: When the Writers Took Power – Germany, 1918*, transl. by Ruth Martin (London: Pushkin Press, 2018 [2017]).

71 Moritz Föllmer, 'The Unscripted Revolution: Male Subjectivities in Germany, 1918/19', *Past and Present*, 241 (2018), 161–92.

72 Sonja Kinzler and Doris Tillmann (eds.), *Die Stunde der Matrosen Kiel und die deutsche Revolution 1918*, Catalogue of Kiel Maritime Museum exhibition (Kiel: Theiss Verlag, 2018).

73 See Corinne Painter and Ingrid Sharp, 'Women of Aktion: Performance, Gender and the German Revolution of 1918', *Feminist German Studies*, 37.1 (2021), 38–60.

74 1917. REVOLUTION. RUSSLAND UND EUROPA, https://www.dhm.de/ausstellungen/archiv/2017/1917-revolution (accessed 4 June 2022).

75 Democracy [DEMOKRATIE 2019, WEIMAR: VOM WESEN UND WIRKEN DER DEMOKRATIE], https://www.dhm.de/ausstellungen/2019/demokratie-2019/weimar (accessed 4 June 2022).

76 Project 100 Jahre Revolution Berlin 1918/19, https://www.100jahrerevolution.berlin (accessed 4 June 2022).

77 See https://www.gda.bayern.de/aktuelles/revolution-und-raeterepubliken-in-bayern-1918-19 (accessed 4 June 2022) and https://www.guardini90.de/schlaglichter (accessed 4 June 2022).

78 Dichtung ist Revolution | Ausstellungen in München, https://muenchen-ausstellungen.de/monacensia-im-hildebrandhaus-dichtung-ist-revolution (accessed 4 June 2022).

79 Officially, the Decade was 2012–22, beginning with the commemoration of the Third Home Bill (which would grant Ireland its own Parliament and a limited freedom) in the Houses of Parliament in 1912 and ending with the establishment of the Irish Free State in 1922 after a violent War of Independence, 1919–21 and the signing of a treaty with Britain. Most people, however, include 2023, to end the decade with a commemoration of the brief but bloody civil war which followed Independence.

80 President of Ireland, Michael D. Higgins, *Machnamh 100: President of Ireland, Centenary Reflections*, Vol. 1 (Department of Tourism, Culture, Arts, Gaeltacht, Sports and Media, 2021), 32. *Machnamh* means *Reflection*.
81 Ibid., 36.
82 *Machnamh 100*, Third Seminar, 'Land Social Class, Gender and the Sources of Violence; Recovering Reimagined Futures', 27 May 2021. The fourth seminar was titled 'Settlements, Schisms and Civil Strife', and took place on 5 November 2021, https://president.ie/en/news/article/machnamh-100-president-of-irelands-centenary-reflections (accessed 4 June 2022).
83 'President of Ireland Centenary Reflections speakers announced', Hot Press, 4 December 2020, https://president.ie/en/media-library/news-releases/machnamh-100-president-of-ireland-centenary-reflections-volume-1 (accessed 9 November 2021).
84 The Expert Advisory Group on Centenary Commemorations, https://www.decadeofcentenaries.com/expert-advisory-group (accessed 11 November 2021).
85 Initial Statement by the Expert Advisory Group on Centenary Commemorations (2012), https://www.decadeofcentenaries.com/publications (accessed 7 April 2021).
86 Ibid., 3.
87 Mary Jones, *Those Obstreperous Lassies: A History of the Irish Women Worker's Union* (Dublin: Gill and Macmillan, 1988), 1.
88 Ibid.
89 Ibid.
90 Donal Nevin, *James Larkin: The Lion of the Fold* (Dublin: Gill Books, 2006), 94.
91 Karen Hunt, 'Women, Solidarity and the 1913 Dublin Lockout: Dora Montefiore and the "Save the Kiddies" Scheme', in Francis Devine (ed.), *1913: A Capital in Conflict – Dublin City and the 1913 Lockout* (Dublin: Dublin City Council, 2013), 107.
92 Ibid., 110.
93 Ibid.
94 Ibid., 111.
95 Ibid., 122.
96 Ibid., 123.
97 Ibid., 124, This was at a rally held at the Albert Hall in London, on 1 November 1913, to fundraise for the scheme.
98 Ibid., 126.
99 Commemorating the Irish Women Workers' Union, 8 March 2013, at https://www.siptu.ie/media/newsarchive2013/fullstory_17051_en.html (accessed 4 June 2022).
100 Angelina Cox, Lisa Connell and Jeni Gartland, 'The Rosie Hackett Bridge Campaign: The Rediscovery of a Forgotten History', in Mary McAuliffe (ed.), *Rosie: Essays in Honour of Rosanna 'Rosie' Hackett (1893–1976), Revolutionary and Trade Unionist* (Dublin: Arlen House, 2015), 15–21.

101 The Rosie Hackett Bridge was opened in May 2014. Affectionately known as the 'Rosie', its city centre location and association with a Socialist and revolutionary woman has meant that many left-wing campaigns now hold media events and protests on the 'Rosie'.
102 Cumann na mBan 100; centenary commemorations of Cumann na mBan, 2–5 April 2014, at https://womenshistoryassociation.com/events/past-events/cumann-na-mban-100 (accessed 4 June 2022).
103 Laura McAtackney, 'Public Memory, Conflict and Women: Commemoration in Contemporary Ireland', in Paul Astoon, Tanya Evans and Paula Hamilton (eds.), *Making Histories* (Oldenburg: DeGruyter, 2020), 99–112 (here 104).
104 Ibid., 104.
105 See Mary McAuliffe, Liz Gillis, Éadaoin Ní Chléirigh and Marja Almqvist, 'Forgetting and Remembering – Uncovering Women's Histories at Richmond Barracks: A Public History Project', *Studies in Arts and Humanities*, 2.1 (2016), 17–32; Mary McAuliffe and Liz Gillis, *We Were There – 77 Women of the Easter Rising* (Dublin: Four Courts Press, 2016); and Mary McAuliffe and Liz Gillis, *77 Women of Richmond Barracks*, https://www.richmondbarracks.ie/exhibitions/77-women-richmond-barracks (accessed 4 June 2022).
106 Mary Moynihan, 'How Waking the Feminists Set an Equality Agenda for Irish Theatre', https://www.rte.ie/brainstorm/2018/1122/1012586-how-waking-the-feminists-set-an-equality-agenda-for-irish-theatre (accessed 11 July 2021).
107 Ibid.
108 'Gender Counts: An Analysis of Gender in Irish Theatre 2006–15', at http://www.wakingthefeminists.org/research-report (accessed 11 July 2021).
109 'Guidance from the Expert Advisory Group on Commemorations to Support the State's Approach to the Remembrance of Significant Historical Events over the Remainder of the Decade of Centenaries', https://irishmuseums.org/uploads/downloads/publications/guidance-from-the-expert-advisory-group-on-commemorations-over-the-remainder-of-the-decade-of-centenaries-eng-1.pdf (accessed 11 July 2021).
110 'Decade of Centenaries 2012–2023 – 2021' Programme, https://www.decadeofcentenaries.com/wp-content/uploads/publications/DOC2012-23 (accessed 10 November 2021).
111 https://www.mna100.ie/about-mna-100 (accessed 4 June 2022). It will also include a section on women's histories over the last 100 years – 'the "100 Year Journey" that Irish women have taken, documenting the actions of individuals and the collective actions of groups', during that time.
112 The Markievicz Award, https://www.artscouncil.ie/Funds/Markievicz-Award (accessed 10 November 2021).
113 Bimpe Archer, 'New exhibits to go on show for Irish Wars 1919–1923 exhibition at National Museum of Ireland', *Irish News*, 23 January 2020, at https://www.

irishnews.com/news/northernirelandnews/2020/01/23/news/new-exhibits-to-go-on-show-for-irish-wars-1919-1923-exhibition-at-national-museum-of-ireland-1821627 (accessed 7 April 2021); Irish Wars, 1919–1923, at https://www.museum.ie/en-IE/Museums/Decorative-Arts-History/Exhibitions/Irish-Wars-1919-to-1923 (accessed 7 April 2021).

114 Women and Violence in Irish Wars, https://www.museum.ie/en-IE/Collections-Research/Collection/Women-and-Violence-in-the-Irish-Wars (accessed 4 June 2022).

115 Other publications include Rosemary Cullen Owens, *A Social History of Women in Ireland, 1870–1970* (Dublin: Gill and Macmillan, 2005); Senia Pašeta, *Irish Nationalist Women, 1900–1918* (Cambridge: Cambridge University Press, 2014); Cal MacCarthy, *Cumann na mBan and the Irish Revolution* (Cork: The Collins Press, 2014); Roy Foster, *Vivid Faces: The Revolutionary Generation in Ireland, 1890–1923* (London: Penguin, 2014); Lauren Arrington, *Revolutionary Lives: Constance and Casimir Markievicz* (Princeton, NJ: Princeton University Press, 2015); Margaret Ward, *Fearless Woman: Hanna Sheehy Skeffington, Feminism and the Irish Revolution* (Dublin: UCD Press, 2019); Leeann Lane, *Dorothy Macardle* (Dublin: UCD Press, 2019); Mary McAuliffe, *Margaret Skinnider* (Dublin: UCD Press, 2020); and Hillary Dully (ed.), *Máire Comerford: On Dangerous Ground – A Memoir of the Irish Revolution* (Dublin: Lilliput Press, 2021).

116 Military Service Pensions Collection (MSPC), https://www.militaryarchives.ie/collections/online-collections/military-service-pensions-collection-1916-1923/about-the-collection/origin-and-scope (accessed 7 November 2021).

117 Report of the Inter-Departmental Committee to Establish the Facts of State Involvement with the Magdalen Laundries (2013), https://www.justice.ie/en/JELR/Pages/MagdalenRpt2013 (accessed 4 June 2022); Final Report of the Commission of Investigation into Mother and Baby Homes, https://www.gov.ie/en/publication/d4b3d-final-report-of-the-commission-of-investigation-into-mother-and-baby-homes (accessed 11 November 2021).

118 Dorothee Linnemann (ed.), *Damenwahl! 100 Jahre Frauenwahlrecht*, Historisches Museum Frankfurt Exhibition catalogue 2019.

119 'Project 100 Jahre Revolution Berlin 1918/19', at https://www.100jahrerevolution.berlin/programm/frauen-in-der-novemberrevolution (accessed 4 June 2022).

120 Wolfgang Niess, *Die Revolution von 1918/19: Der wahre Beginn unserer Demokratie* (Munich: EuropaVerlag, 2017).

121 Gallus (ed.), *Die vergessene Revolution von 1918/19*.

122 See note 67 above.

123 See https://www.bundespraesident.de/SharedDocs/Reden/DE/Frank-Walter-Steinmeier/Reden/2019/02/190206-Weimar-100-Jahre-Reichsverfassung.html (accessed 4 June 2022).

124 Sylvia Paletschek and Sylvia Schraut, 'Introduction: Gender and Memory Culture in Europe – Female Representations in Historical Perspective', in Sylvia Paletschek and Sylvia Schraut (eds.), *The Gender of Memory: Cultures of Remembrance in Nineteenth- and Twentieth-Century Europe* (Frankfurt/Main and New York: Campus, 2008), 26.

Further Reading

This is a list of recommended books, book chapters and articles in English. Those who wish to delve deeper, including into non-English language works, should consult the endnotes at the end of each chapter.

Abolavatski, Eliza, *Revolution and Political Violence in Central Europe: The Deluge of 1919* (Cambridge: Cambridge University, 2021).
Canning, Kathleen, 'Claiming Citizenship: Suffrage and Subjectivity after the First World War', in Kathleen Canning, Kerstin Brandt and Kristin McGuire (eds.), *Weimar Publics/Weimar Subjects: Rethinking the Political Culture of Germany in the 1920s* (New York: Berghahn Books, 2010), 116–37.
Cox, Mary E., *Hunger in War and Peace: Women and Children in Germany, 1914–1924* (Oxford: Oxford University Press, 2019).
Daniel, Ute, *The War from Within: German Working-Class Women in the First World War*, transl. by Margaret Ries (Oxford: Berg, 1997 [1989]).
Eley, Geoff, *Forging Democracy: The History of the Left in Europe, 1850–2000* (Oxford: Oxford University Press, 2002).
Hannam, June and Hunt, Karen, *Socialist Women: Britain, 1880s to 1920s* (London and New York: Routledge, 2002).
Hauch, Gabriella, 'Sisters and Comrades: Women's Movements and the "Austrian Revolution" – Gender in Insurrection, the *Räte* Movement, Parties and Parliament', in Ingrid Sharp and Matthew Stibbe (eds.), *Aftermaths of War: Women's Movements and Female Activists, 1918–1923* (Leiden: Brill, 2011), 221–43.
Helfert, Veronika, 'Between Pacifism and Militancy: Socialist Women in the First Austrian Republic, 1918–1934', *Diplomacy and Statecraft*, 31.4 (2020), 648–72.
Lintunen, Tiina, 'Women at War', in Aapo Roselius and Tuomas Tepora (eds.), *The Finnish Civil War 1918: History, Memory, Legacy* (Leiden: Brill, 2014), 201–29.
McAuliffe, Mary and Gillis, Liz, *We Were There – 77 Women of the Easter Rising* (Dublin: Four Courts Press, 2016).
Painter, Corinne, 'Revolutionary Perspectives: German Jewish Women and 1918–19', *Journal of European Studies*, 51.2 (2021), 93–110.
Scott, Joan W., 'Gender: A Useful Category of Historical Analysis', *American Historical Journal*, 91.5 (1986), 1030–75.
Sharp, Ingrid and Stibbe, Matthew (eds.), *Women Activists between War and Peace: Europe, 1918–1923* (London: Bloomsbury Academic, 2017).
Siegel, Mona L., *Peace on Our Terms: The Global Battle for Women's Rights After the First World War* (New York: Columbia University Press, 2020).

Stibbe, Matthew, Painter, Corinne and Sharp, Ingrid, 'History beyond the Script: Rethinking Female Subjectivities and Socialist Women's Activism during and after the German Revolution of 1918–1919', in Christopher Dillon and Kim Wünschmann (eds.), *Living the German Revolution of 1918–19: Expectations, Experiences, Responses* (Oxford: Oxford University Press, forthcoming).

Szapor, Judith, *Hungarian Women's Activism in the Wake of the First World War: From Rights to Revanche* (London: Bloomsbury, 2018).

Todorova, Maria, *The Lost World of Socialists at Europe's Margins: Imagining Utopia, 1870s–1920s* (London: Bloomsbury, 2020).

Index

Addams, Jane 122
adult suffrage, 9, 11, 14, 15, 16, 18, 51, 99, 100, 102, 114, 116, 119, 131, 199
Agnes, Lore 128
AHRC (Arts and Humanities Research Council, UK) 180-1, 244 n.54
Allied blockade (economic, food), 44, 51, 62, 63, 126
American Commission on Conditions in Ireland, The 88, 226 n.98
Aranyossi, Magda 106, 141, 163-5, 240 n.77
arbeit, die (Austria) 238 n.36
Arbeiterin, Die (Austria) 150
Arbeiterinnen-Zeitung, Die (Austria) 59, 73, 205 n.59, 218 n.137, 223 nn.38-9
Arbeiter-Zeitung, Die (Austria) 22, 153, 159, 201 n.12, 208 n.101, 227 n.124
Arendsee, Martha 6, 24, 44, 151, 214 n.61
Armand, Inessa 36-7
Ashton, Margaret 130, 232 n.67
Atanacković, Milena 121
Austrian civil war (1934) 138-9, 157

Backman, Tyyne 77
Balabanova, Angelica 36, 145, 159
Bang, Nina 10
Barton, Eleanor 102
Bauer, Otto 90, 226 n.104
BBC (British Broadcasting Corporation) 180-1, 244 n.56, 244 nn.59-62
BDF (Bund deutscher Frauenvereine, Germany) 113-14
Beauchamp, Joan 41
Bebel, August 12, 107, 153
Behr, Helene 65, 66, 220 n.6
Beiersdorf, Franz 80, 88
Berliner Tageblatt (Germany) 92, 226 n.103
Bern Peace Manifesto (1915) 35-9, 43, 49
Berner Tagewacht (Switzerland) 36, 212 n.24

Berzeviczy, Gizella 117-18, 232 nn.68-9
Black and Tans (Ireland) 85
Bloch-Bollag, Rosa 54-6
Blood Roses, The 181-2
Blos, Anna, 119, 233 n.73
Bogdanović, Katarina 121, 233 n.77
Bondfield, Margaret 34, 35, 102
Bosch, Yevgeniya 77
Boschek, Anna 25
Brennan, Robert 86
Brennan, Una 86
Brockway, Fenner 35
Budapest Republic of Councils (1919) 117, 118, 145, 146, 156, 164
Bund für Mutterschutz (Germany) 46

Call, The (UK) 115
Casper-Derfert, Cläre 50, 215 n.92, 216 n.96, 224 n.63
censorship 36, 42, 59, 73, 155, 163, 212 n.19
Central European revolutions (1848) 4-5, 201 nn.10-12
Childers, Erskine 86, 225 n.82
Clarke, Kathleen 85, 98, 225 n.80
Clemenceau, Georges 9
CO (Conscientious objector/objection to military service) 7, 41, 60, 64, 180, 185, 244 n.55
Cold War 136-7, 139, 167, 242 n.20
Comerford, Maire 82, 85, 225 n.75, 248 n.115
Comintern (Communist International) 37, 136, 150, 157, 160, 209 n.115, 229 n.28
Communist Party of Yugoslavia 141-2
Conditions in Ireland (1921) 88
Conlon, Lil 85, 89, 225 n.77, 226 n.100
Connelly, May 84
Connolly, James 20, 192, 224 n.51
Connory, Meg 89
Cooper, Selina 60, 172, 184-5, 228 n.13
Courtney, Katherine (Kate) 116

CPGB (Communist Party of Great Britain) 2, 41
Crawfurd, Helen 46, 60, 61
Crimmitschau textile strike (1903–4) 1–3, 201 n.1, 201 n.3
Cumann na mBan – (Republican) Council of Women (Ireland) 70, 75, 76, 83, 84–6, 193, 196, 197, 221 n.15, 225 n.77, 226 n.100, 247 n.102, 248 n.115

Da-Cacodia, Louise 130
Dacre Fox, Nora 119, 233 n.71
Daily Herald, The (UK) 115
Daily Mail, The (UK) 86, 178
Decade of Centenaries (Ireland, 1912–23/2012–23) 67, 171, 172, 177, 178, 188–97, 243 n.44, 247 nn.109–10
Delacroix, Eugène 4
Democratic Alliance of Hungarian Women 163–4
Derbyshire, Ethel 60
deserters (First World War) 5, 7, 60, 64, 72, 165
Despard, Charlotte 126, 192, 233 n.71
disabled ex-soldiers 34, 40, 207 n.95
DORA (Defence of the Realm Act, UK) 125
Dreadnought, The (UK) 116
Dresdner Nachrichten (Germany) 14
Dublin lock-out strike (1913–14) 20, 76, 177–8, 190–2, 243 n.43
Duczynska, Ilona, (married name Polanyi) 13, 117, 141, 143, 145, 148, 149, 155, 156, 157, 164, 204 n.55, 239 nn.56–8
Duncker, Käthe 44

Easter Rising (Ireland 1916) 75, 177, 178, 194, 195, 206 n.89, 221 n.15, 224 n.51, 240 n.2, 243 n.43
Ebert, Friedrich 81
EFF (Election Fighting Fund, UK) 116–17
Eisner, Kurt 12, 56, 188
Ennenbach, Sophie 43–4, 214 n.57, 214 n.59, 214 n.62
Erfurt, Anna 66, 81
Exten-Hann, Florence 41

Fahrenwald, Agnes 44
False Betrayal (Falscher Verrat) 187

Fawcett, Millicent 129, 232 n.65
Federation of Democratic Women (post-1945 Austria) 150
Fellman's Field – A Living Monument of 22,000 People 183
Feminist Association of Hungary 105
Finnish civil war (1918) 69, 74, 75, 80, 87, 174, 220 n.14, 222 n.28, 242 n.20
Fischer, Ruth (aka Elfriede Eisler-Friedländer) 94, 135, 139, 142, 147, 155, 163, 227, 237 n.10, 240 n.76
Forward (Scotland) 46
French revolutions (1789, 1830, 1848) 4, 52
Freundlich, Emmy 148, 150
Frey, Anna (née Schlesinger) 13
Friedländer, Paul 94, 135
FRSI (Federation of Revolutionary Socialists International, Austria) 140, 147
Fürth, Henriette 39–40, 212 n.32

Galileo Circle 13–14, 117, 145–6, 157, 164, 204 n.55
Gaskell, Elizabeth 130
Girls 1918 181–2
Glasgow rent strike (1915) 7, 46, 214 n.71
Glasier, Katherine Bruce 102
Gleichheit, Die (Germany) 10, 15, 36, 103, 111, 119, 131, 212 n.19, 229 nn.24–5, 233 n.73
Gramsci, Antonio 160
Gulag (Soviet Union) 163–5
Gustinčič, Dragotin 153–4, 160

Haase, Hugo 12
Hackett, Rosie 192, 193
hair cropping (Ireland) 83–6, 89
Hammarskjöld, Hjalmar 47, 51–2
Heimburger, Lucie 66
Hentig, Hans von 5, 89, 90, 201 n.14, 226 n.102
Hinden, Rita 238 n.39
HLF (Heritage Lottery Fund, UK) 180, 185, 244 n.55
Hočevar, Pavla 142, 160, 231 n.45, 239 n.67
Hornik-Strömer, Anna 25, 50, 60, 136, 139–40, 149–51, 216 n.94, 218 n.150

Horthy, Miklós 16, 111, 163, 174
Hrstić, Danica 121, 234 n.82
Hungarian Communist Party 111, 115, 141, 146–7, 156–7, 164

IAW (International Alliance of Women, successor to the IWSA) 124
ICA (Irish Citizen Army) 75, 76, 178, 191
ILP (Independent Labour Party, UK) 11, 12, 13, 35, 46, 60
Ingham, Gertrude 184, 185
Inghinidhe na hÉireann (Daughters of Ireland) 190
Interessante Blatt, Das (Austria) 76
International Congress of Women (The Hague, 1915) 37, 102, 116, 125, 126, 232 n.55
International Congress of Women (Zurich, 1919) 61, 113, 125, 126, 218 n.153, 235 n.99, 235 n.107
International Red Aid (*see also* Willi Münzenberg) 160
International Socialist Congress (Stuttgart, 1907) 111
International Women's Day 10, 15, 101, 111, 119, 127, 144, 151, 228 nn.5–6
INTO (Irish National Teachers' Organisation) 97
IRA (Irish Republican Army) 85, 86, 175
Irish Bulletin (Ireland) 85, 225 n.81
Irish Citizen (Ireland) 12, 191
Irish civil war (1922–3) 3, 89, 96, 177, 178, 243 n.43
Irish Free State, 96, 97, 201 n.13, 227 n.131
Irish Volunteers 66, 70, 75
Irish War of Independence (1919–21) 67, 70, 72, 75, 76, 83, 84, 85, 96, 177, 196, 246 n.79
ISK (Militant International Socialist League) 152
ITGWU (Irish Transport and General Workers' Union) 190–1
IWFL (Irish Women's Franchise League) 12, 20, 70, 89, 190
IWM (Imperial War Museum, UK) 180–1
IWSA (International Women's Suffrage Alliance) 2, 11, 18, 129
IWWU (Irish Women Workers' Union) 20, 70, 178, 190–2

January Strike 1918 (Habsburg Monarchy, Imperial Germany) 12, 49–51, 56, 59, 70–1, 72, 138, 147, 149, 151, 155, 216 n.101
Jelovšek, Vladimira 133
Jirku Stridsberg, Gusti 162, 239 nn.45–6
Jogiches, Leo 35, 50
JSDS (Yugoslav Social Democratic Party) 121, 122
Juchacz, Marie 103, 128
Jugendinternationale, Die 22, 208 n.106, 210 n.6
Jung, Cläre 138, 156, 159–60, 165, 239 n.65, 240 n.82
Jus Suffragii 131, 235 n.104

Kádár, János 106
Károlyi, Mihály 140, 146
Keell, Tom 41
Kelen, Jolán 117, 118, 141, 164–5, 240 n.78
Kelley, Florence 126, 235 n.106
Klingelhöfer, Elma 93
Kollontai, Alexandra 34, 74, 113, 119, 209 n.114, 238 n.33
Kos, Leopoldina 123, 234 n.92
Kosovel, Karmela 133
KPD (German Communist Party) 6, 18, 128, 135, 151, 152
KPÖ (Austrian Communist Party) 50, 72, 139, 147, 150, 155, 156
Kramer, Hilde 134, 136, 138, 151–2, 156, 159–60
Kröpelin, Carl 56
Krupskaja, Nadeschda 36
Kun, Béla 17, 62
KUNMZ (Communist University of the National Minorities of the West, Soviet Union) 162

Labour Leader (UK) 11, 35, 115, 117, 218 nn.143–7
Landová-Štychová, Luisa 25
Lansbury, George 46
Le Bon, Gustave 90
Leach, Lydia 184
League of Nations 127, 185
Ledebour, Georg 93, 219 n.1

Leichter, Käthe (née Pick) 75, 139, 142, 148–50, 154, 156, 238 n.30, 238 n.32, 239 n.55
Lenin, Vladimir Illych 18, 36, 37, 49, 62, 107, 208 n.106, 210 n.6
Lerch, Sonja (aka Sarah Rabinowitz) 12, 19, 56–7, 204 n.51, 217 nn.124–6, 217 n 127
Leviné-Meyer, Rosa 6, 18, 202 n.20, 206 n.79
Liebknecht, Karl 22, 32, 35, 60, 208 n.106, 210 nn.5–6
Lindhagen, Anna 35, 47
Lloyd George, David 9
Lokar, Anica 142, 152–4, 159–62, 239 nn.47–51, 237 n.53, 240 n.68, 240 n.73
Longman, Mary 35
Luxemburg, Rosa 23, 35, 93, 100, 101, 112, 119, 146, 227 n.1, 240 n.83
Lynn, Kathleen 85, 98

Macarthur, Marcy 119, 233 n.71
Machnamh 100 189
Macmillan, Chrystal 126
Majerová, Marie 25
Markievicz, Countess Constance 14, 119, 178, 179, 190, 195, 205 n.57, 233 n.71, 243 n.46–7, 248 n.112, 248 n.115
Markievicz Award 178, 195
Marković, Branislava 162
Marković, Sima 162
Mehring, Franz 35
Menzi, Hildegard 93
Meyer, Ernst 6, 18
MI5 (The Security Service, UK) 150, 184
Milčinović, Adela 121
Mink, Paule (aka Adèle Paulina Mekarska) 19
Mitchell, Hannah 11, 12, 204 n.48
Montefiore, Dora 2, 14, 191–2, 201 nn.1–2, 205 n.61, 246 n.91
Morgonbris (Sweden) 35
Müller, Irén (née Singer) 141, 144–5, 147, 152, 237 n.23, 238 n.27
Munich Republic of Councils (1919) 71, 73, 80, 81, 186–8
Munkásnő (Hungary) 144
Münzenberg, Willi 36–7, 60, 160

Muskete, Die (Austria) 93, 94

Nádas, Péter 164, 240 n.77
Naprej: Glasilo jugoslovanske socialno-demokratične stranke (Yugoslavia) 234 nn.86–7, 240 n.81
National Assembly (Germany, 1919) 103, 104, 119
NCAS (National Council for Adult Suffrage, UK) 116
NCF (No-Conscription Fellowship, UK) 35, 41, 212 n.37
Neue Freie Presse (Austria) 72
New York Times, The 126, 235 n.105
Niedermeyer, Amma 56
NMI (National Museum of Ireland) 196
NUWSS (National Union of Women's Suffrage Societies, UK) 102, 116, 117, 185

O'Malley, Ernie 85
Östlund, Agda 47
Outrage (Ireland) 89

Pankhurst, Christabel 9, 129
Pankhurst, Emmeline 9, 129, 130, 134
Pankhurst, Sylvia 102, 185
Paris Commune (1871) 17, 19
Paris Peace Conference (1919–20) 8, 17, 61, 125, 218 n.153
Pärssinen, Hilja 74, 94, 95
Pethick Lawrence, Emmeline 126
Petković, Leposlava 121
Pfülf, Toni 151
Phillips, Marion 35
Polanyi, Karl 14, 145, 157, 205 n.55
Polish-Soviet War (1920–1) 77
Pollak, Marianne 4, 201 n.12
Pölz, Berta (married name Pollak) 139–40, 147, 154–6, 239 n.54
Popp, Adelheid 68. 221 n.21
POWs (Prisoners of War) 81, 82, 87, 219 n.155
Proclamation of Independence (Ireland) 70, 223 n.51

Quast, Cläre, 66, 78, 224 n.63

Raffald, Elizabeth 130

Red Guard (Finland) 76, 78, 79
Red Terror (Finland) 140
Red Women (Finland) 80, 87, 90, 91, 92, 95, 173, 183
Regent, Malka 162
Reich Conference of Workers' Councils (Austria) 136
Republikanischer Schutzbund (Austria) 78, 138, 157
Résistance 156, 163
revolutionäre Proletarierin, Die (Austria) 74, 223 n.44, 238 n.28
Richmond Barracks, '77 women' of 1916 quilt 193, 194
Robinson, Annot 61, 126
Roland-Holst, Henriette 17, 35, 206 n.74
Rote Fahne, Die (Austria) 136
Rote Fahne, Die (Germany) 104, 229 n.26
Russell, Dora 238 n.39
Russian civil war (1917–20) 77, 156
Russian revolutions (1905, 1917) 4, 12, 15, 17–19, 26, 56–8, 69, 74, 105, 169, 188, 205 n.70

Salomon, Alice 1
Salter, Ada 35, 102
Samoilovna Salkind, Rosaliya 77
Saran, Mary (Maria) 133, 138, 151–2, 156–8
Saumoneau, Louise 113
Scheidemann, Philipp 71
Schmitt, Carl 64, 219 n.165
Schwager, Irma 151, 238 n.37
Schweizer Illustrierte Zeitung (Switzerland) 55
Schwimmer, Rosika 105, 111, 129
SDAP (Austrian Social Democratic Party) 148, 155, 156
SED (Socialist Unity Party, East Germany) 67, 212 n.27
self-determination 3, 9, 17, 19, 64, 203 n.33, 205 n.72
Sender, Toni 38, 39, 43, 44, 128, 151, 212 n.29, 213 n.51, 214 n.58, 219 n.156
Sheehy Skeffington, Hanna 88. 98, 192, 221 n.15, 248 n.115
Sighele, Scipio 90
Sinisalo, Rauha 77

Skinnider, Margaret 96, 97, 248 n.115
Sklarz, Heinrich 82
Smith, Lydia 41
Snowden, Ethel 102, 126
Söderhamn hunger protests (1917) 49, 52–3, 216 n.108, 217 n.114
Sontheimer, Josef 57
sovereignty 2, 5, 8–9, 16, 17, 19, 22, 38, 58, 64, 203 nn.31–3, 219 n.165
Spanish civil war (1936–9) 79
Spanish Flu pandemic (1918–20) 57
Spartacist League 50
Spartacist Uprising, Berlin 65, 78, 91, 93
SPD (German Social Democratic Party) 12, 14, 15, 35, 43, 44, 50, 103, 104, 111, 114, 120, 152, 188
State Socialism 106, 129
Štebi, Aljozija 121–2, 231 n.45, 233 n.79, 233 n.81, 234 nn.81–4
Steinbring, Charlotte 65, 66, 78, 219 n.1
Sterky, Anna 47
Stimme der Frau (Austria) 150
Stopford Green, Alice 85
Strasser, Isa 135, 159
Stritt, Marie 1–2
Sturm, Hanna 78
Svensson-Vessman, Signe 47
SWI (Socialist Women's International) 113
Swiss general strike (*Landesstreik*) (1918) 16, 57–8, 213 n.39, 217 n.129–30, 218 n.134, 218 n.136

Tägliche Rundschau (Germany) 92, 93, 224 n.56, 226 n.115, 226 nn.117–18, 227 n.120
teenagers 5, 7, 13, 32, 34, 40, 42, 43, 47, 48, 64
Tillard, Violet 41
Toller, Ernst 56, 148, 188
Treaty of Rapallo (1920) 141
Treaty of Trianon (1920) 129, 140
Treaty of Versailles (1919) 62

Unterleitner, Hans 56
USPD (Independent Social Democratic Party, Germany) 12, 13, 44, 50, 51, 56, 71, 93, 104, 120, 213 n.54, 216 n.104

Västervik Manifesto (1917) 52
veterans 21, 96, 120, 207 n.96
Vode, Angela 122–3, 142, 158, 165,
    234 nn.85–91, 239 n.45, 240 n.81
Völcker, Gertrud 152
Volk, Bertha 41, 58, 213 n.39
Volksrecht (Switzerland) 57, 218 n.131
Vorkämpferin, Die (Switzerland) 36, 55,
    212 n.19, 212 n.21, 214 n.67, 217 n.122,
    218 n.133
Vorwärts (Germany) 65, 79
Votes for Women (UK) 116

Waking the Feminists 195
Weckruf (Austria) 72
Weimar Republic (Germany) 70, 72, 138,
    151, 199, 202 n.20, 214 n.70, 220 n.7
Wengels, Margarete 44
Wertheim, Hilde 136
WHAI (Women's History Association of
    Ireland) 193
White Terror (Finland) 99, 111, 140, 141,
    147, 174
Wibaut, Mathilde 35
WIDF (Women's International
    Democratic Federation) 150
WIL (Women's International League, UK)
    116, 117, 125, 235 n.100

Wilkinson, Ellen 2, 61, 130, 218 n.151,
    239 n.63
WILPF (Women's International League
    for Peace and Freedom) 61, 102, 113,
    114, 124, 125, 127, 132
Wilson, Woodrow 9, 17, 62
Winterbottom, Elsie 184
Wolfe, Lilian 41
Women of Aktion 188
Women's Cooperative Guild (UK) 185
WPC (Women's Peace Crusade, UK) 60,
    117, 184, 185
Workers' International Relief 138, 160
WSPU (Women's Social and Political
    Union, UK) 2, 11, 46, 119
Wurm, Mathilde 128

Ženski pokret (Yugoslavia) 120
Zetkin, Clara 2, 9, 10, 11, 12, 14, 15, 23, 34,
    35, 36, 37, 49, 74, 101, 104, 107, 111–13,
    114, 119, 124, 125, 127, 128, 131, 144,
    150, 151 203 n.34, 204 n.52, 211
    nn.14–16, 212 n.22, 212 n.24, 212 n.28,
    216 n.104, 228 n.5, 229 n.26, 232 n.54,
    232 n.56, 234 n.96
Zietz, Luise 128
Zimmerwald Manifesto (1915) 37, 145,
    212 n.25

www.ingramcontent.com/pod-product-compliance
Lightning Source LLC
Chambersburg PA
CBHW062124300426
44115CB00012BA/1808